THE NEW CAT OF BUBASTES

Rebecca Balder

Copyright © 2023 Rebecca Balder

All rights reserved

The characters and events portrayed in this book are fictitious. Any similarity to real persons, living or dead, is coincidental and not intended by the author.

No part of this book may be reproduced, or stored in a retrieval system, or transmitted in any form or by any means, electronic, mechanical, photocopying, recording, or otherwise, without express written permission of the publisher.

ISBN-13: 9798379306977

Cover design by: Ruth Balder
Library of Congress Control Number: 2018675309
Printed in the United States of America

Dedicated to my family.

INTRODUCTION

When I began rewriting these books, someone asked me why I would take on such a gigantic project. The problem back then (and today) is that G.A. Henty's writing style is hard to absorb. I would never compare myself to him as a writer, but his tone is complex. He wrote long sentences in the passive voice and used colloquialisms that don't translate. By (hopefully) putting the same meaning into modern English, I would be happy if readers became engaged enough to tackle the original.

Another reason to rewrite old English texts is that it allows us to tell stories in a way that helps students remember important facts. When I taught (both in the classroom and at home), I used stories to cement concepts. One of my first teaching mentors told me that "your students won't remember the facts you tell them, but they always remember a story." Telling stories can benefit those who struggle with memorization or understanding complex concepts.

It is essential to acknowledge that Henty's books contain instances of racism and sexism that are unacceptable in our modern world. As we read and learn from the past, we must recognize these wrongs and use them as teaching points for our present and future generations. Rather than eliminating their stories, we can use them to help define our worldview. We use stories to build empathy and understanding for people from different backgrounds, cultures and periods of history. We can develop an awareness of the mindset that created the worldviews we don't accept. We can teach the importance of respecting all individuals (even those with differing worldviews) regardless of background and identity, and inspire the next generation to be agents of positive change.

Lastly, when my children were young (almost all of them are in their thirties now!), I read books as I put them to bed. Under the covers, they'd hear stories of Hobbits and Narnia, which created worlds outside of our own. I would be grateful if families would use this book in the same way.

BECKY BALDER, MARCH 1, 2023

CHAPTER I

The King of the Rebu

The sun was blazing down upon the Western Caspian city. It was a primitive city, yet its size and population made it seem more significant. It consisted of a vast grouping of buildings, which were primarily huts. Even though they were more extensive and solidly built, these buildings could have been more impressive. Instead, they were little more than large huts, and even the king's palace was a group of these buildings.

A lofty wall with battlements and loopholes surrounded the city, and a similar but higher wall surrounded the king's dwellings and his principal captains' houses. The streets were alive with the busy multitude, and it was evident that they didn't spend much time working on their peacemaking skills. Nevertheless, they had everything a man would need to wage war. Most men wore helmets closely fitting to the head with a spike. These were made of hammered brass, although some of the headpieces had rugged, tough knobs of metal. All of them carried round shields—the soldiers had leather shields with metal fittings, and the captains had decorated brass shields. In their belts, everyone wore daggers, while at their backs were slung quivers of iron; painted bows hung over one shoulder, and some slings and a pouch of stones at their waist. Their main outfit was a kilt falling to the knee. Above the waist, some wore only a thin vest of white linen; others wore a long white shirt like a nightgown with short sleeves. They wore the kilt over this. Some had breastplates of thick leather tied with straps in the back, while in the case of the officers, pieces of metal covered the leather in a breastplate and backplate.

All carried two or three lances in the left hand and a spear ten feet long in the right. Horseback riders galloped about at full speed to and from the royal palace, while occasionally chariots, drawn sometimes by one, sometimes by two horses, dashed along. These chariots had wheels only about 3 feet high. Between them was the vehicle's body, only big enough for two men to stand on. It consisted only of a small platform, with a semicircular rail running eighteen inches high around the front. Anyone in the front could have seen that all the city's men weren't just going out on a military journey but going to a battle on which everyone's safety depended.

Women were crying as they watched the men going out of the gates. The men themselves had a stubborn and determined look, and no one was cheerful. Inside the palace, the people were as busy as the warriors outside. The king, his principal councilors, and leaders assembled in the great hall hut, which formed the audience room and council chamber. The room was filled with news enemy's strength and progress or with messages from the neighboring towns and tribes telling how many men they had sent and the time at which these had set out to join the army.

The king himself was a warlike figure in the prime of life. He had led his warriors on many successful expeditions far to the west and had pushed back the Persians who tried to take his territory. Standing behind him was his son, Amuba, a fifteen-year-old young man. The king and his councilors, along with the city's wealthier inhabitants, wore, in addition to the kilt and linen jacket, a long robe highly colored and ornamented with intricate designs and having a broad, rich border. It was fastened at the neck with a large brooch, fell loosely from the shoulders to the ankles, and was open in front. The belts which held the kilts and the daggers were also highly ornamented, and the ends fell in front and ended in large tassels.

All wore a profusion of necklaces, bracelets, and other gold ornaments; chiefs wore feathers in their helmets, and most men had figures tattooed on their arms and legs. They were light-skinned, with blue eyes; their hair was mostly golden or red, and they wore their beards short and pointed. The young Prince Amuba dressed for the field; his helmet was gold, and he covered his armor with plates of the same metal. He listened impatiently to the arguments of his elders, for he was eager to be off, this being the first time that the elders permitted him to take part in the military expeditions of his country.

After listening for some time and perceiving no prospect of the council breaking up, he returned to the adjoining council chamber. This was the dwelling place of the ladies and their families. It was divided into several apartments by screens formed of hide sewn together and hidden from sight by colored hangings. In one of these, a lady was seated on a low couch covered with panthers' skins.

"They are not done talking yet, mother. The question is where we will gather for battle. It does not make much difference to me where we fight, but they seem to think that's the most important point, and of course, they know more about it than I do. They finally found a place—about fifteen miles from here. They say that the ground in front is marshy and the enemy's chariots can hardly get across, but if they cannot get at us, it seems we cannot get at them. So we sent messengers to order all the contingents to assemble at that spot. Of course, six thousand men will remain behind to guard the city, but as we are going to win, I do not think there can be many occasions for that; for you think we shall beat them—don't you, mother?"

"I hope so, Amuba, but I am very fearful."

"But we repulsed them several times when they invaded our country, mother; why wouldn't we do it this time?"

"They are much stronger than they have ever been before when they have come against us, my boy, and their king is a great warrior who has been successful in almost every enterprise he has undertaken."

"I cannot think why he wants to conquer us, mother. They say the riches of Egypt are immense, and we can't even imagine the splendor of their temples and buildings. We won't fight with them if they will just leave us alone."

"No country is so rich that it does not desire more, my son. We have gold, so they undoubtedly think they will get a lot of treasure. Therefore, their monarch believes he will get more honor if he defeats us. As to their not fighting us, haven't we made many trips to the west, returning with captives and much booty? And yet the people did not quarrel with us—many didn't even know us when our army appeared among them. Someday, my son, things may be different; but at present, kings with power make war upon weaker people, take their goods, and make slaves of them.

"I hope, Amuba, you will not overexpose yourself in the conflict. You don't have a man's strength yet; remember, you are my only child. See that your charioteer covers you with his shield when you have entered the battle, for the Egyptians are fierce archers. Their bows carry much further than ours, and their arrows will pierce even the strongest armor. Nevertheless, our spearmen have always shown themselves as good as theirs —maybe even better- for they are more robust in body and full of courage. The strength of Egypt lies in the skill of its archers and the multitude of her chariots. Remember that although your father, as king, must go into the middle of the battle to encourage his soldiers, there is no reason why you, still a boy, should expose yourself like that.

"It will doubtless be a terrible battle. The Egyptians have the memory of past defeats to wipe out, and they will fight under their king's eye. I am terrified, Amuba. I have never doubted the result when your father has gone out to battle. The Persians weren't enemies we feared, nor was it difficult to force the hordes passing us from the eastward toward the setting sun to respect our country, for we had the advantage in arms and discipline. But the Egyptians are strong foes, and their king's armies have succeeded everywhere. My heart is filled with dread at the thought of the approaching conflict, though I try to keep up a brave face when your father is with me, for I wouldn't want him to think I'm a coward."

"I trust, mother, that your fears are groundless, and I cannot think that our men will give up when fighting for their homes and country on the ground we chose."

"I hope not, Amuba. But there is the trumpet; it signals that the council has broken up and that your father is about to start. Bless you, my dear boy, and may you return safe and sound from the conflict!"

The queen fondly embraced her son, who left the apartment hastily as his father entered so that the king might not see the traces of tears on his cheeks. Then, a few minutes later, the king, with his captains, started from the palace. Most of them rode in chariots, the rest on horseback. The town was quiet, and the streets were almost deserted. Except for the garrison, all the men capable of bearing arms had gone out; the women with anxious faces stood in groups at their doors and watched the royal party as it drove off.

The charioteer of Amuba was a tall and powerful man; he carried a shield far bigger than the rest, and the king selected him specifically for this service. His orders were not to rush into the front line of fighters and that he was even to disobey the Prince's orders if he wished to charge into the enemy's ranks.

"My son must not avoid danger," his father said, "and he must fight well; but he is still but a boy, not ready to enter upon a hand-to-hand contest with the best warriors of Egypt. I hope he will fight next to me someday, but today you must restrain his enthusiasm. I don't have to tell you to protect him as well as you can from the arrows of the Egyptians. He is my eldest son, and if anything happens to me, he will be the king of the Rebu; his life is precious."

Half an hour later, they came upon the tail of the stragglers making their way to the front. The king stopped his chariot, sharply scolded some of them for delaying their exit, and urged them to hurry to the appointed place. In two hours, the king arrived at this spot, where some forty thousand men were assembled. The scouts reported that although the advance guard of the Egyptians might come in an hour, the main body was some distance behind and would only be up in time to attack after dark. This was welcome news, for before night, the rest of the forces of the Rebu, fully thirty thousand more, would have joined. The king at once set out to examine the ground chosen by his general for the conflict. It sloped gently down in front to a small stream that ran through soft and marshy ground and would oppose a formidable obstacle to the passage of chariots. Moreover, the right wing rested upon a dense wood, while the left wing held a village a mile and a half distant from the wood.

They broke up a passageway from the marsh and scattered stones to stop the chariots. The archers were placed in front to harass the enemy attempting to cross. Behind them, the spearmen were ready to advance and aid them if pressed. The chariots were on the higher ground in the back, prepared to dash in and join in the conflict should the enemy succeed in forcing their way through the marsh. The inspection was scarcely finished when they saw a cloud of dust rising over the plain. It approached rapidly. The sun reflected a flash of arms, and many horses were seen coming in an even line.

"Are they horsemen, father?" Amuba asked.

"No, they are chariots, Amuba. Like us, the Egyptians do not fight on horseback, although there may be a few small bodies of horsemen with the army; their strength lies in their chariots. See, they stopped; they see our ranks drawn up in order of battle."

The chariots drew up perfectly, and as the dust clouds blew away, they could see four lines of chariots at a distance of a hundred yards.

"There are about a thousand in each line," the king said, "and this is but their advance guard. We have learned from fugitives that there are fifteen thousand chariots with their army."

"Is there no other place to pass this swamp, father?"

"Not so well as here, Amuba; the valley gets deeper the further we go, and the passage would be far more difficult than here. Then there is a bigger lake; after that, the ground is rough, so chariots don't cross it. Besides, they have come to fight us, and their king's pride would not permit them to make a detour. See, some great personage, probably the king himself, is advancing beyond their ranks to inspect the ground."

A chariot approached the valley's edge; two figures were in it. Numerous figures who appeared to be the attendants and courtiers of the king walked next to it. Great fans carried on wands and shaded the king from the sun's heat.

He drove slowly along the edge of the brow until he reached a point opposite the wood and then, turning, went the other way till he reached the causeway that passed through the village. After this, he rode back to the line of chariots and gave a word of command, for instantly, the long line of figures seen above the horses disappeared as the men stepped off the chariots to the ground. No movement took place for an hour; then there was a sudden stir, and the long lines broke up and wheeled round to the right and left, where they took up their position in two solid masses.

"The main army is at hand," the king said. "Do you see that great cloud, ruddy in the setting sun? That is the dust raised by their advance. In another hour, they will be here, but by that time, the sun will have set, and they will likely not attack until morning."

He ordered the front line to remain under arms; the others were told to fall out and prepare their food for the night. The Egyptian army halted about a mile distant, and as soon as it was evident that they intended no further movement, all of the soldiers were ordered to fall out. They placed a line of archers along the edge of the swamp, and before long, a party of Egyptian bowmen took up their post along the opposite crest. Great fires were lit, and they slaughtered several oxen for food.

"If the Egyptians can see what is going on," the king said to his son, "they must be filled with fury, for they worship the oxen as among their chief gods."

"Is it possible, father, that they can believe that cattle are gods?" Amuba asked in surprise.

"They do not exactly look upon them as gods, my son, but as sacred to their gods. Similarly, they reverence the cat, the ibis, and many other creatures."

"How strange!" Amuba said. "Do they not worship, as the Persians and we do, the sun, which, as all must see, is the giver of light and heat, which ripens our crops and gives fertility in abundance?"

"Not so far as I know, Amuba, but I know that they have many gods they believe give them victory over their enemies."

"They don't always give them victory," Amuba said, "since they have been repulsed in their fight to invade our land four times. Perhaps our gods are more powerful than theirs."

"It may be that, my son, but so far as I can see, the gods give victory to the bravest and most numerous armies."

"That is to say, they do not interfere at all, father."

"I do not say that, my son; we know little of the ways of the gods. Each nation has its own, and as some nations overthrow others, it must be that some gods are more powerful than others or do not interfere to save those who worship them from destruction. But these things are all beyond our knowledge. So we have to do our part bravely, and we need not fear the bulls and the cats and other creatures in which the Egyptians trust."

The king, his leaders, and his captains spent some time among the troops seeing that all the contingents had arrived well-armed and in good order. Then, they notified the leaders of each delegation of the position they should take up in the morning and did all in their power to animate and encourage the soldiers. When he finished, the king sat down on a pile of skins prepared for him and talked long and earnestly with his son, advising him on his conduct in the future if aught should befall him in the coming fight.

"You are my heir," he said, "and as is customary, the throne goes down from father to son. If I survive for another eight or ten years, you will succeed me, but things may happen otherwise if I fall tomorrow and the Egyptians overrun the land. In that case, the people need a military leader who would rouse them to prolonged resistance and repeatedly lead them against the Egyptians until the perpetual fighting wears them out. We want them to abandon the idea of subjecting us and turn their attention to less stubborn-minded people.

"You are too young for this; the people would look to Amusis or one of my other captains as their leader. Should success crown his efforts, they may choose him as their king. In that case, I would say, Amuba, it will be far better for you to approve the public's choice than to struggle against it. A young man like you would have no prospect of success against a victorious general, the will of the people, and you would only bring ruin and death upon yourself and your mother by opposing him.

"I can assure you that there is nothing so very significantly to envy in the job of a king, and as one of the land nobles, your position would be far more pleasant here than as king. A cheerful concession on your part to their wishes will earn the goodwill of the people, and at the death of him whom they may choose for their king, their next choice may fall upon you. Therefore, do everything in your power to win the goodwill of whoever may take the leader's place at my death by setting an example of prompt and willing obedience to his orders. It is easy for an ambitious man to remove a lad from his path, and your safety demands that you give him no reason to regard you as a rival.

"I hope that you won't need all this advice and that we may conquer in tomorrow's fight, but if we lose, the probability that I will escape is minimal. Therefore, you should be prepared for whatever may happen. Suppose you find that despite following my advice, the leader of the people, whomever he may be, is ill-disposed toward you, withdraw to the country's borders, and collect as large an army as possible. In that case, plenty of restless spirits are always ready to take part in any adventure. Journey with them to the far west, as so many of our people have done before, and establish yourself there and found a kingdom.

"None of those who have ever gone in that direction have returned, so they must have found space to establish themselves. Had they lost to people skilled in war, some at least would have found their way back, but so long as we know, tribes from the east have poured steadily westward to the unknown land, and no band has ever returned."

His father spoke so earnestly that Amuba lay down that night on his couch of skins in a very different mood to that in which he had ridden out. He had thought little of his mother's forebodings and looked upon it as sure that the Rebu would beat the Egyptians as they had before, but his father's tone showed him that he, too, felt by no means confident of the issue of the day.

As soon as daylight broke, the Rebu stood to their arms, and an hour later, dense masses of the Egyptians were seen advancing. As soon as they reached the slope's edge and descended toward the stream, the king ordered his people to move to the swamp's edge and open fire with arrows.

A shower of missiles flew through the air and fell among the ranks of the Egyptian footmen who had just arrived at the swamp's edge. So terrible was the discharge that the Egyptians recoiled and, retreating halfway up the slope, where they would be beyond the reach of the Rebu, they discharged their arrows. The superiority of the Egyptian bowmen was at once apparent. They carried mighty bows, stood sideways, drew them to the ear, and shot their arrows vastly farther than their opponents. The Rebu usually drew their bows only to the breast.

Scores of the Rebu fell at the first discharge, and as the storm of arrows continued, they, finding themselves powerless to damage the Egyptians at that distance, retreated halfway up the side of a slope. Now from behind the lines of the Egyptian archers, a column of men advanced a hundred abreast, each carrying a great bundle of sticks. Their object was evident: they were about to prepare a wide passageway across the marsh by which the chariots could pass. Again, the Rebu advanced to the swamp's edge and poured in their showers of arrows, but the Egyptians, covering themselves with the bundles of sticks they carried, suffered only a little harm. At the same time, the Rebu the Egyptian archers mowed down the Rebu, shooting calmly and steadily beyond the range of their missiles.

As soon as the front rank of the Egyptian column reached the edge of the swampy ground, the front line's men laid down their sticks in a close row and then retired in the intervals between their comrades behind them. Every new group did the same. Rebu arrows killed many, but the operation went on steadily, the sticks being laid down two deep as the ground became marshier. The Rebu saw, with a feeling approaching dismay, the gradual but steady advance of a passageway two hundred yards wide across the swamp.

Descending from their chariots, the king and his bravest captains went down among the footmen and urged them to stand firm. They pointed out that every yard the causeway advanced, their arrows inflicted fatal damage among the men forming it. Their requests, however, were vain; the ground facing the causeway was already thickly covered with the dead, and the hail of the Egyptian arrows was so fast and deadly that even the bravest shrank from withstanding it. At last, even their leaders stopped urging them, and the king ordered them to retreat beyond the Egyptian arrows' range.

They made some changes in the formation of the troops, and they placed the best and most disciplined bands facing the passageway to receive the charge of the Egyptian chariots. The two front lines were of spearmen, while on the higher ground behind them were the archers who had orders to shoot at the horses and to ignore those in the chariots. Then came the chariots, four hundred in number. Behind was a deep line of spearmen; on the right and left, extending to the wood and village, were the main body of the army, who were there to fight the Egyptian footmen advancing across the swamp.

The last portion of the causeway cost the Egyptians heavily. They were exposed to the arrows of the Rebu archers for a while, but now they were beyond the range of the Egyptians. At last, the work was completed. Just as they finished and the workers left, the king leaped from his chariot and dashed down the slope, leading a body of a hundred men carrying blazing brands. When the Egyptian archers saw the Rebu, they ran forward and poured arrows into the little band. Two-thirds fell before they reached the causeway; the others applied their torches to the sticks. The Egyptian footmen rushed across to extinguish the flames while the Rebu poured down to push them back. A desperate fight ensued, but the bravery of the Rebu prevailed, and the Rebu drove the Egyptians back. The attack served its purpose because the struggle in the passageway made the sticks sink deeper into the muddy ground, and the fire was extinguished. The Rebu returned to their first position and waited for the Egyptian attack. It was over an hour before it began. Finally, a long line of Egyptian footmen appeared, and their chariots lined up in fifty rows. With a mighty shout, the whole army advanced down the slope. The Rebu replied with their war cry.

At full speed, the Egyptian chariots dashed down the slope to the causeway. This signaled the Rebu archers to draw their bows, and the Rebu confused the first line of chariots. The wounded horses fell, and the Rebu stopped the advance momentarily. But the Egyptian footmen, entering the swamp waist-deep, opened such a terrible fire with their arrows that they forced the front line of the Rebu to fall back, and the aim of their archers became wild and uncertain.

The king tried to steady them. But, while he was doing so, the first Egyptian chariots had already made their way across the passageway, and behind them, the others poured on in an unbroken column. Then through the broken lines of spearmen, the Rebu chariots dashed down upon them, followed by the host of spearmen. The king's object was to stop the first onslaught of the Egyptians, overwhelm the leaders, and prevent the mass behind from emerging from the crowded passageway.

The shock was terrible. Horses and chariots rolled over in wild confusion, javelins were hurled, bows twanged, and the shouts of the fighters and the cries of the wounded as they fell beneath the feet of the struggling horses created a terrible noise. Light and active, the Rebu footmen mingled in the fray, diving under the bellies of the Egyptian horses and inflicting vital stabs with their long knives or engaging in hand-to-hand conflicts with the dismounted Egyptians. Amuba had charged down with the rest of the chariots. He fought in the second line, immediately behind his father; and his charioteer, mindful of the orders he had received, strove, despite the angry demands of the boy, to keep the chariot stationary; but the horses, accustomed to maneuvering in line, weren't holding back. So he charged down the slope with the rest.

Amuba, who had hunted the lion and leopard, remained calm and shot his arrows among the Egyptians with steady aim. For a time, the contest was doubtful. The Egyptian chariots bunched up on the passageway could not move forward, and in many places, their weight forced the sticks so deep in the mire that the vehicles couldn't move. Meanwhile, a terrible contest was going on along the swamp on both sides. Finally, the Egyptians, covered by the fire of their arrows, succeeded in making their way across the swamp, but here they were met by the Rebu spearmen, and the fight raged along the whole line.

Then two thousand chosen men, the bodyguard of the Egyptian king, made their way across the swamp close to the causeway, while at the same time, there was a movement among the densely packed vehicles. A mass of the heaviest chariots drawn by the most powerful horses forced their way across the causeway over all obstacles.

In their midst was the King of Egypt himself, the great Thotmes.

The weight and impetus of the mass of horses and chariots pressed all before it up the hill. This gave the chariots behind an opening to the right and left. The king's bodyguard shook the solid formation of the Rebu spearmen with their thick flights of arrows, and the chariots dashed in among them. The Rebu fought with the courage of their race. The Egyptians who first charged among them fell pierced with arrows while their horses were stabbed in innumerable places. But as the chariots poured over without a break, the infantry broke into groups, each fighting doggedly and desperately.

At this moment, the officer in command of the Rebu horses, a thousand strong, charged down upon the Egyptian chariots, drove them back toward the swamp, and stopped the fighting for a time. But the breaks between the Rebu center and its two flanks enabled the Egyptian bodyguard to thrust themselves through and to fall upon the Rebu chariots and spearmen, who were still maintaining the desperate conflict. The Rebu king had throughout fought in the front line of his men, inspiriting them with his voice and valor. Many times his chariot was so jammed in the mass that all movement was impossible. Yet the king leaped to the ground, passed through the crowd, and killed many Egyptian charioteers.

The efforts of the king and his captains were unavailing because the weight of the attack was irresistible. The solid phalanx of Egyptian chariots pressed onward and forced the Rebu back. Their chariots, enormously outnumbered, were destroyed rather than defeated. The horses fell pierced by the terrible rain of arrows, and the wave of Egyptians passed over them. Looking around in his chariot, the king saw that all was lost here and that the only hope was to lead the infantry off the field. But as he turned to give orders, a shaft sent by a bowman in a chariot a few yards away struck him in the eye, and he fell back dead in his chariot.

CHAPTER 2

The Siege of the City

Amuba saw his father fall off the horse, and he leaped from his chariot to get to the spot. Jethro was close behind, having noticed the king had fallen. He understood what Amuba didn't, that the Rebu had lost their ruler. Jethro was determined to rescue the monarch, but Amuba was already out of reach. An Egyptian archer shot an arrow right then, and Jethro put a shield between Amuba and the projectile. The arrow pierced the shield and the arm that held it. Jethro immediately snapped off the shaft of the shield and, in one motion, pulled the arrow out of the wound.

It was a swift task, yet in that brief moment, Amuba was almost killed. The archer, who leaned forward, dropped the back of his bow over the boy's head—an action common among Egyptian bowmen—and pulled him to the ground in no time. Jethro rushed forward with a roar of anger and swung his blade, cutting off the spearhead as it dropped. Then, he shortened his sword and hopped into the chariot, stabbing the bowman and struggling with the spearman.

The fight was brief. Jethro put his sword in the archer's body and quickly killed him. Then he leaped down and lifted Amuba, who had been knocked out by the bowstring around his throat and the impact of the fall. Jethro managed to get the chariot away from the battle, which had become even more intense. The Rebu, seeing the death of their king, rushed forward to take his body and avenge him. They cleared the area around him and carried his body away from the horses, broken chariots, and fighting men since they couldn't get the chariot out.

Jethro watched as the chariot he was in sped toward the city. He quickly realized the Rebu had lost the battle. The Egyptian chariots were stuck in the swamp, and the footmen formed a new causeway. It was clear the Rebu had no chance.

Jethro saw that the Egyptians were close to completing a causeway that would allow them to cross the Rebu's rear and attack. He ran up to two wounded, mounted men and told them to ride to each flank and inform the captains that their only chance to save their troops was to retreat quickly and in good order to the city.

This would be finished soon, for they were now working without interruption, and Jethro understood that as soon as it was done, the Egyptian army would pour over and assail the rear of the Rebu. Jethro ran up to two horsemen, gravely hurt, who had managed to escape the fighting like him.

"Listen," he exclaimed, "the new causeway will be completed in a quarter of an hour, and the Egyptians are about to swarm it. If that transpires, we won't be able to oppose them and will be defeated. So someone needs to speed to both sides and inform the commanders that the king is no more and that nobody is issuing instructions here. The only way to rescue their army is to retreat to the city quickly and coordinate."

The horsemen dashed away immediately, for Jethro, the king's charioteer, was slightly restless. After sending out the messengers, he returned to his chariot and drove away. Amuba was beginning to recover, and the jerky motion of the carriage as it raced along at full speed stirred him.

"What is it, Jethro? What has taken place?"

"It's all over now, prince, and I'm taking you back to the city. You had a tough time and a close call, and you can't do any more fighting even if it was useful, which it isn't."

"And the king, my father?" Amuba said, standing up. "What happened to him? Did I not see him go down?"

"I don't know anything definite about him," Jethro answered. "There was a fierce fight, and since I had you to protect, I couldn't join in. Plus, I am wounded in the left arm—if I had been any later, it would have hit you instead. So now, if you don't mind taking the reins, I will wrap it up. I haven't had the chance to process it yet, but it's bleeding heavily, and I'm starting to feel faint."

It was indeed true; Jethro meant to distract Amuba's mind from worrying about his father by pointing out his injury. But, as Amuba drove, he glanced back. The landscape was filled with a multitude of people who had fled.

"It's clear that everything is lost," he said sadly. "But why aren't they chasing us?"

"It won't be long before they start chasing us," Jethro responded. "But I'm guessing that few Egyptian chariots can pursue us. Most of them have lost horses or drivers. Many were destroyed in the battle. But they're making a new causeway, and those who cross over will take up the pursuit when it's finished. As for their infantry, they don't have much chance of catching the Rebu."

"Our soldiers should retreat in an orderly manner, Jethro. Spread apart like they are, they will be cut down by the Egyptian chariots by the thousands."

"They couldn't put up much of a fight anyhow," Jethro responded. "On an open field, footmen have no chance against a chariot attack. Many will certainly be killed, but they will disperse to the left and right; some will make it to the hills, a few will hide in forests and jungles, and some will outrun the chariots. The new road is narrow, so only a few can pass at a time, and therefore, even though many of our men will be overtaken and slain, I'm hoping that the majority will get away."

"Let's wait here for a bit, Jethro. I see a few carriages and a few riders behind, and since they're with the main group of refugees, they're probably allies. Let's join them and travel together to the town. I don't want to be the first to show up with the news of our defeat."

"You're right, prince. Our horses are so fast that we don't have to worry about being caught. We can wait a few minutes."

Suddenly, a group of chariots pulled up, and everyone stopped when they saw Amuba. Amusis, the head of the army, jumped out of his chariot when he saw Amuba and strode towards him.

"Prince," he said, "why are you still here? I'm so glad you made it out of the fray unharmed - I watched you fighting courageously - but I must urge you to start moving. The Egyptian charioteers are just a few minutes away."

"I'm ready to go, Amusis, now that you're here. Have you heard anything about my father?"

"The sovereign has been grievously hurt," the leader declared, "and was taken away from the fight; yet come, Prince, we must be quick. Our presence will be desperately required in the city, and we should make all arrangements for protection before the Egyptians arrive."

As the chariots continued their journey, they reached the city without being noticed by the Egyptians, who only arrived an hour later due to the chaos caused by the fleeing troops. When the group arrived, they found the town in disarray. The people had heard the news of the king's death and the army's defeat, and everyone was distressed. Women cried out in grief and terror, some wandering, others sitting in despair with their faces hidden in their hands, and some tearing their clothes in desperation. It was a heartbreaking sight.

As they made their way to the palace, Amuba and Amusis encountered the troops who had been left behind to defend the city. They marched on in solemn silence, ready to take their positions along the wall. During the journey, Amusis broke the terrible news to Amuba that his father had passed away. When they arrived, the royal enclosure was filled with sorrowful wailing from the women.

"I'll visit my mother," he told Amusis, "and then I'll come down with you to the walls and do whatever job you think is best for me in the defense. We need to rely on your experience and courage."

"I'll do whatever I can, Prince. The walls are strong, and if, as I hope, most of our army makes it back, I'm sure we'll be able to defend ourselves effectively against the Egyptian army. Let your royal mother know I'm sorry for her sorrow and devoted to her."

The general drove away, and Amuba entered the royal dwellings. The King's body was placed on a couch in the center of the main room. The queen stood there in sorrowful silence while the attendants let out loud wails, wrung their hands, and filled the air with their cries of grief and praises of the King's character and courage. Amuba moved to his mother's side. She turned and embraced him.

"Thank goodness, my son, you're back safe with me, but this is a huge loss for us!"

"It certainly is, Mother. No one could have been a better father than mine. But please, Mother, try to put your sorrow on hold for now; we'll have time to grieve for him later. We need all the courage we can get. The Egyptian army will be at our gates in a few hours, and everyone must fight for our defense. I'm going down to join the men and do my best to encourage them, but the chaos in the city is terrible. No one knows who has lost a husband or a father, and the women's cries and lamentations will only weaken the men's morale. I think, Mother, you could do a lot to help, and I'm sure that my father, in his resting place with the gods, would much rather see you trying to secure the safety of his people than mourning here."

"What shall I do?"

"I'd recommend, mother, that you take the wheel of a chariot and drive through the city's streets; urge the women to follow in the footsteps of their queen and postpone their mourning for the dead until the enemy is pushed back. Ask each of them to do their part in protecting the city; there are tasks for everyone—moving stones to the walls, preparing food for the combatants, tanning hides to be taken to the ramparts where the attack is fiercest, to protect our soldiers from arrows. These and other jobs are available, and, in helping to defend the city, the women would find relief from their grief and worries."

"Your advice is sound, Amuba, and I'll take it. Have a chariot brought down. My handmaids will accompany me and ensure two trumpeters are ready to lead us. This will guarantee interest and quiet, and my words will be heard as we go along. How did you survive the battle?"

"The loyal Jethro got me away; mother or I would have been killed; now, with your permission, I will go to the wall."

"Do so, Amuba, and may the gods keep you safe. You ought to eat something before you go, for you'll need all your energy, my son."

Amuba quickly devoured the meal before him in another apartment and took a sip of wine before dashing down to the wall.

The sight was devastating. All across the plain, men rushed toward the city while Egyptian chariots pursued them, killing and destroying. But the Rebu put up a fight; they organized in small groups, shields overlapping and spears jutting out. The ones inside the circle fired arrows or hurled stones from their slings. The horses wounded by the arrows often ran wildly across the plain, while others charged only to be impaled by spears. The chariots were often empty of their occupants as they broke into the phalanx.

Despite heavy losses, many Rebu forces could make it to the town's gates and bolster their numbers. As night fell, Egyptian chariots had yet to make their appearance. In the meantime, many of the Rebu who had fled to the hills returned to the town. The six thousand men who had stayed behind to defend the city had been joined by four times as many more by morning. The Rebu secured the city against the invading Egyptians through courage and perseverance.

Although this was only a little more than half the force that marched out to fight, the return of so many refugees reduced the terror and suffering that had taken hold. The women whose husbands or children had returned rejoiced in the ones they had feared lost, while those whose friends had not yet returned found hope in the stories of the newcomers that their beloved might still be alive and would soon make their way back. The queen's example had already done a lot to restore confidence. Everyone knew how much the king and she loved each other. The women all understood that if she could set aside her deep sorrow and show such serenity and bravery at such a moment, everyone else should put aside their worries and do their best to protect the town.

Amusis commanded that all soldiers returning from battle should spend the night in the comfort of their homes while the troops who had remained in the city kept watch over the walls. Everyone mustered the following day again, organized according to their respective companies and battalions. Sadly, many companies that had faced the most combat were down to few survivors. Weak divisions were merged with the strong to compensate for this, and new officers were appointed to replace any missing ones. In addition, the weapons were inspected, and any shortages were replenished from general stores.

Ten thousand men were assigned as a reserve to reinforce the points most at risk, while the rest of the force was spread out to occupy designated wall sections. As soon as the morning dawned, women quickly returned to work, making their way to the walls in long lines, carrying baskets of stones on their heads. Disused houses were dismantled for their stones and timber, and women with ropes dragged the latter to the walls, ready to be thrown onto the enemy's leaders. Even the children took part in the effort, carrying small baskets of dirt to places that Amusis had identified as needing reinforcement.

The strategic location of the city was deliberately selected for its defensive purposes. It sat on a rocky plateau roughly fifty feet from the surrounding plains. The Caspian Sea lapped at its eastern edge, and on the other three sides, a high wall of dirt and stones ran along the plateau's edge. Every fifty yards or so, towers rose above the walls. The circumference of the walls was about three miles. Since its foundation by the grandfather of the late king, the town had never been breached, despite several sieges. The Rebu believed they could form a formidable defense against enemy forces now that the Egyptians' chariots were no longer a threat.

At noon the Egyptian army approached, and the city's defenders couldn't help but feel a sense of dread at the enormous force they saw. The army was an impressive three hundred thousand strong and was organized according to their arms and nationality; Nubians, Sardinians, Etruscans, Oscans, Dauni, Maxyes, and Kahaka from Iberia, along with other foreign mercenaries. It was a sight to behold.

The Egyptians were organized by their weapons. They had units of bowmen, who carried a slightly curved club for close combat; other groups of archers utilized hatchets. All the heavy infantry had the traditional Egyptian shield, roughly three feet long. The top of the shield was semi-circular, while the bottom was flat. There was a round boss near the top. Some battalions equipped themselves with spears and heavy maces, others with axes. Their helmets snugly fit their heads, many with metallic fringes dangling from the top. The helmets were primarily padded and quilted, as they provided better protection from the sun's heat than metal.

Each company had its banner; these were all of a religious character and depicted creatures holy to the gods, sacred ships, emblematic designs, or the names of the king or queen. These were metal and were hoisted at the ends of lances or staffs. The banner-bearers were all officials of demonstrated bravery. Behind the military trailed a tremendous baggage train, and the moment this had arrived on the ground, the tents of the king and the primary officers were pitched.

"What an amazing host!" Jethro exclaimed to Amuba, who had joined the young prince at the walls after having his arm bandaged on his arrival at the palace. "It looks like a nation more than an army. No wonder we were defeated yesterday, but we stood our ground for so long, and many survived the battle."

"It's incredible, Jethro! Look at the procession of vehicles moving in perfect formation. It's a good thing they'll be powerless now. Even though they're numerous, they can't do much against our walls. Their towers on the fields won't match our elevation here, and the cliff is so steep that it can be scaled only in a few places."

"It appears impossible for them to take it, Prince; however, we must remain vigilant. We know that the Egyptians have taken many cities that thought themselves invincible, so we should be prepared for even the most daring of attempts. The gates have already been shut, and such a large amount of rocks have been piled up against them that they have become the most fortified part of the wall; the details of the roads that were made of wood have been set ablaze, and they can now only reach the gates by scaling, like at other points. Moreover, we have enough food to last nearly a year since the entire region has brought in its harvest and many thousands of livestock; there are plenty of wells too."

"I heard about the arrangements they were making, Jethro, and I'm sure that if we can withstand the initial attack of the Egyptians, we can stay much longer than they can since supplying such a large army will be hard. How do you think they will attack us? I can't find any approach that could work."

"I can't tell you that. We assume our cities and those of our neighbors are unconquerable, but the Egyptians are highly experienced in war tactics. They've laid siege to and taken many cities and must have plans we're unaware of. However, we'll find out tomorrow. So no actions will be taken today. The generals must first assess our walls and decide where the attack should be launched, and the troops will get at least one day of rest before they're asked to storm the post."

In the afternoon, a procession of vehicles circled the walls from the sea's shoreline to the elevated plateau and back again, staying just beyond the reach of the arrows.

"If we had only a couple of their archers here," Jethro said, "the Egyptian king wouldn't dare to get so close. It's amazing how accurately they shoot. Their arrows have nearly doubled our range, and their strength is enough to penetrate the most resilient shields, even when reinforced with metal. If I hadn't seen it with my own eyes, I would have thought it inconceivable that ordinary people, no bigger or stronger than us, could fire arrows with such power. They take a different stance than our archers, and even though their shafts are almost a foot longer than ours, they can draw them back. I thought I was a good archer before encountering the Egyptians, and now I feel like a little child when witnessing a man doing feats of strength that I never even dreamed of being possible."

In the evening, all the key figures of the army, the priests, the royal councilors, and the leading influencers of the state gathered for a great council. After a discussion, it was concluded that it would be best to postpone appointing a successor to the late king until the present crisis was resolved. Amusis was then granted absolute powers so that no time would be wasted on consulting. Amuba was at the council with his mother, although neither actively participated. Before the council began, Amuba and his mother stated that they were willing to abide by whatever the council decided and hoped the person best suited to take the command in such an emergency would be chosen.

That night the king's body was cremated in a grand funeral ceremony. Under normal conditions, the event would have been held on a cliff overlooking the sea, about five miles from the city. This was where all past kings had been cremated, in full view of their people, and buried beneath large dirt mounds. The priests had long deemed this spot spiritually significant, forbidding anyone from stepping on the hallowed ground. But due to the current circumstances, the king's ashes could not be laid with those of his ancestors, so the ceremony was held within the royal enclosure with the priests, the queen, and the prince in attendance. After the ritual, the ashes were collected and placed in a casket that, in more favorable times, would be placed on the sacred cliff in full view of the people.

Early the following morning, the trumpets sounded from the city's walls, calling all the troops to take up arms. Amuba, when he arrived at his post, saw the Egyptian army marching against the city. The archers leading the attack opened fire when they were within bow range. Most of their shots fell short, but the attackers on the wall still managed to rain arrows on them with deadly accuracy. The attackers were forced to retreat temporarily, and many foot soldiers poured through and charged the walls, running forward in an irregular formation to find shelter from the arrows.

"What are they going to do now?" Amuba exclaimed, laying aside his bow.

Jethro shook his head.

"They are working with a plan," he said. "We will see soon. Listen."

Even amidst the bustle of the immense crowd, a distinct metallic ringing could be heard - like thousands of steel hammers clanging away.

"Surely," Amuba exclaimed, "they're not thinking of taking the rock away! That is too great a task even all of Egypt was here."

"It certainly isn't that," Jethro agreed, "and yet I can't imagine what else they're up to."

After almost an hour, the mystery was solved. At the sound of a trumpet and the Egyptian king's command, many people appeared on the edge of the rock at the base of the walls. The Egyptians had been busy hammering metal spikes into the crevices of the rock and using them as a staircase up to the top. They then threw down ropes and ladders to help the rest of the soldiers climb up. In no time, the ledge, barely wide enough to fit a few people, was crowded with soldiers.

The ladders were now hauled up and placed against the wall, and the Egyptians scrambled up in huge numbers, but the Rebu were ready for the attack, and a barrage of stones, logs, arrows, javelins, and other projectiles came raining down on the Egyptians. Despite being crowded with men, many of the ladders were pushed back by the defenders and crashed over the edge of the rock to the ground below. Here and there, the

Egyptians managed to take hold of the wall before the Rebu could gather their shock and respond; but as soon as they regrouped, they charged the Egyptians with such force that all the latter were slaughtered in combat or thrown from the ramparts.

The Egyptians fought for hours but ultimately had to retreat due to heavy losses and the trumpet's call.

"That wasn't too serious, Jethro," Amuba said, wiping away the sweat from his forehead; for he had been invigorating the crew by helping to hoist and throw over the hefty stones and lumber.

"It wasn't hard to push them back in those circumstances," Jethro commented, "but their attack was certainly a shock to us, and they fought with great courage. You'll find that they'll have learned from the experience next time, and we'll have to devise something else to cope with. But, unfortunately, we won't get any peace now that they've found a way to climb the rock."

The conflict was restarted in the evening when many Egyptians ascended the rock as the darkness descended. As earlier, the Rebu pelted them with missiles; but this time, only enough had climbed up to form a line close to the base of the wall, where they were, to a great extent, shielded from the projectiles from above. The night was dark, and the Rebu continued to bombard their unseen enemy.

When the defenders awoke to the morning light, they were shocked that the Egyptians had used the night to their advantage. Ropes were used to hoist up a mass of timber to build a shelter for the siege operations. The timber was cut and ready for construction; the Egyptians could even fit it together in the darkness. As a result, defenders saw an array of about forty or fifty shelters right against the base of their walls. These shelters were built in a way that sloped down like a lean-to and were covered with thick hides.

The Rebu were astounded to discover that the walls were so strong that the projectiles they threw at them just bounced right off. The Egyptians had also connected each shelter to the ground below with ladders to switch out workers or bring in reinforcements as necessary.

To no avail, the Rebu launched missiles and spilled boiling oil over the walls. The timber beams were too intense for the missiles, and the overlapping hides prevented the oil from reaching those below.

"These are terrible foes, your highness," Jethro declared. "I warned you that we could anticipate fresh tactics and techniques, but I didn't anticipate that the day after the siege started, they would have conquered all the strengths of our natural fortifications and would already be in a safe position at the bottom of our walls."

"What should we do, Jethro? The workers in those shelters will soon remove the stones that make up the walls and then easily excavate the earth behind."

"The situation is grave," Jethro agreed, "but there is no need to panic. Most of our forces will be gathered behind the barrier, and if the Egyptians manage to breach it, we can pour through the gaps, and since they can only be reinforced slowly, we would quickly force them off the edge of the precipice. That is not something I am worried about."

"What are you afraid of, Jethro?"

"I'm afraid, Prince, because I have no idea what to expect. We're like children fighting against the Egyptians, who have thrown us off. I'm afraid they could do anything next, and I wouldn't know. It's obvious to everyone that if they breach the walls, we'd rush in and take them down."

"Perhaps they intend to go under the walls until large portions of them fall over, and they make their way in."

Jethro shook his head.

"That would devastate the Egyptian shelters and bury their workers; even if they managed to escape before the walls crumbled, they wouldn't gain anything. I wish we could cause the walls to collapse, for in that case, the mound of dirt and stones would form right at the precipice of the rock, and as the Egyptians could only climb up in small numbers at a time, we could obliterate them with ease. Now I understand that our architects made a mistake in constructing a tall wall around the city; it would have been better to have built a low barrier right at the cliff's edge. Here comes Amusis; we'll see what he thinks of this situation."

Amusis looked flushed and anxious, but his expression changed to calm when he saw the Prince.

"The Egyptians are going to dig through our walls," he said, "but we will drive them like rats out of the holes when they do. Don't you think so, Jethro?"

"I do not know," Jethro said gravely. "If they dig through our walls, we shall certainly, as you say, drive them out of their holes; but I don't believe that that is what they will do."

"What do you think they are going to do?" Amusis asked roughly.

"I have no idea, Amusis. I wish I had, but I am sure they haven't gone to all this trouble for nothing."

CHAPTER 3

Captive

The Rebu were so sure they could fend off the Egyptians, even if they managed to tunnel through the walls or even demolish them, that they paid little attention to the shacks placed at the foot of the wall, leaving only a large group of personnel standing behind the walls, half of whom were always at the ready to combat the Egyptians if they managed to break through. This trust, unfortunately, resulted in their downfall. The Egyptians were more than familiar with excavation operations and knew that if they penetrated the wall, the Rebu could easily overpower the small working teams; thus, after getting to a significant depth in the embankment, they branched off to either side, creating a sizeable opening, which was held up with beams and planks hoisted at night.

The number of those employed on the job expanded rapidly as space allowed, and while the Rebu believed that each of the protected places had at most twelve workers, in only a day and a half, close to two hundred men were working in the center of the embankment at each point. The Pharaoh of Egypt had commanded his chief engineer to have everything ready to take the city by the end of the third day.

Every night, the workforce expanded, delving deeper and deeper. Instead of picks, they used large knives to cut into the ground. They were commanded to remain silent, allowing them to tunnel close to the surface without alerting those on the defense. They pushed spears through at night to measure the distance to the inner wall. After three days, the dig had progressed so much that only a foot of earth remained, kept in place by a lining of boards and beams. This way, the Egyptians were prepared to burst through the unsuspecting defenders at twenty points.

Once night fell, the preparations for the assault began. First, stagings of enormous length, paired with an abundance of broad and lofty ladders, were noiselessly moved to the base of the cliff. Then, with a deafening roar, the Egyptian army advanced, with thousands of laborers quickly getting the stages in place to scale the cliff. Finally, the moment of truth was near – the Egyptians were ready to storm the walls.

The city's defenders rushed to the walls to protect it, and all sorts of projectiles were hurled at the Egyptians as they attempted to scale the ladders and structures. With everyone preoccupied and the noise of battle so loud, no one noticed the small encampments at the base of the wall, and the work of digging a tunnel through was utterly unnoticed. The troops assigned to watch these spots joined their fellow soldiers on the walls, unaware of the mass of dark figures that had begun to emerge from the mound at twenty different points.

The Rebu, elated by the Egyptians' weakening defense, was suddenly stunned by a trumpet behind them. Turning around, they were met with a line of footmen and a barrage of arrows. Without hesitation, the Rebu charged down to fight off the unexpected invaders. But their efforts were hindered by the Egyptians' strength—each company was composed of 400 well-trained soldiers, making it difficult for the Rebu to overpower them.

Amusis and the other Rebu leaders worked quickly to get their troops into formation, knowing that they would need to be organized to stand a chance against the phalanxes of the Egyptians, but, unfortunately, the chaos was too great.

While this was happening, the Egyptians outside had seized the opportunity to set up their ladders and stagings in mass numbers. Some were dragging up ladders and planting them against the walls, while others were climbing the embankments from behind and attacking the Rebu, who were still defending the wall.

The tribesmen never fought with more courage; however, the unexpectedness of the attack, the number of Egyptians who had taken up positions in their rear, and the continuous pushing in of forces both through and over the wall made it impossible for them to reverse the tide. Moreover, they could not tell allies from enemies in the disorder and darkness. The different battalions and companies were blended; the commands of their directors and officers were inaudible in the clamor.

In the face of the Egyptian onslaught, the defenders were overwhelmed. The assailants had devised a clever plan, stealthily making their way to one of the gates and taking it by surprise. Great fires were lit, and engineers rapidly bridged the gaps in the roadway. The Egyptians poured into the city, leaving the Rebu in confusion. It seemed as if their enemies had arisen from the ground, and with no option to regain their lost position, the Rebu began to flee, some for their homes and some for the water facing the city, the only option open to them. Boats lining the sand were quickly filled with desperate fugitives, and those who arrived later found no means of escape. Some reluctantly lowered their arms and returned home; others ran forward to face the Egyptian forces and meet their fate.

It was several hours before the struggle ended, as the darkness threw the Egyptians off balance. Many fierce fights occurred between different regiments before they realized they were allies. Illumination was obtained by burning down some of the dwellings closest to the walls. Yet, as soon as the Egyptians stepped beyond the halo of light, they were ferociously attacked by the Rebu. Eventually, the trumpet blasted the order for the troops to stay in their respective locations until dawn.

When the sun rose, a sizable group of women emerged from

the middle of the town. As they got close to the Egyptians, they prostrated themselves on the ground and begged for mercy. A moment of silence passed before some Egyptian officers stepped forward and took about twenty women to meet the king. Thotmes had joined the troops who had forced their way into the city through the gate, but after the officers begged him not to risk getting killed in the chaos - maybe by an arrow from his own army - he moved back to the plain and had just returned to take part in the occupation of the city.

The Rebu females were guided towards him across the land, greatly blanketed with corpses. Nearly half of the city's defenders had perished, while the Egyptians' fatalities were almost as significant. The women prostrated before the illustrious ruler and begged for mercy for themselves, their children, and the surviving citizens.

Thotmes was filled with joy. He had conquered a city that was thought impossible to take; he had put down the people who had beaten his predecessors; he had increased his fame and the fame of the Egyptian forces. The Egyptians had a kind attitude. Human sacrifices were not part of their religion, and they didn't usually kill prisoners of war without cause. Life was held in high regard in Egypt more than in any other ancient nation, and their laws were designed to foster a merciful mindset.

An interpreter translated the women's messages to the king.

"Has all the fighting ended?" the king asked. "Have all the men laid down their weapons?"

The women exclaimed that there wasn't an armed man in the city; all the weapons were collected during the night and placed in piles in front of the entrance to the palace.

"Then I grant everyone their life," the monarch announced graciously. "When I battle with cowards, I have little leniency for them, for men who are not courageous are unworthy of living; yet when I struggle with men, I treat them as men. The Rebu are a valiant people; the jackal could battle the lion as the Rebu go up against the might of Egypt. They fought valiantly in the field and have courageously defended their walls; consequently,

I grant life to all in the city—men, ladies, and children. Where is your ruler?"

"He died in battle four days ago," the women replied.

"Where is your queen?"

"She drank poison last night, preferring to join her husband than to survive the city's capture."

Thotmes had now commanded the people to be taken to the plain and put under guard. The town was then thoroughly searched, and all valuable items were taken. The king allocated a portion of the golden vessels for the Temple, kept some for himself, and gave others to his generals. Afterward, he commanded 100 captives—50 young men and 50 maidens of high rank—to be chosen as slaves for Egypt and imposed the tribute the Rebu were to pay from then on. The army then vacated the town, and the inhabitants were allowed back.

The following day, news of the capital's fall came flooding in from the other Rebu towns. Unbeknownst to them, the seemingly-invincible city had been taken down after a short siege, leaving the townsfolk terrified. In response, they sent messengers to the king, offering unconditional surrender and willingness to pay any tribute he demanded.

The king, delighted with his success and eager to return to Egypt, from which he had been away for over two years, warmly acknowledged the various delegations. Then, he announced that he had already determined the required yearly tax from the nation and demanded immediate contributions from each city based on their size. Soon enough, the funds arrived in money, gold vessels, embroidered robes, and other valuable items. After collecting the entire amount, the army left for the long journey back to Egypt, leaving a high-ranking officer and ten thousand soldiers behind to guard the newly acquired province.

Amuba was one of the fifty slaves chosen. Amusis had managed to escape the chaos, like many others. Jethro was also part of the selected group. Initially, Amuba didn't care about what would happen to him. However, the news of his mother's death, which he learned after fighting until the end and returning to the palace, was a disastrous blow, following so closely on his father's death and his nation's defeat. His mother had left him a message that, as life had no allure for her anymore. She preferred death to the humiliation of being taken as a prisoner to Egypt; she hoped he would deal with the misfortunes that had befallen him and his people with acceptance and patience; he was young, and no one could predict what the future had in store for him.

"You may be taken away into captivity in Egypt, my son," her message began, "but you could still have a chance to escape, reunite with your family, and find a life where you can be content or even happy. So my final words to you are: no matter what happens, stay strong and be loyal to your heritage - you were born a king, and you can still be respected even when you're a slave. May the gods of your country watch over you and give you the strength to make your happiness because you can be happy no matter your station in life - be it a throne or a cottage. May you be blessed always."

The message was delivered by an elderly lady who had been with the queen since birth. Despite being filled with sorrow due to Amuba's mother's passing, he still acknowledged that this sorrow was less painful to endure than the possibility that his mother, who had been so beloved and respected by the people, was being dragged as a slave in the Egyptians' procession of conquest. His grief was so intense that he followed the order to leave the city without protest. He was barely affected when the Egyptian officer responsible for choosing slaves picked him to be part of the group taken to Egypt.

Prostrate as he was, he found comfort in that Jethro was also part of the conscripted crew. "It's selfish of me to be pleased that you're going to be taken away too, Jethro," he remarked, "but it'll be a great comfort to have you with me. I know most of the others in the group, but none of them can. I share my thoughts about my parents and my home the way I can with you, whom I've known for so long."

"I'm not sorry to be chosen," Jethro said, "for I have no

relatives, and now that the Rebu are defeated, I won't find much joy in my life here. When we get to Egypt, we'll probably be split up, but there's a long stretch of months ahead of us, and during that time, we can at least be together; so, if me being with you, Prince, makes you feel better, I'm pleased to have been chosen. I thought it was a cruel blow when my wife died a few weeks after we married. Now I'm glad it happened, and I can go off without anyone's heart being broken. Prince, you and I are probably the least miserable of those chosen. Most of the others are leaving wives and children; some of the youngest are still single but have fathers and mothers they'll be separated from. Let's not complain because it could have been worse, and our life in Egypt might not be so terrible."

"That is just what my dear mother said, Jethro," Amuba replied, repeating the queen's message.

"My dear mistress was right," Jethro said. "We may find as much happiness in Egypt as anywhere else, and now let's try to cheer up our companions, for by cheering them up, we might forget our misfortunes." Jethro and Amuba went among the rest of the captives, most prostrated with grief, and did their best to get them out of their misery.

"The Egyptians have seen that the Rebu are resilient in the face of adversity," Amuba said to some of them. "Let's show them that we can handle our difficulties with strength. Worrying won't make it any better and will only worsen our situation. If the Egyptians see that we remain courageous, they'll be more likely to show us compassion. We have a long and grueling journey ahead of us, and we'll need all the strength we can muster. Our hardships pale in comparison to those of the women. So let's show them the power of courage and fortitude. Even though we have been defeated, our spirit remains unbroken; we are prepared to defy fate and not bow to it."

Amuba's words had a powerful impact on the prisoners. They admired him as the son of their late king and as one who would have been the king himself had not this misfortune befallen them; his poise and bold speech encouraged them to battle against their anguish and to confront their destiny with more optimism. As long as the military stayed in camp, the prisoners' hands were bound behind their backs, but when the march began, they were released from their restraints and were situated in the middle of an Egyptian unit.

It was a long and tiresome journey. On the way, people taken in past military operations were added to the procession of captives who had been left in the care of the troops sent to the various territories controlled by the Egyptians until the army could return. Supplies had been pre-arranged to provide it with sustenance along the way. As the distance traveled each day was limited, the captives suffered minimal hardship until they reached the arid area between the southern tip of Syria and the delta of the Nile.

Here, although a considerable amount of water was brought along with the army, the amount of water given to the captives was minimal. Moreover, the scorching heat of the sun, combined with the thick dust clouds kicked up by the thousands of soldiers around them, made the captives' suffering even more intense. Nevertheless, the Rebu captives earned the admiration of the troops escorting them through their brave and stoic attitude, in stark contrast to the grief displayed by other prisoners. Moreover, the regiment consisted of Libyan mercenaries, hardy and active men accustomed to the heat and fatigue.

The march to Egypt had taken three months, during which time most of the captives, including Amuba and Jethro, had learned the Egyptian language. Jethro insisted that this was crucial for the prisoners, as it would keep their thoughts from dwelling on the past and make life in Egypt more bearable.

"Remember," he said, "that we will be slaves, and masters aren't known for their patience. They'll give us orders, and things won't go well if we don't understand them. It will make us more valuable and get better treatment if we can speak their language."

Amuba was genuinely thankful when the vibrant green of Egypt's plains replaced the desert's dull monotony. As soon as they entered the land, the order they had marched was switched, and the long line of prisoners followed closely behind the king's chariot. Everyone was carrying a portion of the loot taken from their homeland. Amuba had a large golden vase on his head that had been used in temple rituals. Jethro had a fancy helmet and armor that belonged to the king.

Amuba was astounded the moment they entered the city. Everywhere they looked, there were signs of prosperity and comfort. The streets were filled with people who prostrated themselves to the ground in reverence for the king as he passed and who stared at the procession of captives from the different nations that his military power had subdued. But what truly stunned him were the temples with their long avenues of sphinxes, the grandiose statues of the gods, the tall rows of pillars, and the sheer magnitude and grandeur of the entire structures.

"How were they built, Jethro?" he exclaimed repeatedly. "How were these massive stones put up? How did they drag these huge sculptures across the plains? What tools could they have used to carve them out of the solid granite?"

"I'm worried, Amuba," Jethro said gravely, for Amuba had strictly prohibited him from calling him prince anymore, pointing out that the name for a slave would only be mocking. "We'll soon find out firsthand how these wonders were built, for that's exactly what they are. It would have taken hundreds of people to get one of these statues here, and although the citizens helped, it's clear the slaves did the lion's share of the work."

"What could all these figures mean, Jethro? In this day and age, there are no creatures with the faces of women and lion-like bodies, human faces and bull-like bodies, or even bird-like heads and human bodies. How strange!"

"There's no way these can exist, Amuba. It's surprising that the Egyptians, a smart and wise people, would choose such unusual figures as their gods. I think they must represent their qualities, as the head stands for their intelligence, the bodies of the lions or bulls for their strength and power, and the birds' wings for their speed. I'm not sure, but it seems like a plausible explanation. We know their gods are powerful because they give them victory over all other nations. Hopefully, we'll learn more about them and other things soon."

The journey went on for an additional three weeks, full of unexpected wonders. The captives were particularly amazed by the land's extraordinary fertility. The Rebu practiced essential cultivation, yet everywhere they looked, they saw an abundance and variety of crops that seemed miraculous. They were familiar with irrigation in Persia, but the enormous projects in Egypt - including massive river embankments, a network of canals and ditches, and the remarkable order and method - filled them with awe and admiration.

Many of the cities and temples were much more grandiose and splendid than the ones they had initially encountered, and Amuba was in awe when they came to Memphis, the capital of Egypt not long ago. The captives were taken aback by the city's riches and size, but they were most astounded when they observed the huge pyramids a few miles away from the city and were told that these were the tombs of the kings.

The terrain changed as the army marched forward. On the left were a series of rolling hills, and similar, but not as high, hills were seen on the right.

After two weeks, a jubilant cheer rose from the troops as they spotted Thebes, the capital of Egypt and the end of their long and arduous journey, in the distance.

Thebes stood on both sides of the Nile. The river's eastern bank was home to the most significant portion of the population, mainly the poorer class. The west bank of the river, known as the Libyan side, was densely populated with houses close to the river's edge. Behind them were impressive temples and palaces, while the tombs of kings and queens were carved out of the valley's steep sides, surrounded by the rock sepulchers of the wealthy. The low-rise dwellings of the city gave way to grand temples, palaces, and public buildings, presenting a stunning sight to visitors.

The royal army entered the city from the western bank of the river, marching towards the tremendous Libyan suburb and its palaces and temples. An enormous crowd welcomed the king and the returning army as they arrived. Cheers and applause filled the air, musical instruments blared, and religious processions of the great temples moved through the crowd. Everyone stopped to watch the gods, priests, and attendants bearing emblems pass by.

"Indeed, Jethro," Amuba exclaimed with excitement, "it's almost worth it to be made a slave if it just means witnessing this fantastic sight. What remarkable people! They have such knowledge, power, and magnificence! My father's palace would be considered a mere hut in Thebes, and our temples, which we were so proud of, are tiny compared to these massive structures."

"That's all very true, Amuba, and I'm not saying I'm not filled with admiration. But you know the Rebu have pushed back their forces several times, and man for man, our people are more than a match for their soldiers. We're taller than them by half a head. We don't have as much luxury, but we don't need it. All of this has to make people weak."

"You may have a point," Amuba conceded. "But it's not long ago that we lived in tents and wandered for pasture. We haven't turned soft despite settling down and building towns. No one can deny that Egyptians are brave - even if they aren't as physically strong as us. Look around, Jethro. I bet they've never seen a race like ours with blue eyes and fair hair - even though there are many shades of darkness within their people. The nobles and upper classes are generally lighter than the common people."

The amazement of the Egyptians was incredible at the appearance of their captives, and the design of their walls has been passed on in works of art which still show the blue eyes and fair hair of the Rebu. The festivities upon the ruler's arrival lasted for a few days; the sovereign's order a. A few were given to the military officers who had most prominent themselves.

Numerous were delegated to the ministers, while most were sent to work on public projects.

The Rebu captives, whose fair skin tone and beauty made them stand out, were passed out among the king's particular favorites. Many girls were assigned to the queen and princesses, and some to the wives of the priests and generals who formed the king's council. The men were mostly given to the priests to assist in the temples.

Much to his joy, Amuba found that he and Jethro were two of the eight hostages chosen to work in the service of the priests at one of the grand temples. This was no coincidence, as the hostages were lined up, and the number assigned to each temple was chosen together, so that they would be distributed evenly between the temples. Since Jethro always stood close to Amuba, they ended up in the same place.

When the captives arrived at the temple, the high priest, Ameres, a serious and respectable man, inspected each of them. Then, he gestured for Amuba to move forward and declared, "From now on, you'll be my servant. If you act properly, you'll be treated well." He continued inspecting the line, and Amuba noticed that he would pick someone else, so he got down on his knees.

"May I beg your forgiveness for being so forward?" he questioned. "But, can I implore you to pick that man beside me? We have been friends since we were children, he protected me in battle, and he's been like a father to me since I lost mine. Please, my lord, don't split us up now. You'll find us both willing to do whatever task you give us."

The priest paid attention solemnly.

"It will be done as you ask," he replied. "It's every man's duty to make those around him happy if it's in his power, and as your friend is strong and hearty and has an honest face, he'll surely do as well as anyone else; therefore, you two follow me to my house."

The other captives respectfully saluted Amuba as he and Jethro prepared to leave. The priest noticed and asked the boy: "Were you an important person among your people who warranted such a respectful goodbye rather than your elder companion?"

"I am the son of the former king," Amuba answered. "He was killed in battle with your forces, and had it not been for the Egyptians capturing our city and overcoming our nation, I would have inherited the throne."

"Is it so?" the priest said. "Truly, the changes and fortunes of life are strange. I wonder that since you were their king's son, you were not specifically kept by Thotmes himself."

"I don't think he was aware of it," Amuba said. "We were not familiar with your customs, and my fellow captives thought that perhaps I might be executed if it became known that I was a son of their king, and so avoided showing any outward signs of respect, which, of course, would have been silly for someone in the same position as them."

"Perhaps it's for the best," the priest said thoughtfully. "We don't kill our captured prisoners; it may be easier for you to live in a priest's house than in the king's palace. But don't tell anyone about your previous rank, or you may be summoned to the court. Unless you'd rather be an observer of the court's splendor than a humble servant in a humble house."

"I would much rather stay with you, my lord," Amuba responded excitedly. "You have already demonstrated the kindness of your heart by granting my request and selecting my companion Jethro as my fellow slave. I already feel my circumstances will be much more fortunate than expected."

"Don't make quick judgments based on appearances," the priest said. "At the same time, here in Egypt, slaves aren't treated as in the wild places of Nubia and the desert. Everyone is subject to the law, and anyone who kills a slave is punished as if they killed an Egyptian. But I can say that your life won't be hard; you're intelligent, as evidenced by how quickly you've picked up enough of our language to speak it fluently. Can you speak it too?" he asked Jethro.

"I can manage a few words," Jethro declared, "but not nearly as fluently as Amuba. My age makes it difficult for me to learn a new language as quickly as he can."

"You speak well enough to comprehend," the priest said, "and you'll master our language eventually. This is my home."

The priest went through an awe-inspiring gateway with tall walls on either side. Fifty yards away was a large estate, much grander than the royal abode in which Amuba had grown up. Inside the walls was a garden of around three hundred yards square, with avenues of fruit trees, a vineyard, and a vegetable garden, separated by an avenue of palm trees.

Ahead of the house was a large body of water, with a brightly painted boat drifting in it and aquatic plants of every type framing its edges. Graceful palms spread their foliage over it, flat lily leaves gliding on the surface, and the white blossoms of the lotus - which Amuba had seen carried in religious processions and by many of the upper class - rising above them. The two captives were amazed and awed by the beauty of the view, momentarily forgetting their status as slaves as they looked around them at a greenery more beautiful than they'd ever seen. A smile spread across the priest's face.

"No man has perfect happiness," he said, "yet I think you might learn contentment here."

CHAPTER IV

An Easy Servitude

Just as the priest got done speaking, a boy about the same age as Amuba appeared at the front of the house and ran down to his father.

"Father!" he exclaimed, "you brought two of the captives home? We saw them in the procession and were amazed at their hair and eye color. Mysa and I especially noticed this boy's hair is almost like gold."

"As usual, Chebron, you speak faster than you think. This young man understands enough Egyptian to know what you are saying, and it's rude to talk that way, especially in front of him."

The boy blushed.

"I'm sorry, " he said to Amuba kindly, "I didn't think that since you had just arrived, you would be able to understand any of our language."

"Don't apologize," replied Amuba, smiling. "It makes sense that our appearance is strange to you, and even compared to the people of Lydia and Persia, we have fair hair and eyes. I appreciate that you even regret saying anything; people don't usually think that their captives have any feelings."

"Chebron was correct to apologize," his father declared. "In our culture, politeness is essential, and every Egyptian is taught to be respectful to those around them. It is much simpler to be polite than rude, and people respond far better to kindness than intimidation."

"Are they going to stay here, father," Chebron asked, "or have you just brought them for today?"

"They are to remain here, my son. I selected them from those set aside for our temple. I chose the younger because he was about your age; it is beneficial for a man to be surrounded by someone who has been raised with him and is attached to him, although their station in life may not be the same. I hope you find Amuba, as he tells me in his name, to be a friend and companion. I must say that circumstances are everything. This young man, in his own country, held a higher position than you here, for he was the king's son, and, since his father fell in battle, he would currently be the king of his people had they not been subjugated to us. Therefore, Chebron, always remember that, although misfortune has put him as a captive among us, he is your superior in birth, and treat him as you would want to be treated if you were to be a captive of a hostile nation."

"I'll be more than happy to count you as a friend," the young Egyptian said sincerely to Amuba. "Though we're from different backgrounds, I can see you're loyal and honest just by looking at you. What's more, my father wouldn't have asked me to trust you so much if he hadn't been confident that you'd be a good friend to me."

"You and your father are both a gift to me," Amuba responded. "I know how hard the life of war captives can be since we Rebu had many slaves we took during different campaigns, so I was prepared for anything. So you can imagine how thankful I am to the gods for putting me in different hands than I had expected, and I promise you, Chebron, that I will be loyal and devoted to you. The same goes for my friend here, who can assist you much better than I could if you ever need help. He was one of our fiercest warriors. He drove my chariot during the battle we had with your people and saved my life multiple times, and if you ever need a strong and brave man, Jethro will be able to aid you."

"And you have been in a battle?" Chebron asked in surprise.

"That was the first time I had ever engaged in combat with other men," Amuba said, "but I had often hunted lions, which are almost as fearsome opponents as your troops. I was young to join the fight, but my father was determined to get me to join our nation's warriors as soon as possible."

"By the way, Chebron," Ameres said, "I must caution you not to disclose the position Amuba held in his native land. He could be removed from us to serve at the palace if revealed. His fellow captives, who were taken with him, refused to say anything about his rank for fear that harm would befall him if it were known, and hence it was assumed that he was of the same standing as the other captives, all of whom were of noble birth among the Rebu. So, keep this to yourself, not even telling your mother or your sister Mysa. The fewer people who know it, the better it will be kept safe."

As they talked, Amuba looked closer at the young man who had promised to be his friend.

Like his father, he was much fairer in complexion than most Egyptians, with a lighter color of the upper class. However, at a much shorter and slighter stature than Rebu, he carried himself regally and had the distinctive calm and nobility of Egyptians born to high rank. One difference was that he had his head shaved Egyptian style, with a single lock of hair falling over his left ear. Amuba later found out that this indicated a young man, and it would be shaved off when he reached adulthood, married, or entered a profession.

At present, his head was bald, but when he went out, he wore a close-fitting cap that held in a lock of his hair that hung down to his shoulder. He had yet to adopt the common practice of wearing a wig that was popular among the upper and middle classes. Initially, the baldness was strange for Amuba, but he eventually became accustomed to it. The Egyptians likely adopted the custom of shaving their heads for coolness and cleanliness. However, to Amuba, keeping his natural hair free from dust was much easier than attempting to manage the complicated wigs the Egyptians wore. The priest now led them into the house. They entered a large hall with walls covered with marble and colorful stones and a floor paved with the same material. A fountain played in the middle of the room and threw its water up high. The hall was open to the sky, with majestic columns running along its sides and a colorful pattern painted on the ceiling. A lady was seated on a long couch with no back but one end raised and carved into the shape of an animal head. Around the room were seats of all kinds and large pots filled with palms and other plants of graceful foliage. It was an opulent and awe-inspiring sight. It left them with a feeling of grandeur and elegance.

The priest ushered them inside the house. As they passed through the entrance, they stepped into a grand hall. A line of solid columns ran along its side, holding up the ceiling, which extended twelve feet from each wall. The walls were decorated with marble and various other stones; the floor was tiled with the same material; a fountain stood in the middle and sprayed water high into the air since the area between the columns was open to the sky. Various types of seats were scattered around the room, and large pots contained palms and other plants with graceful foliage. The ceiling was painted with a vibrant pattern of colors. A lady sat on a long couch with no back, but one end was raised to support the arm, and the ends were carved into animal heads.

Two Nubian slave girls stood behind her, fanning her, and a girl about twelve years old was seated on a low stool studying from a roll of papyrus. She threw it down and jumped to her feet as her father entered, and the lady rose with a languid air as if the effort of even so slight a movement was a trouble to her.

"Oh, Father…" the girl began, but her father stopped her with a wave of his hand.

"My love," he said to his wife, "I have brought home two of the captives our great king has taken as a sign of his victory. He has given many to us and the temples, and these two have been given to me. They were of high rank in their homeland, and we'll do our best to make them forget the unfortunate transformation of their status."

"Your ideas are always so eccentric, Ameres," the lady said more irritably than her lazy mannerisms would suggest. "They're prisoners; I don't think it matters what they were before as long as they're prisoners now. So do whatever you want with them; just don't put them close to me; the contrast between their bright hair, eyes, and pale skin makes me shudder."

"Oh, Mother, I think their hair is wonderful," Mysa exclaimed. "I wish my hair was golden like that boy's instead of black like everyone else."

The priest shook his head at his daughter in disapproval, but she wasn't embarrassed because she was her father's favorite and knew full well that he was never distraught with her.

"I'm not suggesting you have them close to you, Amense," he replied calmly to his wife. "It appears you have more assistants around you than you can use. The young man I have assigned to Chebron; as to the other, I haven't decided what his obligations will be."

"Can't you give him to me, Father?" Mysa pled sweetly. "Fatina is not fun at all, and Dolma, the Nubian girl, can only look pleasant and display her pearly whites, but since we don't understand each other, I don't see how she's of any help to me."

"What would you do with this tall Rebu?" the priest asked her.

"I don't know yet," she said as she examined Jethro, "but I like his looks, and he looks like he can do all sorts of things. He looks like a good guard when I go out; he could row in my boat and help me care for my pets."

"You mean when you're too lazy to feel them yourself. Very well, Mysa, we'll try this experiment. Jethro will be your servant, and when you don't have anything for him to do (which will probably be a lot of the day), he can take care of the waterfowl. Zumbro never takes care of them properly. Do you understand that?" he asked Jethro.

Jethro responded by coming forward, taking Mysa's hand, and bowing until his forehead touched her hand.

"There is your answer, Mysa."

"You're too lenient with the children, Ameres," his wife stated with annoyance. "I don't think there are children as spoiled anywhere in Egypt as much as ours. Other men's sons never speak unless asked a question and never even think of sitting in the presence of their father. I'm surprised that you, considered one of the wisest men in Egypt, allow your children to be comfortable around you."

"Perhaps, my love," Ameres said with a slight grin, "it's because I am one of the wisest men in Egypt. My children honor me in their hearts as much as those forced to obey many rules. How will a child's brain grow if he doesn't pose inquiries, and who should be so well-prepared to answer his inquiries as his father? So there, children, you can leave. Bring your new friends to the garden and your animals."

"We're fortunate, Jethro," Amuba said as they followed Chebron and Mysa into the garden. "When we imagined our lives before we arrived here, we never thought it would be anything like this. We expected to be toiling the land, helping to build dams and embankments, and quarrying stones for public buildings. Instead, we all wanted to work together and see how generous the gods have been to us! Instead, we've found friends in our masters and a home in this strange land."

"This is wonderful, Amuba. This priest is excellent and seems to be loved by everyone near him. We are so fortunate to be chosen by him."

The brother and sister led them through the avenue of fruit trees, and at the end, there was a gate that went through an area surrounded by trees and shrubs. There were several wooden structures in the shade. The third area had a pool in the center, and like the large pond they had seen before, there was a house surrounded by wooden structures. At the pond's edge stood two ibises, and at the same time, many beautiful birds were swimming or cleaning their feathers on the bank.

As soon as the gate closed, the waterfowl threw a considerable commotion. The ibises walked gracefully to meet Mysa, the ducks quacked loudly, and those on the water came to shore. But the first to approach the group were two gazelles from one of the huts. They pushed their soft noses into Chebron and Mysa's hands. The other huts also had a chorus of sounds like the dogs barking.

"It's not food time, you know," Chebron said, looking at the gazelles, "and I know you're not used to us coming empty-handed. We will give you something anyhow. See, Jethro, this is their food pantry," and he led the way into a building that was larger than the rest, full of large boxes and bins. He pulled out one of the bins, took a handful of fresh grain, and put it in front of the gazelles. "This is their special food," he told Jethro, "collected from our farm six miles away every morning. The container next to it holds the seeds for the waterfowl. Wheat, peas, pulse, and other seeds are mixed here. Mysa, why don't you give them a few handfuls; their clamor is so loud I can hardly hear myself think!"

"In this box, you can see a pan of soggy bread for the cats. It's mixed with water, but just a bit, for it won't last long. Those cakes are for them as well. The large, plain, hard-baked cakes in the following box are for the dogs; they get some meat and bones a couple of times a week. The frogs and toads in the cage are for the crocodile; he has an entire tank. All the other boxes contain different kinds of food for the other animals. Each box has a picture of the appropriate creature so you won't make a mistake. We usually feed them three times a day when we're here, but it's up to you when we're away.

"Please," Mysa said, "above all things, ensure they all have access to fresh water; they love it so much, and sometimes it gets so hot that the pans are dry within an hour. The gazelles can go to the pond to drink when thirsty, but the other animals must remain confined since they don't get along as they should. We let them out for a while when we're here. The dogs are always scaring the waterfowl, and the cats will take the ducklings, even when there's plenty of food; and the ichneumon will fight with the snakes if we let him into their house. They can be troublesome, but they're all so good with us. The houses need to be cleaned and made nice each morning."

Chebron and Mysa led the party from house to house, introducing them to the animals all lovingly cared for. The Nubian hunting dogs were particularly impressive. The real stars were the three large cats dozing contentedly on their cushioned beds, who rose to greet their visitors with affectionate rubs and loud purring. A group of playful kittens added to the scene, mewing in excitement. Amuba noticed that Chebron and Mysa showed respect to each animal they encountered – the dogs, the ichneumon, and the crocodile – a reminder of their importance to the people of Thebes.

Mysa gave many specifics about the special care each of her animals needed to Jethro, and when they had finished their duties, they took a stroll through the garden. Amuba and Jethro were taken aback by the immense array of plants grown from seeds and roots brought from all the places the Egyptian army had conquered.

Amuba had a pleasant and peaceful time in the priest's household for an entire year. His and Jethro's work was not demanding. When Amuba and Chebron went for a walk or a trip, they left their social class behind. Amuba learned how to row a boat on the Nile when they went out fishing. However, when they were in Thebes, it was difficult to disregard their distinctions in class, as Chebron could not take Amuba with him to the homes of his father's many friends and relatives among the priests and military. When the priest and his family went out to a gathering, Jethro and Amuba were always part of the group of attendants who escorted them home with torches. Jethro and Amuba's job was easy, but others did not have an easy task as they did because the Egyptians often drank heavily at these gatherings, and many slaves had to carry their masters on light couches. Drunkenness was common among the ladies who usually ate separately from the men at these events.

When Amuba was at home, he was often present when Chebron was studying. He was very eager to learn as much of the knowledge of the Egyptians as he could, so Chebron taught him the hieroglyphic characters. Soon enough, he could read the inscriptions in the temples and other public buildings and explore the papyrus scrolls stored in one of the largest rooms in the house.

Once Chebron's studies were complete, Jethro educated him on using weapons, and Amuba was his practice partner. A tutor specializing in archery was a frequent visitor to the house — all Egyptians, regardless of class, were experts at their nation's signature weapon — and the Rebu captives, who were already proficient in the bow as part of their own culture, picked up a few tips by observing the instructor's lessons to Chebron on using the longer, more powerful bow favored by the Egyptians. In addition, whenever Mysa ventured out of the house, Jethro was right behind her, waiting outside the dwelling she entered or returning to pick her up if her stay was prolonged.

The family loved visiting their farm and watching the fields' cultivation and the grapes' conversion into wine. To extract the juice, the grapes were piled in a large vat, ropes were suspended above it, and a dozen barefooted slaves entered and pressed out the grapes by using the ropes to lift themselves and drop back with more force onto the fruit. Chebron had told Amuba that while he was going to join the priesthood as a requirement for his career, he was not intended to become a priest but instead have a role in the state.

"My older brother is the most likely candidate to succeed my father as the high priest of Osiris. My father may not think he's particularly clever, but it isn't necessary to be exceptionally intelligent to serve in the temple. I had assumed I'd also reach a high rank in the priesthood; after all, most positions are typically passed down from generation to generation. But I have no interest in it and was overjoyed when my father told me that I didn't have to pursue priesthood and that there were other ways I could serve my country and its citizens. Members of priestly families tend to fill almost all government positions, from provincial governors to military generals."

"'Some are born to minister in temples, and it is certainly

a great honor and privilege,' he said. 'But for others, a more active life and a bigger purpose are better. We need engineers for canals and irrigation systems, judges to enforce laws, diplomats to handle foreign relations, and governors for the many peoples we rule. So, my son, if you don't feel a strong inclination to serve in the temple, by all means, pursue studies that will prepare you for a government position. I can easily get you a posting from the king, where you can start and if you prove yourself, rise to higher positions.'"

During the reign of Thotmes III, Ameres was held in high esteem by the Egyptian people. He was a man of deep piety and learning, a revered high priest in the temple of Osiris, and a trusted counselor to the king. He deeply understood the sacred laws and the innermost mysteries of the faith. Ameres was blessed with great wealth, which he used to live a luxurious lifestyle that fit his status - but he was generous with his resources, using most of his riches to help those in need.

If the Nile rose higher than usual and spread ruin among farmers, Ameres stood by to help the suffering. But, on the other hand, if the river's rise was insufficient, he always led by example, reducing the tenants' rents of his vast lands and offering to lend money without interest to tenants of more stringent landlords.

Yet among the high priesthood, Ameres was viewed with doubt and even animosity. Rumors circulated that, even though he was learned and devout, Ameres had beliefs different from those of the other priests. He completed his duties and participated in the rituals and parades, but he seemed to have a different kind of reverence. His views were said to be at odds with most of his peers.

Ameres was the type of person who wouldn't accept the ideas and beliefs of other people, and he always had to use his judgment on every issue presented to him. His father, who had been a high priest earlier – as most significant roles in Egypt were passed down in the family – was both glad to see his son's enthusiasm for gaining knowledge and studying yet was often taken aback by the openness with which he made his opinion known as he was gradually brought into the sacred mysteries.

From the start of his priesthood, Ameres had already mastered geometry, astronomy, and architecture. Not only that, but he had overseen the construction of canals and irrigation works on temple grounds. His father was proud of his achievements and the respect Ameres had earned from his peers. But the liberal stance Ameres took on religious matters was a cause for concern for his father.

The Egyptians were highly traditional in their ways. Nothing changed in their constitution, customs, and habits for thousands of years. It was deeply ingrained in every Egyptian that their country was far superior to any other and that their laws and customs were nearly perfect. Everyone, from the highest to the lowest, was bound by the same rules. Even the king was not exempt; the time he rose, how he spent his day, and the quantity and quality of food he ate were all predetermined by custom. He was always surrounded by young men his age—sons of priests who were chosen for their virtue and holiness.

Ameres was free from the influence of bad advisors, and even if he wanted to, he didn't have the means or power to oppress his people, whose rights and privileges were protected. In a country where everyone followed in their father's footsteps, it was a surprise that Ameres, the son of the high priest of Osiris and heir to the same position, had different opinions than the priesthood leaders. Yet, his piety, benevolence, intelligence, and scientific knowledge enabled him to take office without resistance.

Even back then, the higher-ranking priests would have opposed Ameres' election. But he was so popular with the lower classes of the priesthood and the people at large that their votes outweighed those of his opponents. The crowd had never heard any criticism of the high priest of Osiris. They saw him leading the sacrifices and processions, and they knew he was tireless in his temple services and devoted his free time to acts of kindness and charity. As they bowed reverently when he passed them on the streets, they never guessed that the high priest of Osiris was seen by his colleagues as a dangerous innovator.

He was part of a religious order, but his views mainly differed on one subject. Through his knowledge of the more profound mysteries, he understood the true meaning behind the religion he served. He knew that Osiris, Isis, and the other gods the Egyptians worshiped were merely different aspects of one all-powerful deity - a God so vast and unknowable that it could only be comprehended when each element was given its own identity and worshipped separately.

Ameres and a select few were aware of the mysterious inner workings of the Egyptian religion. Though opinions varied, the rest of the population worshipped the animal-headed gods and their associated animals. In some parts of the kingdom, the crocodile was sacred; in others, it was seen as an enemy. Similarly, some worshipped the goat while others consumed it as food. Respect for animals varied from group to group, depending on the gods honored in that area.

Ameres believed that the knowledge given only to those in the know should be shared more widely, and, not wanting to share it with the uneducated rural and working classes just yet, he was willing to let all informed and intelligent people of Egypt understand the real gods they worshipped and the inner secrets of their faith. He realized it had to be done gradually and that slowly expanding the number of those initiated was essential. His thoughts were met with fear and shock by his peers. They argued that if others besides the higher clergy were to become aware of the profound secrets of their religion, it would have terrible repercussions.

It would completely undermine the power and reverence held by the priesthood and reduce their influence. The temples would become deserted, and, without their belief in the gods, people would soon abandon religion altogether. "No other people on the planet are as moral, content, happy, and easily governed as the Egyptians," they argued, "But what would happen if you took away their faith and cast them into an ocean of doubts and questions? They would no longer have access to wisdom.

Ameres was silenced, though not convinced. He knew there was much truth in his colleagues' views and that the consequences of the people discovering they had been worshipping false gods for thousands of years would be catastrophic. The system had worked well up until now, and it couldn't be said that worshipping these imaginary gods had done any harm. Nevertheless, he was alone and had no power to do anything. Widening the initiated circle would need the higher priesthood's consent, so any action on his part would only bring disgrace and death. After voicing his opinion in a council of the higher initiates, he stayed quiet and returned to his everyday life.

Enlightened as he was, he felt he did no wrong in presiding over the sacrifices and taking part in the services of the gods. He was not worshiping the animal-headed idols but the qualities which they embodied. He pitied the unenlightened crowd who would place offerings on the altar, and yet he knew that it would break their joy instead of adding to it were they to discover that the deity they praised was fiction. So he permitted his wife and daughter to join with the priestesses in the service in the temple and in his heart, conceded that there was much in the statement of those who argued that the diffusion of the knowledge of the inner mysteries would not be beneficial to the joy of all who obtained it. In truth, he would have recoiled from agitating the minds of his wife and daughter by notifying them that all their devout ministrations in the temple were offered to nonexistent gods, that the holy animals they nurtured were not any more sacred than others, except that in them were recognized some hint of the attributes of the undiscovered God.

His eldest son was not one to be troubled by the difficulties that weighed on his father's mind. On the contrary, he would do well in his duties as priest and councilor to the monarch. He was level-headed but lacked imagination. Knowledge of the more profound mysteries was unlikely to disturb him, and he likely never questioned whether the deception of the people by the enlightened was anything but correct.

Ameres noticed that Chebron was structured in a completely different way. He was brilliant and had a burning passion for understanding all sorts of knowledge, but he also had his father's habit of looking at things from every angle and thinking for himself. The way Ameres had overseen his studies and taught him to use his mind and make sure each rule and command was valid before going on to the next had sharpened his thinking skills. All in all, Ameres saw that the questions that filled his mind about the fairness, or even practicality, of keeping everyone in the dark and wrong would likely be experienced more intensely by Chebron.

He had decided that his son should not work his way up through all levels of the priesthood but instead should gain enough knowledge and experience to be ready for a leadership role in one of the central government departments.

CHAPTER 5

In Lower Egypt

"I'm heading out on a trip soon," Ameres told his son a few days after returning from the farm. "I'd like you to come with me, Chebron, to check out the progress of the new canal built on our Goshen estate. The supervisor doubts whether it will work as intended when the floodgates open, and I'm afraid there may have been a miscalculation in the levels. I've already taught you the basics of this work; it would be good for you to get some practical experience. There's no more useful or honorable profession than engineering projects that help the Nile reach thirsty soil."

"Thank you, father, I want to go," Chebron replied with delight, for he had never been far south of Thebes. "And can Amuba go with us?"

"Yes, I was planning to take him," the high priest replied. "Jethro can come too. I usually take a small group with me. If it were up to me, I'd much rather travel without all the pomp and ceremony, but as a state official, I must adhere to the customs. And even in Goshen, it's always wise to travel with ceremony. The people there are from a different culture. Although they've lived there for a long time, they're notoriously stubborn, and it takes a lot more effort to get any public work done in that region."

"I have heard of them, father. They come from the same ethnic group as the shepherd kings, who were oppressive rulers in Egypt. What happened to them to make them stay here when the shepherds were expelled?"

"They are of the same race but were not part of the group that conquered this land and were never a part of the shepherds' armies. You may remember from your history studies that the shepherds from the region east of the Great Sea had been here for a while before these people arrived. They were related to Joseph, the chief minister of Egypt."

"He was a slave when he arrived here, coming from the same country our oppressors had. But it's said that he wasn't a part of their race and that his forefathers had come from a far eastern land. Nevertheless, he won the king's trust, became his minister, and ruled wisely, with the people having little to thank him for. During his rule, a devastating famine happened, and they say he had predicted it, and his gods had warned him. Large granaries were built and filled up to cope with this, and when the famine arrived and people were starving, the grain was distributed. In return, the people had to give up their land. This transformed the land tenure in the nation, and it all became the state's property, with the people staying as renters on the land they used to own. The state then granted large plots to temples and other military orders, and currently, all farmers have to pay rent to the king, temples, or the military order."

"In this way, the army can remain in peak condition, with tens of thousands of troops living in the cities assigned to them. This ensures that the royal treasury remains full and the rituals of the temples are maintained. Moreover, this measure increases the power and grandeur of the nation. Also, it benefits the farmers by allowing extensive irrigation projects to be undertaken - a feat that would not be possible if the land was owned by many small proprietors, each with narrow interests."

"But you said it doesn't do the people any good!"

"Especially in one respect, Chebron, for it created a large divide between the aristocratic classes and the bulk of the people who can never own land. Because of that, they don't push themselves forward."

"Father, they're just ignorant and nothing more."

"Chebron, I believe they could be something more in other situations. However, that's not the topic we're discussing. Joseph brought his family out of the east side of the Great Sea to Goshen, where they settled and flourished quickly. Thanks to Joseph's contribution to the state and their shared heritage, they were favored while the shepherd kings were in charge. When Egypt rose and expelled the shepherds, these people - who by then had increased a lot - stayed behind. Naturally, they were seen as suspicious because of their connection to our former oppressors situated to the east, which could be a gateway to a new invading army."

"With our far-reaching conquests, fear of Joseph's people has subsided. But unfortunately, prejudices are slow to dissipate among the general public. These people's tendency to stay together, marrying within their own and keeping to themselves, has unfortunately sustained this negative perception of them. In my opinion, this is unjustified. They are hardworking and driven, albeit they can be resistant to authority. Collecting the required number of workers from Goshen for public works is more challenging than from any other region of Egypt."

"Do they look different from us, father?"

"Chebron, they're substantially fairer than us, have a more defined nose, and are much stronger. They don't shave their heads as we do and often let their facial hair grow. After settling down, they practiced their religion but eventually adopted ours."

"That can't be right," Chebron exclaimed. "Every country has its gods, so if a population turns away from their gods, it's unlikely that other gods would look after them as they do for their own people."

"It's a tricky question, Chebron, and one you're probably better off not tackling right now. Soon, you'll join the lower levels of the clergy, and even if you don't rise to the higher levels, where you'd get to know the more profound secrets, you'll still gain enough knowledge to give you an idea of the situation."

Chebron was respectful enough not to press his parent with more questions, but he brought up the topic again while taking a leisurely walk with Amuba in the garden afterward.

"I wonder how each nation found how which gods were the ones that cared specifically for them, Amuba?"

"I have no idea," replied Amuba, who'd never even thought about that subject. "You are always asking strange questions, Chebron."

"But there must be some explanation," Chebron insisted. "Do people know what the gods look like? Are some gods more powerful than others? Why do people offer sacrifices and ask for their help before battle? Why do some win and some lose? Do the gods change in power on different days? And why don't the gods protect their temples and images? It's all so confusing."

"It's all quite odd, Chebron. I was recently asking Jethro a similar query, but he was unable to provide me with a response. Have you thought about asking your father? He's one of the most knowledgeable Egyptians."

"I questioned my father, but he refused to answer me," Chebron said, pondering the situation. "I suspect he's trying to prevent me from becoming a high priest because of my curiosity. I didn't mean any disrespect to the gods. However, when I inquire, and he doesn't answer me, I can tell he's regretful that he can't answer my questions."

"Have you ever asked your brother Neco?"

"Oh, Neco is different," Chebron said scornfully. "He tends to get very passionate and makes all sorts of threats, but I can tell he's just as lost as I am because whenever I ask him, he looks confused. He even put his hands over his ears on more than one occasion and ran off as if I had said something blasphemous against the gods."

The high priest and their group set out for Goshen the following day. They used a large boat with a wood pavilion and two masts bearing sails of many colors to begin their travels.

Influential individuals often had two or three musicians playing harps, trumpets, or pipes. Egyptians were passionate about music; no celebration was considered complete without music. Consequently, their instruments were varied and included stringed instruments ranging from tiny zither-like instruments to large harps, trumpets of many shapes, reed instruments, cymbals, and long and narrow drums.

Ameres, however, while not against music after supper, was too practical to care for at other times. He thought it was too often an excuse for not doing anything, so he only enjoyed it on special occasions. As they sailed down the river, he explained to his son the various things they passed; he described how the fishermen in their high boats made of wooden boards held together by rushes or in smaller crafts shaped like punts constructed entirely of papyrus tied together with bands of the same plant, caught the fish; showed him the entrances to the various canals, and explained the working of the gates which let in the water; gave him the history of the multiple temples, towns, and villages; named the many waterfowl sunbathing on the river, and told him of their customs and how the fowlers hunted them; he pointed out the giant tombs to him, and told him who had built them.

"The most significant monuments are a reminder of the age-old struggle for power and immortality. One such example is the pyramids, built by an ambitious king who wanted to be remembered for eternity. But unfortunately, the people suffered terribly during its construction. It was so bad that when the king eventually died, the people were asked if he ruled them well. If the answer was yes, he was buried in the mausoleum he had built for himself; however, if the answer was no, then the mausoleum stood empty, and the king was denied his rightful burial. This ancient practice demonstrates how powerful the people's voice can be, even after the death of a king.

"Most of our rulers do not deserve the hatred of their people since they are carefully educated by youths chosen for their holiness and academic prowess, and they must obey the laws of the land just like any of their subjects. This understanding that their actions will be judged by the people even after death keeps them from being too reckless."

"I want to see the pyramids,' Chebron said. "Are they made of brick or stone? I have been told that their surface is so smooth and shiny they look as though they're cut out of a single stone."

"They're made of huge blocks and stone, each of which took hundreds of men to carry from the stone quarries after they were cut."

"Was it the slaves or the citizens that did the work?"

"Many slaves captured in warfare were utilized to construct these pyramids," the priest answered. "But, despite their numbers, they were insufficient for the project. Nearly half of the population of Egypt had to leave their homes to contribute to the effort. The people were so overburdened and distressed that even today, those who built the pyramids are not spoken of without curses, and rightfully so. Just think, the same labor could have been put to better use. Imagine the number of canals that could have been built and the soil fertility improved. Enormous tracts of land could have been recovered from the swamps and shallow lakes, and the land output could have been doubled."

"And they might have made splendid temples!" Chebron said enthusiastically.

"Without a doubt, my son," the priest said, pausing momentarily. "The gods should have temples worthy of them, of course. But we also believe that the gods love Egypt and want to see the people prosper. So, I think they'd be more pleased if we could improve the people's condition through ambitious projects rather than just building long avenues of sphinxes and lavish temples for their honor."

"Yes, it would seem so," Chebron remarked thoughtfully. "Yet, Father, we are always taught that it's our highest obligation to revere the gods and that there's no better way to spend money than constructing new temples and enhancing the magnificence of the ones that already exist."

"Respecting the gods is our foremost obligation, Chebron; however, understanding how to carry out that respect is a more complex inquiry beyond your years. You can contemplate it when you're older. See that temple over there on the right bank of the river? We'll stay there for the night. My messenger will arrange everything for our arrival, and everything will be ready."

As they made their way to the temple, they saw a large group of people on the giant stone steps leading to the water's edge and heard music. When they arrived, the priests welcomed Ameres with great respect, and all bowed before him, while those of lower status knelt and didn't look up until he had gone past. As soon as he entered the temple, a procession was formed. Priests carrying holy vessels and symbols of the gods went first, followed by the sound of unseen musicians playing a ceremonial song. Priestesses and maidens, who also had offerings and emblems, followed after Ameres. He naturally took the lead role in the sacrifice at the altar, killing the animal and presenting the parts meant for the gods.

After the ceremonies were completed, the procession moved along in an orderly fashion to the residence of the chief priest. All the attendees greeted Ameres, whom his son and attendants then followed. A festive banquet was prepared, and Ameres took his seat along with the other principal priests. Chebron was then taken to the room prepared for him, where food from the high table was served. Amuba and the remaining high priest's entourage were served in another room. After Chebron had finished his meal, he joined Amuba.

"Let's leave," he said. "The feast will last hours, and music will play all night. My father hates these lavish meals; he prefers plain food and thinks the priests should too. But, since it's not polite for a guest to complain about the food served, he'll have to suffer through it. He's said it's one of the worst parts of his job; everywhere people think they need to throw a feast for him everywhere he goes. He'd rather have a bowl of boiled lentils and water than the most expensive dishes."

"Will it be like this the whole trip?" Amuba asked.

"Oh, no! I'm aware that while traveling down the river, we must take a break at a temple, or else the priests would consider it an insult; afterward, we'll get off the boat and go on chariots or carts. When we get to Goshen, we'll live in a small house my father had built for himself, and we won't have to deal with any ceremonies as we do at our farm. He'll be busy with the duties of his estate and the irrigation projects; yet, even though we'll be accompanying him on his trips, as I'm starting to learn the tasks of a superintendent, I'm sure we'll have plenty of time for entertainment and fun."

They took a leisurely walk along the riverbank, basking in the full moon's light and admiring the boats going up and down the stream. While poles propelled some, others were towed by men on the bank. When they returned to the house, they stopped to listen to the music before turning in for the night. Amuba lay on a comfortable couch made of bulrushes and thick woolen cloth, with a pillow filled with bulrushes that Jethro had put together for him. Unfortunately, neither Rebu had adopted the Egyptian tradition of using a stool as a pillow.

These stools were elongated and slightly curved to fit the neck. For ordinary people, they were roughly made of wood, which was sanded down where the head lay. However, the head-stools of the well-off were crafted from rare materials like ebony and cedar and exquisitely decorated with ivory inlays. Amuba had tried to sleep on one of these head-stools a few times, but his neck usually started to ache within half an hour, so he usually reverted to his regular pillow of rushes. To sleep on the stool pillows, one had to lie on the side with an arm propping the head up to the exact height of the stool. Since Amuba was accustomed to flinging himself onto the bed and conking out in any position, the rigid posture needed for sleeping on a hard stool was utterly intolerable.

The journey down the river continued for a week, and then they arrived at Memphis, where they remained for some days. Ameres passed the time in ceremonial visits and performing sacrifices in the temple. Chebron and Amuba visited all the temples and public buildings and one day went out to inspect the great pyramids attended by Jethro.

"This is greater than anything I have ever seen," Jethro said as they stood at the foot of the great pyramid of Cheops. "What a fantastic structure, but a huge waste of human labor!"

"That's incredible," Amuba exclaimed. "What wealth and power must a monarch have had to construct such a gigantic structure! You mentioned, Chebron, that laws restricted your kings like everyone else. If that's true, how could this ruler have demanded such massive labor and effort from his subjects for this project?"

"Rulers should be held accountable to the law," said Chebron, "but some are so powerful and arrogant that they lord over the people. Cheops oppressed the people to build this grand tomb for himself. But he got his comeuppance, for at his funeral, he was judged by the court of public opinion, and the people judged him as a bad and oppressive ruler. Consequently, he was not allowed to be buried in the lavish tomb he had built for himself. I do not know where his remains lie. Still, this grand pyramid is a permanent reminder of the futility of human ambition—the most expensive tomb in the world, but without an occupant, save that Theliene, one of his queens, was buried here in a chamber next to the one meant for the king."

"The people did well," Jethro said enthusiastically, "but it would have been better if they had gone against him in the beginning when they understood the magnitude of the task he was going to have them do."

As the group left Memphis, they continued the journey by boat. The following day, they started again on land. Ameres traveled in a chariot similar to a war chariot but had higher sides to provide a deep open box to lean against. Amuba and Chebron rode in a wagon pulled by two oxen while the rest of the party walked. They took in the countryside's beautiful sights, sounds, and smells along the way

After two days, they arrived at their destination. The house was small compared to the grand mansion near Thebes but shared the same design. A tall wall surrounded a quarter-acre area. The house had one main room for general activities in the middle and two small bedrooms on either side. The garden, although limited in size, was meticulously maintained. Rows of fruit trees gave off a pleasant shade. A tiny pond was in front of the house with lilies and rushes. A Nubian slave and his wife kept everything ready for the owner's arrival. As a cook and a barber were part of Ameres' entourage, a large staff of servants was not required. Instead, the estate's supervisor was in place to greet the high priest.

"I have brought my son with me," Ameres declared when the ceremonies and greetings were complete. He is going to begin his lessons in irrigation. However, I won't have enough time to teach him right now. I'd like him to become proficient in outdoor activities, so I ask you to get specialists in fishing, hunting, and fowling so that he can fill his free time with sport. In Thebes, he doesn't have many of these activities, except in the reserves, wildlife is nearly extinct, and there's no fowling available in Upper Egypt, while here in the swamps, there are plenty of birds."

The superintendent promised that suitable men would be available for the job, one for each profession. In Egypt, people usually followed the same job as their fathers, and the same trade was passed down along family lines. Therefore, people only married those within their profession and rarely considered switching to something different. This meant that the fowler would not know how to catch fish, and the fishermen would not be familiar with fowling. However, they both had some knowledge of hunting, as it was necessary to protect their village from hyenas, hippopotami, and other animals that threatened their crops.

The countryside where they traveled at the moment was good farming land watered by canals, which filled up when the Nile was high.

A day's journey to the north sat Lake Menzaleh—a massive

shallow lagoon that stretched to the Great Sea, divided by just a narrow bank of sand. If the Nile rose higher than usual, threatening to flood the land, great gates at the end of the canals would open, allowing the water to flow into the lagoon. Some of the lower arms of the Nile are also connected to the lake, making the salt water slightly less salty than the sea. The lake was teeming with waterfowl and fish, making it a sight to behold.

These lakes stretched along the entire northern coast of Egypt, providing an abundant source of fish and fowl for the Egyptians. Further southeast was another string of lakes, with saltier water than the sea. Legends tell of a time when these lakes were connected to both the Great Sea to the north and the Southern Sea, and even now, when the south wind is strong, the salt water from the Southern Sea is driven up into Lake Timsah - aptly named for the number of crocodiles it holds.

"I will be busy for a few days, to begin," Ameres said to his son on the evening of their arrival, "giving you a great chance to explore the different kinds of sport available in this part of Egypt. The steward will provide you with people, and you can take Amuba and Jethro with you. He will ensure that there are slaves to bring supplies and tents since much of your sport will require you to rise early, and you may even have to sleep nearby."

Chebron talked with the steward in the morning, who told him he had a plan for their adventure.

"My lord, there is not much to be found here beyond what you can find in Thebes. However, venture northward for a day's journey, and you will be at the lake's edge. You can do whatever you want - fish, trap waterfowl, hunt hippopotami in the wetlands, or pursue hyenas in the bush on the dunes. I have made the necessary preparations, and in an hour, the slaves with the provisions will be ready to set off. Unfortunately, the local hunters are useless to you, so I have asked one of my top aides to accompany you."

"When you get here, you'll find the best men for the job, familiar with the terrain and wildlife. Your father said you'd be away for about a week, but you'll have some days for hunting here and there. He thought you should start this adventure since you'll be busy afterward."

Roughly an hour later, approximately twenty slaves arrived at the house, hauling supplies, tents, and other necessities on their heads. A horse was available to Chebron, but he opted to walk with Amuba. "There's no benefit to riding a horse," he said, "when you have to move as slow as the foot soldiers, and we may even find something to hunt along the way."

Upon hearing Chebron's decision, the head of the troop told him that game would be found when they exited the prepared nation, which reached out just a few miles further north. Six canines went with them. Four were incredible creatures, kept for pursuing the more threatening animals, such as the hyena or lion. Although there were no lions in that area, they overflowed in the complex grounds at the base of the slopes to the south. The other two were more delicately worked and fit to run down a deer. Canines were held in high respect in Egypt. In some parts of the country, they were born to be sacred. The season was chilly, and the warmth was less than they were used to at Thebes. In Thebes, the slopes around the city cut off a great deal of air and appeared to reflect the sun's beams down upon it. This made the walk agreeable.

Chebron and Amuba strode ahead, chatting merrily as they carried their bows. Jethro and Rabah, the foreman, came next, followed by two slaves with their dogs on leashes. The carriers trailed behind, and as they moved along, they passed through villages where the women peered out of their doorways to glimpse the strangers. Often, they were greeted with offerings of milk and fruit. The men were usually out in the fields, doing their daily tasks.

"They are sturdy looking. Strong and bonier than our people," Chebron remarked to the group's leader.

"They are hard to manage," he said. "They cultivate the land well and pay their share of the harvest without complaint, but if you ask them to do some extra work, there's sure to be trouble. It's much simpler to handle a thousand Egyptian peasants than a hundred of these Israelites, and if compulsory labor is needed for public works, you have to send in the troops before you can get it done."

"But they have not been treated fairly and have endured a lot. During the rule of Usertuen I, they arrived in Egypt and were allocated land. During the rule of the king and the following Pharaohs, they were favored, and their population grew immensely. But when the Theban dynasty replaced the one from Memphis, the kings felt threatened by the presence of these foreign people. As a result, they viewed them with hostility and treated them like prisoners of war instead of as a part of the population. In addition, they were forced to bear an unfair amount of work for public projects, such as making bricks and constructing royal tombs and pyramids," the leader replied.

"Isn't it strange that they don't shave their heads like us?" Chebron asked.

"Well, I don't," Amuba laughed, "or Jethro either."

"You're different," Chebron replied. "You don't work with the soil and get dirt in your hair. And you do keep it short. But I think you'd be more comfortable cutting it our way."

"It's all a matter of routine," Amuba replied. "To us, when we first arrived here, the sight of all the poor people with their heads shaved was quite unpleasant—and as far as comfort is concerned, surely one's hair must be more comfortable than the large wigs that all people of a higher class wear."

"They protect from the sun," Chebron said, "when you're outside, and they're rarely worn inside, and then when you come in, you can rinse off the dirt."

"I can get the dirt out of my hair," Amuba said. "Still, I think these Israelites have their hair way too long; the long braids their women wear down their back look graceful, and the women themselves are beautiful."

Chebron shook his head. "They may be beautiful, Amuba, but I'd think they would make difficult wives. They don't have the subdued and obedient look of our women. I'd say they'd have their own thoughts and aren't obedient to their husbands; is that correct, Rabah?"

"The women have just as much spirit and fire as the men," the foreman said. "They certainly have a say in all domestic matters and know how to use their voices when needed. For example, when soldiers came to collect gangs of men for public works, they often had more trouble with women than men. The men knew they had to submit, but the women would gather a little away and scream curses and abuse at the troops, sometimes even throwing stones. The soldiers wouldn't raise their weapons against them, but sometimes taking a few women's leaders to prison was necessary to prevent chaos."

"I thought they were aggressive," Chebron said with a laugh. "I would rather hunt a lion than fight one of those women who set out for me."

In a few miles, cultivated farms became scarce; sand dunes replaced the level fields, and only a few spots in the valleys had developed patches. Rabah commanded the slave leading the two quick dogs to stay near and be ready. "We could spot deer any time now," he said. "They thrive in these sandy wastelands which provide them a refuge, and yet, they can access fields with vegetation and food when the resources here are insufficient." A few minutes later, a deer emerged from a shrubbery. The dogs were immediately released and began their pursuit.

"Hurry on a hundred yards and take your spot on that hill!" Rabah shouted to Chebron, and at the same time, he gestured to the slaves behind him to stop. "The dogs understand their jobs, and you'll soon see them pushing the deer into range."

Chebron asked Amuba to accompany him, and they ran forward. The deer was far away when they reached the mound, and the dogs struggled to catch up. It seemed they weren't progressing much, and soon everything was out of sight among the sandhills. Despite Rabah's assurance, the young men were doubtful that the dogs would be able to drive the animal back to where they were standing, and it took a full fifteen minutes before the hunters and their prey came back into view. The pace had slowed significantly, with one of the dogs lagging about twenty yards behind the stag and the other circling around it about the same distance away, obviously trying to direct it toward the spot where the boys were waiting.

"Let's take the shot together," Chebron said. "The stag will be within fifty yards of us." The two hunters waited for the perfect moment as the stag ran toward them. The dog had fallen back to the side, leaving the stag undisturbed by their arrows. As the stag approached, they fired their arrows simultaneously. However, it was moving faster than they had anticipated, and the arrows soared behind it. They let out disappointed sighs, but before the deer could run twenty yards, Jethro had crept up and was ready in the bushes at the left of the clump. His arrow shot perfectly, and the stag fell over.

"Well done, Jethro!" Amuba shouted. "It's been so long since I've been hunting. I may have lost the talent, but you haven't!"

The dogs stood quietly next to the deer on the ground because they were too well-trained to interfere with it. Jethro ran over and slit its throat. It was a smaller animal than they were used to, with two long straight horns.

"It will make a good addition to dinner tonight," Raba said, "although there are better varieties for eating."

"Don't the dogs ever kill the animals on their own?" Amuba asked.

"Rarely. These two are particularly fast, but I doubt they'd catch it. Deer can run for long stretches, and though they'll let dogs get close, they can easily outpace them. I've seen this pair run down a deer when they couldn't drive it within bowshot, but they know that's not allowed since deer aren't fit for food unless killed and bled correctly."

Several other deer were startled but managed to escape, as the dogs had already exhausted themselves with their first chase. The other dogs were let loose to wander around the area. They stumbled upon several hyenas, some of which they killed, while others were brought to bay until the boys ran up and shot them with arrows. The ones that managed to flee in time managed to get away, for the hyena can outrun heavy dogs like the ones the party had with them for a reasonable distance.

After walking about fifteen miles, the boys abruptly stopped and discovered a vast expanse of water in front of them, surrounded by a strip of vegetation. Long rushes and aquatic plants lined the shoreline, and various huts with cultivated land could be scattered across the area.

"We have finished our journey," Rabah stated. "Hunters and anglers mostly occupy these cabins. We will set up camp at the bottom of this mound. We shouldn't go too close to the water's edge, as the air isn't good for those not used to it. The best hunting grounds are a few miles to our left. When the river is high, floods come through a valley that is always wet and marshy. We should anticipate finding plenty of wildlife in abundance there."

CHAPTER VI

Fowling and Fishing

The tents, made of lightweight fabric meant to shelter them from the night's dew rather than keep them warm, were swiftly set up. They quickly lit fires with their pre-packed fuel, saving time to focus on other matters. Rabah searched for fish and fowl and returned with a local carrying four ducks and an impressive fish catch.

"Let's get going," he declared; "with these and the deer, our provisions are ready. We've brought everything apart from the meat."

Chebron, having kept up courageously, was worn out from his hike and was happy to collapse on the beach and take in the beautiful sight, which was unfamiliar to him, for he'd never set eyes on such an extensive body of water before.

From the top of the hill, he could spot a faint dark line in the distance - the sandbank that divided the lake from the Great Sea. From his position, however, it was invisible, replaced by an endless stretch of water that seemed to reach the sky. Rabah pointed out the dark patches that were clumps of waterfowl, and in the shallow water near the shoreline, a quarter of a mile away, he could spot vast numbers of wading birds, white cranes, and white and black ibises. Meanwhile, smaller waterfowl were darting around among them.

Now and then, a flock of birds would take off in the air with a loud chorus, some flying away in a straight line while others just circled the area before settling back down, realizing that the commotion was unnecessary.

"It's simply beautiful, isn't it?" Chebron exclaimed, glancing over to Amuba, who stood beside him, supporting his bow and gazing longingly at the horizon.

Amuba was silent until Chebron noticed the tears in his eyes.

"What's wrong, Amuba?" Chebron asked with concern.

"It's nothing, Chebron, but the sight of this wide ocean brings back memories of home. They say this Great Sea is way bigger than the one I used to see every day from the palace walls back home, but no matter how big it was, it was still too vast for the eye to take in."

"Who knows, Amuba? Maybe you'll see it again one day," Chebron said encouragingly.

Amuba sadly shook his head.

"Chebron, our chances of success seem slim. Jethro and I talked it through many times and figured if we ever found ourselves in the hands of an oppressive master, we'd attempt an escape. But the journey is long and would take us through countries under Egyptian rule. People there speak languages we don't understand, and it's almost impossible to make it there alive. So we're content with our current situation, and it would be foolish to give this up on a slim chance of finding our way back to the land of the Rebu. Who knows who might rule there now and if I'd be welcomed back?"

"If you could get back and were sure of getting there safely, would you exchange all of the comforts of this life here for the life you described among your people?"

"There's no denying, Chebron, that your existence here is much more lavish, and you are much more civilized than the Rebu. Compared to your palaces, our houses are a little more than huts. We are even lacking in reading and writing. Our furniture is just a pile of rushes for our beds and a simple table and chairs, but maybe you aren't happier because of the possessions you have. Everyone loves their country the most, but I don't think we can love ours as much as you do. For starters, we've only been living there a few generations, with lots of us constantly migrating west, either by ourselves or together with one of the groups that push past us from the far East; besides, wherever we go, we take our country with us, building houses similar to the ones we left behind, living off the hunt or fishing in one place as well as another. In contrast, the Egyptians could never find a place like Egypt. I think it's the people rather than the country, the familiar language, the familiar faces, and ways. I freely agree the Egyptians are an incomparably greater people than us, more powerful, more knowledgeable, masters of many crafts, owners of many comforts and luxuries; yet, one still yearns sometimes for the free life among the Rebu."

"Amuba, you were once a prince, but not anymore. If you were just a common man, born to work, labor, or fight for your king, you might find that the life of an Egyptian peasant is more comfortable and enjoyable than your previous life."

"It may be," Amuba said thoughtfully, "but I believe the poorest among us were freer and more independent than the wealthiest Egyptian peasants. They didn't bow down to the king as he passed by. If they were braver than others, they could rise through the ranks. They could fish, hunt, farm, or make weapons as they wished; their lives weren't confined to customs or rules. They were humans, poor perhaps—even a little uncivilized—but they were people, whereas your Egyptian peasants, as free as they may be on paper, are slaves to legislation and conventions. But it seems the meal is ready, and I'm starving!"

"I agree, Amuba! It was worth the long journey just to enjoy this incredible meal. Everything is incredible - one of the servants is an amazing cook, and the fish, birds, and venison were all amazing. Plus, we left out the vegetables that make up a big part of the average Egyptian meals!"

"What are we going to do tomorrow, Rabah?" Chebron asked after they finished eating.

"Tomorrow, if that pleases you, my lord, I have organized a fowling trip for you. First, a boat will take you to the lake's edge, about three miles away, where you will have the best chances for success. Then, after you are done, it will take you another eight miles to the spot I told you about, where you will have more luck. Finally, I will wait for you to arrive and set everything up."

"That is well," Chebron said. "Amuba and Jethro, you'll be joining me, of course." So, at dawn, Rabah took Chebron down to the lake, and the boy with Amuba and Jethro boarded the boat, which was made of rushes sealed with pitch and barely created a ripple. Two men with long poles were already in the boat; they were bird catchers by trade and experts in all the various methods by which waterfowl were snared. They had, during the night, been getting the boat ready for the journey by fixing rushes all around it; the lower ends of these dipped into the water, the upper ends were six feet up, and the rushes were so densely stuck together as to form an impenetrable barrier.

The boat had a square stern, and there was only a tiny opening in the weeds for the boatman at the stern to propel the boat with his pole. One of the men stood there, and the other was at the bow, peering through a gap in the weeds and guiding his companion in the stern. Two cats lay at the bottom of the boat, seemingly aware of what was about to happen, and watched keenly. The basket was filled with food, and a jar of wine was placed on board before the boat was pushed away without making a sound.

"Do you stay this distance the whole time?" Chebron asked the man with the pole.

The man nodded.

"As long as we remain near the reeds, the waterfowl won't notice our arrival. Although we can also capture them by pushing out into the middle, it's better to get to the upwind side of the flock we want to reach and slowly drift down on them. There's plenty of birds here, and you'll be busy in no time."

In five minutes, the man in the bow gestured to his passengers that they were coming up on a flock of waterfowl.

Each of them grabbed their bow and arrows and got ready while the man in the stern poled the boat even more quickly and silently than before. Then, suddenly, he stopped poling at a signal from his crew. There were soft sounds around the boat - low, satisfied quacks and wings fluttering as the birds rose and shook the water off their backs. Then, parting the reeds in front of them, the two lads and Jethro peered through.

They were right in the middle of a flock of waterfowl foraging without suspicion of danger from the tuft of reeds. The arrows were already in their notches, the reeds were parted a little further, and the three shafts were fired. The twangs of the bows alarmed the ducks, and stopping their meal, they looked at the reeds with heads on one side. Three more arrows glided out, but this time one of the birds aimed at was injured only, and crying out a cry of distress and terror, it flapped along the water's surface.

In an instant, with frantic cries of fear, the flock took off; but before they had gotten away, two more were shot down with arrows. The cats, who had been on the lookout, jumped off the back of the boat and began to gather the dead ducks, including the one that had initially flown away, as it had dropped into the water about fifty yards from the boat. This scene was repeated about a dozen times until approximately sixty ducks and geese were in the boat. At this point, the group had had enough fun and lost most of their arrows, as those that didn't hit their intended target flew deep into the muddy bottom and couldn't be recovered.

"Now let's see the experts show us their skill at throwing sticks," Chebron said. "You will see they do better than us with the arrows."

The men steered the boat towards a patch of rushes growing from the shallow waters a hundred yards away in the lake. Ducks and geese were swarming around, searching for food, as the reeds were seeding. The birds were so preoccupied that they didn't notice the approaching vessel. The men removed the cover from the far side of the boat and prepared themselves, each holding six two-foot-long sticks made from curved and bent wood.

When the boat drew near the birds, it was swung around, and the birds took off with loud cries; but the men quickly threw their sticks at them, the last being targeted at the birds that were foraging in the reeds and were not able to flee as fast as the others. The youths were shocked by the power of these simple projectiles. After hitting one, the birds were so tightly packed that each stick scattered among the others, often taking down three or four birds.

The cats sprang into action. The flapping and squawking was immense, for although many birds were killed outright, others were injured in the leg or wing. Some flew away from the surface of the water, and some managed to take off into the air, but the majority were killed by the cats or knocked unconscious with the poles of the two hunters. In total, twenty-seven birds were added to the haul in the boat.

"That puts our arrows to shame, Amuba," Chebron said. "I have always heard that the hunters on these lakes were very skilled with their throwing sticks, but I had no idea that two men in such a short time could accomplish such a kill; I had no clue about the immense numbers of birds on these lakes." Jethro was inspecting the sticks and the ducks, which the cats had recovered.

"They are interesting things," he said to Amuba. "I thought before the men used them that straight sticks would be much better and wondered why they chose curved wood, but I do not doubt that the shape has something to do with it. As the men threw them, they gave them a strong spinning motion. That appears to be the secret of their effectiveness. It was incredible to observe how they whirled through the birds, striking one on the head, another on the leg, another on the wing until they fortuitously hit one squarely on the body; that seemed to stop them. One of those sticks I kept my eyes fixed on must have taken down six birds. I will practice with these devices, and if I ever get back home, I will demonstrate their use to our people.

There are nearly as many waterfowl on our sea as there are here. I have seen it almost black with them down at the southern end, where swamps and reed-covered marshes surround it."

"How do they catch them, Jethro?"

"They net them in decoys, and sometimes they wade out with them and have their heads hidden by floating grass and stick disguises. That way, their get near enough to grab them by the legs and pull them under the water. That way, a man can catch twenty of them before the other birds have figured it out."

"We catch them the same way here," one of the fowlers who had been listening remarked. "We weave little covers just large enough for our heads and shoulders and leave three or four of them floating around for a few days before we will go to catch them. The birds get used to them, and then it's no problem to go and capture quite a few."

"I think fowling must be a good profession," said Chebron.

"It's good enough at times," the man answered, "but the ducks aren't here all year round. The long-legged birds always stay here in large quantities, but the ducks and the geese are unreliable. They all leave us during specific periods of the year. Some say they travel to the north across the Great Sea; others believe they go south to Nubia. They aren't always here either. At times they are in abundance, then suddenly none can be found, and we hear they are swarming on the lakes further west. The wading birds can't be consumed, so we're in trouble when ducks and geese are scarce. But, even when we've got a boatload, we have to take it a long way to market, and when it's hot, everything may be ruined before we can sell it. The price is so low in these parts when the flocks are here that it's hard to save money to sustain ourselves and our families during the lean period. It would be different if the great cities of Thebes and Memphis were close to us. They could consume all we could catch, and we would get better prices, but unless under great conditions, there is no hope of the fowl remaining fresh during the long journey up the river to Thebes. If it weren't for our decoys, we would starve. So we take them alive and send them in baskets to Thebes, and because of that, we get a fair price."

"What type of decoys do you use?" Jethro asked.

"There are several different techniques," the man answered. "Sometimes we construct a bridge over the reeds, connecting them at the top to create a long channel through the reeds; then we spread corn over the water and set ducks close to the entrance, which are trained to swim around the outside until a flock arrives; then they enter the passage eating, and the others follow. Finally, there is a door they can easily push aside as they go in but can't open on their way out."

"That's exactly the type we use in our country," Jethro said.

"An alternate method," the fowler continued, "is to locate an area where the reeds form a dense shelter twenty yards wide along the bank; then a thin net a couple of hundred feet long is pegged to the shore behind them, and extended across the top of the reeds, going as close as a foot or two of the water. It is then curled up to sink into the water as it is spread out. People are positioned among the reeds at either end of the net while another goes out in a boat. When they observe a flock of ducks swimming near the shore, they propel the boat in their direction, but not speedily enough to scare them away, but just enough to get their attention and cause distress. They go back and forth, gradually getting close to the shore and naturally maneuvering to push them toward where the net is situated. They move faster when they are right above it, and the ducks swim into the reeds. Immediately they are in, the people at either end of the net lower the curled-up portion, and then the entire flock is captured. After that, the fowlers need to enter the reeds and pick them up as they try to fly upward and are impeded by the net. With luck, two or three catches can be made in a day, and a thousand ducks and sometimes twice as many can be taken. Then they are put into flat baskets just high enough to stand in with their heads out through the openings at the top. We put them on board and take them up the Nile."

"Yes, I've seen those baskets taken out of the boats, and I thought it was bad to pack them in so tight. But how do they feed them? It must take several weeks to make the trip?" asked Chebron.

"The merchant who has procured these and other feathered creatures from other hunters and us wait until they have obtained enough to fill a large vessel - since it wouldn't be profitable to operate on a small scale - brings them up the river and sustains them routinely with little pellets made of moistened flour. This is similar to how they are done in Upper Egypt, where they breed poultry and stuff them for the markets. On the off chance that the boat is a large one and is taking up forty or fifty thousand birds, of course, he takes two or three young men to assist him, for it is no little undertaking to feed such an enormous number, and each should have a little water in addition to the dinner. It appears odd here, where fowl are so plentiful, that individuals should raise and sustain them like cattle. But, in any case, I suppose it is true."

"It is quite true," Chebron replied. "Amuba and I visited one of the great hatcheries a few months ago. This kind of facility usually consists of two parts - the hatching process and the fattening process. The one we went to had both. Collectors gather eggs from local fowl keepers and purchase eggs from more distant locations. The eggs are placed in a low chamber with a sand-filled floor heated with flues from a fire underneath. It requires careful regulation to maintain the perfect temperature. However, the staff at this facility have mastered the art of keeping the temperature exactly right."

"We recently visited a facility where eggs are hatched in batches of eight or ten. The eggs are ready to be swapped with fresh eggs every two or three days. In return, people who send the eggs receive several chickens, with one chicken given for every two eggs. Some hatchers offer more, while others provide less, with any surplus going towards their wages. It's a lucrative business if they can hatch ninety chickens out of every hundred eggs. On the other hand, if the temperature is too high or too low, this number drops to twenty or thirty. To compensate for losses, hatchers often add their eggs to the mix before returning the final number of chickens to their customers."

"Once the breeders have provided the necessary number of chickens to the farmers, they can sell the remaining chickens to others. The process of fattening the chickens differs greatly. First, long rows of small boxes are stacked to form a wall five feet high. Each box has a small door with a hole and a shutter that can be closed. A chicken is placed inside each box. The attendants, working in pairs, carry a basket filled with meal balls. One attendant lifts the shutter and grabs the chicken's neck, making it open its beak. The other then quickly pushes the ball of meal down its throat. It is an exact process that takes only a few seconds. The attendants work their way down the rows until the last chicken is fed. Then, they start again from the beginning."

"Why do they keep them in the dark?" the fowler asked.

"They told us they did it because they aren't restless in the dark, so they sleep all the time between meals. Then each time the flap is lifted, they think it's daytime and come out. So it only takes about ten days for them to get fat, and then they're ready for market."

"That seems like a lot of work," the fowler said. "But I suppose it works since they have a good market nearby and get good prices. That makes more sense than the hatching business. Why they don't let the birds hatch their eggs is a mystery to me."

"Birds will lay many more eggs than they can hatch," Chebron noted. "A well-nourished bird ought to lay two hundred and fifty eggs in the year; if left alone, she won't incubate more than two batches of fifteen eggs each. Thus, you can see, as it's more worthwhile for the farmers to breed poultry than to sell eggs, it's monetarily beneficial to send their eggs to the incubation facilities and, in this way, get a hundred and twenty-five chicks a year instead of thirty."

"I suppose it does," the fowler agreed. "Here we are, my lord, at our destination. We will land over there, and the servant who hired us is waiting for you. I hope you are happy with the day's adventure."

Chebron said they were pleased, and in a few minutes, the boat reached the landing where Rabah was waiting for them. One of the fowlers, carrying a dozen of the finest birds they captured, brought them to the spot Rabah had chosen for their camp. Like the last one, it stood at the foot of the sand hills, a few hundred yards from the lake.

"Are we going to hunt near here?" was Chebron's first question.

"No, my lord; it is two miles away. But, in accordance with your order last night, I have arranged for you to fish tomorrow. In the afternoon, I will move the tents a mile nearer to the country where you will hunt, but it is best not to go too close, for near the edge of these great swamps, the air is unhealthy to those who are not accustomed to it."

"I can't wait to start hunting," Chebron said, "but it is better, like you said, to have a day of fishing first because the work would seem boring after the excitement of hunting the hippopotamus. We'll be glad to have dinner as soon as possible because even though we did justice to the food you put on board, we're quite ready to eat again. Twelve hours of this fresh air from the sea gives one the appetite of a hyena."

"Everything is already ready, my lord. I thought it better not to wait for the game you brought home, which will be fine tomorrow, so I bought fish and fowl from the peasants. Since we saw your boat for the last two or three hours, we were able to calculate the time of your arrival and thus have everything ready."

The dinner was similar to the previous day, except that a rabbit replaced the venison—a change for the better, as the rabbit was a delicacy much appreciated by the Egyptians. The following day was spent fishing. For this purpose, a long net was used, similar to modern times. One end of the net was fastened to the shore, and the net itself was coiled in the boat. The boat was rowed into the lake, the fishermen paying out the net as it went. A circuit was then made back to the shore, where the men seized the two ends of the net and hauled it to land, capturing the fish enclosed within. After seeing two or three hauls made, the lads went with Jethro on board the boat. The fishermen provided them with long, two-pronged spears.

They quietly rowed along the edge of the rushes, where the water was deeper than usual. It was, however, so clear that they could see to the bottom, and with their spears, they struck at the fish there. At first, they were unsuccessful, as they didn't know that allowance must be made for diffraction and were puzzled because their spears seemed to go at an angle to the fish at the water's edge. The fishermen, however, explained that they had to adjust for the water creating a bend in their vision and that it was only when the fish were exactly under them that they could strike directly at it. But even after being told what was happening, they still weren't very successful, and they finally laid down their spears and simply watched the boatmen, who almost always got their target.

Their attention was drawn to four boats carrying six to eight individuals. Two had arrived from opposite directions, and the people in them shouted insults at each other as they came close.

"What's this all about?" Chebron asked as the two fishermen laid down their spears and, with faces full of excitement, spun around to observe the boats. "The boats are coming from two villages, my lord, which are currently in a quarrel over some fishing nets that were taken away. As customary here, they issued a traditional challenge to one another a couple of days ago, and their representatives are about to fight it out. You can see that the number of men on one side is the same as those on the other, and the boats are roughly the same size."

Amuba and Jethro stared on with great enthusiasm since they had seen depictions of these fights between boatmen on the walls, which were quite common since the Egyptians were a very combative population and often had long-standing feuds between neighboring villages. The men were armed with poles about ten feet in length and an inch and a half in diameter, their preferred weapons for this type of event. The boats had now come into close contact, and a fierce battle began immediately, the clattering of the sticks, the heavy thuds of the blows, and the shouts of the combatants creating an uproar that caused all the waterbirds within a radius of half a mile to fly off screaming across the lake. The men handled their heavy weapons skillfully, warding off most of the blows. Nevertheless, some strikes were successful, causing some combatants to fall into the water, others to collapse in their boats, and others to drop their long staves after a powerful hit on the arm.

"Incredibly, they don't all kill each other," Jethro said. "This head-shaving tradition, Amuba, which has always seemed strange to us, clearly has a purpose—it must strengthen their skulls. Without breaking like glass, no one else's heads could withstand these hits." Herodotus later confirmed this hypothesis, wrote about the intense battles between Egyptian villagers, and mentioned that they had thicker skulls than others.

Many men who plunged into the water climbed back into the boats and continued the fight; however, some went under immediately and were never seen again. In the end, after half of the men on each side had been incapacitated, four or five killed or drowned, the boats split apart, no one having a definite advantage, and still shouting insults and taunts at each other, the men paddled toward their respective towns.

"Are these types of fights common?" Chebron asked the fishermen. "Yes; there are often a few quarrels," one of them replied, quietly resuming his fishing as if nothing had happened out of the ordinary. "If they are water-side villages, their champions typically fight in boats, as you witnessed; if not, equal parties meet at a spot halfway between their villages and decide it on foot. Sometimes they fight with short sticks, with a basket hilt protecting their hands, while on the left arm, a piece of wood is strapped on, extending from the elbow to the tips of the fingers, serving as a shield; but more commonly, they fight with the long pole, which we call the neboot."

"It's an excellent weapon," Jethro said, "and they protect their heads well, holding their hands far apart. If I were back home again, Amuba, I would love to form an army with these weapons. To make them even better, we could add light iron on the part used as a guard, so swords or axes don't cut through it. That way, they'd become even more formidable, and it would be incredibly tough for foot soldiers with swords and shields to repel an attack with them."

"The downside would be," Amuba remarked, "that each individual would need so much space to wield their weapon that they must stand far apart, and each would be up against three or four swordsmen in the enemy's formation."

"That is true, Amuba, and you have certainly come up with the weak spot in utilizing such a weapon; however, they would be great for one-on-one fighting or battling broken lines. When we return to Thebes, if I can discover any peasant who can educate me in using these neboots, I will, without a doubt, gain proficiency with it."

"You have the potential to be a great athlete," one of the fishermen remarked, looking at Jethro's muscular physique. "I wouldn't want to get a whack on the head from someone like you. But the sun is setting, and we should go to the spot where you will be dropped off."

"We had a fantastic day, Rabah," Chebron said when they reached their new camp. "I hope the rest of the days will be as successful."

"I'm sure they will, my lord. I've been asking around the village, and I heard the riverbed swamp is teeming with hippos."

"Do you hunt them on foot?"

"No, my lord. The river bed has enough water for flat boats made of rushes to pass through, and there are many deep pools where the animals can take refuge during the heat of the day."

"Are they aggressive animals?" Amuba asked. "I have never seen one; they are said to be common higher up the Nile and in swamps at its mouth, but there are none near Thebes. So I assume they are too intimidated by the activity here and do not dare show themselves in this water."

"There would be no food for them," Rabah uttered. "They

can be found in swamps like this one or in spots on the Upper Nile where the stream is shallow and bordered by water plants, on whose roots they generally live. They are bashful animals and can just be seen in barely visited spots. When struck, they normally attempt to make their escape; for even though now and again they will dash with their tremendous mouth open at a vessel, tear it separated, and murder the hunter, this happens just every once in a while. They just try to fly."

"They must be cowardly creatures!" Jethro said disdainfully. "I would preferably chase an animal, be it ever so little, that will battle for its life. But, in any case, we shall see."

They set out toward their destination when they woke up the following day. When they reached the top of a sand dune, they saw a broad, flat plain stretching out before them, covering a mile in each direction. The terrain was filled with reeds and other water-loving plants, and the scene extended southward as far as the eye could see.

"For one month each year," Rabah said, "this is a river, but for the other eleven months, it's not much more than a swamp. Shallow boats can make their way up quite a few miles, but there's usually little water. It's one of the few spots in Northern Egypt where the hippopotamus can still be found, but you need the governor's permission to hunt them unless you are of a high enough rank. The steward knew you were accompanying your father, so he wrote and got that permission as soon as he heard."

"Are there crocodiles there?" Amuba asked.

"Many," Rabah replied, "although there aren't many in the lakes anymore. The people here are not like those of the Theban zone, who hold them in high respect—here, they regard them as dangerous enemies and kill them without mercy."

CHAPTER VII

Hippopotamus and Crocodile

Guided by Rabah, the group descended to the swamp's edge, where they spotted three boats - or rafts - made from bundles of bulrushes. These had a swan-necked bow and were shaped like modern skates. Each was manned by a person who used a pole to propel it and had several spears. These were peculiar because their blades were loosely attached to their shafts so that when an animal was struck, the shaft would drop off, leaving the head embedded in its flesh. Attached to the head was a cord wound around a handle with a spindle running through it.

"Those rafts don't look like they can hold three," Chebron remarked.

"They can manage it, but they're better with two," the man replied.

"If it's all right with you, Chebron, I'll stay onshore with the rope-holders," Jethro said. "I suppose they're here for a reason, so I'll come with them."

"The ropes pull the creatures out of the water after we've hit them," the man explained.

"Well, I'll go and lend a hand with the hauling. I can do my part and would be useless on one of those small rafts; I believe my weight would sink it in the water."

"We were out this morning, my lord," the boatman said, addressing Chebron, "and we discovered a hippopotamus wallowing in a pond a mile up the river. I think it's large and will give us some good fun."

Chebron and Amuba then took their spots on the two rafts, and the men, setting down their spears and taking the poles, pushed away from the shore. Quietly they made their way amidst the reeds. Occasionally the channels were too narrow that the reeds almost brushed the rafts on both sides; then they opened up into large pools, and here the water was so deep the poles could hardly reach the bottom. Not a word was spoken, as the men warned them that the slightest sound would unsettle the hippopotami and make them sink to the bottom of the pools, where they would be hard to catch. Finally, after half an hour of poling, they reached a pool bigger than any they had passed before, extending along one side almost to the bank of the river.

The man on the raft now signaled to Chebron to grab one of the spears, but the lad shook his head and gestured to take on the challenge, for he realized that, lacking knowledge of the creature's behavior, it would be reckless of him to do so. The man nodded, for he had indeed been questioning which approach the situation would take, for it required a thrust with a powerful arm to thrust the spear through the tough hide of the hippopotamus. Amuba followed Chebron's lead, preferring to be a spectator rather than a participant in this unfamiliar sport.

Chebron and the boatman fixed their eyes on the glassy water, which was still as can be. Then suddenly, they saw two lumps of black mud that seemed to be rising out of the surface. Ripples started to appear, and the hunter knew there was something nearby. He swiftly moved the boat closer and realized it was a giant hippopotamus. The hunter threw his spear with all his might, but the animal's tough hide barely budged. The hippo ran into the rushes, and the hunter knew it would take another spear to defeat it. Nudging the reeds out of the way, they maneuvered the boat until they saw the hippo standing in the water. Chebron now had a spear ready, just in case.

"Is he going to charge?" Chebron asked, grasping a spear.

"No, that is highly unlikely. If he were to do so and rock the boat, jump into the reeds, and lie there with only your head above the surface. I will divert his attention and return to put you into the boat after he's gone."

Another spear was thrown, and it was successful. Then, a roar followed by a loud splash occurred. Chebron believed the animal was about to get them, but he veered off and hastened back to the pool where he initially rested.

"I assumed that's what he'd do," the hunter said. "They always look for refuge in the depths of deep pools, and here you see, the water is not deep enough to cover him."

The boat pursued the hippopotamus again. Amuba was still on his raft in the pool.

"What happened to him?" Chebron asked as they moved away from the reeds.

"He has sunk to the bottom of the lake," Amuba answered. "He gave me a scare, I can tell you. First, we heard him crashing through the reeds, and then he appeared with his mouth wide open—a mouth like a cave; and then, just as I thought he was going to attack us, he switched direction and descended to the bottom of the lake."

"How long will he stay there?" Chebron asked the hunter.

"A long time if he is left alone, but we will stir him up."

After saying this, he pointed the boat toward the reeds closest to the shore and drove the vessel through them.

"Ah, here you are, Jethro!" Chebron exclaimed, noticing the Rebu and the people he had come with standing on the shore.

"What's going on, Chebron—have you taken one of them down? There was a kind of rumble and a huge splashing."

"We haven't killed him, yet two spearheads are buried in him."

The hunter passed the ropes to the men and instructed them to pull steadily yet not hard enough to snap them. Then he took the end of the rope they were carrying from them and poled them back into the pool.

"Those ropes aren't tough enough to haul the large animal to the shore, right?" Chebron asked.

"Oh, no, they wouldn't move him; however, tugging on them causes the spearheads to cause him pain; he gets uneasy and rises to the surface in anger. I toss this lasso over his head at that point, and they can draw on that."

The creature's head appeared over the water in two or three minutes. The second it did as such, the hunter tossed the lasso. His aim was right, and he tightened it around the neck with a yank. "Now pull!" he shouted.

Despite the hippopotamus' attempts to swim the other way, the peasants gradually pulled it closer to the bank.

As soon as the animal's feet touched the ground, it threw its full weight onto the rope. The peasants, unprepared for the force, fell to the ground but didn't give up. Instead, they pulled on the rope and cords, again and again, until the hippopotamus was finally dragged into the shallow. This went on for eight or ten tries.

"He's tiring out now," the hunter declared. "It's just a matter of time before we can get him onto shore. Then, we can use spears and arrows to take him down when we do."

Sure enough, the hippo was exhausted and allowed itself to be pulled onto shore without resistance. As soon as it was there, the hunters, Jethro, and the boys attacked it with spears. But the thick hide made it impossible for the boys to penetrate, so they resorted to their bows and arrows. Another rope was slung over its head when it emerged from the water, and the peasants yanking on the ropes stopped it from launching a counterattack. A few more thrusts from the hunters and one of the spears hit a crucial spot - the hippo kneeled and fell over dead.

The peasants cheered, for hippopotamus meat is good for eating, and there was enough for everyone in the area.

"Shall we look for another one, my lord?" the hunter asked Chebron. "No. I think I've had enough of this. Killing an animal that can't fight back is not very enjoyable. What do you think, Amuba?" "I completely agree with you, Chebron. It's like killing a cow. What was that?" he asked suddenly as a scream came nearby. "It's a woman's voice."

Chebron sprinted off with Amuba and Jethro in pursuit. After running about a hundred yards, they saw the cause of the outcry: an immense crocodile was dragging a woman along with it.

Without hesitation, Chebron slammed his spear into the crocodile's nose. Jethro and Amuba joined the attack. The crocodile, seeing the reinforcements, dashed to the river, snapping its jaws.

"Watch out for its tail!" one of the hunters shouted, running up.

Unfortunately, the warning was too late, and Amuba felt a powerful strike that threw him to the ground. The hunter thrust his spear into the animal's back leg through its soft skin. Jethro followed his lead on the other side. The beast halted its flight and spun around, flailing its tail.

"Stay away from it!" the hunter shouted. "It's fatally wounded; it won't need more spears." It was true; the crocodile had been dealt its death blow. Its movements slowed and stopped thrashing its tail; though it still tried to bite those closest to it, that eventually stopped. Finally, its head drooped, and then it was dead. Jethro, after delivering the blow, ran to Amuba.

"Are you hurt?" he asked, concerned.

"No, I don't think so," Amuba exclaimed, entirely out of breath. "That brute hit me so hard he knocked the wind out of me, but it's better than if he'd hit me in the leg—I'm sure it would have been broken. How's the woman—is she dead?"

"I haven't had a chance to check yet," Jethro replied. "Let me help you and see if your ribs are broken. I'll look into her afterward."

Upon getting to his feet, Amuba declared that he didn't think he was seriously injured, though he couldn't stand up straight. "I just got bruised, Jethro. That was a huge hit he gave me, and I doubt I'll be able to do any sports for the next few days. That crocodile was worth way more than a dozen hippopotamuses. He was fearless."

They now went to Chebron, who was bent over the figure of the crocodile's victim.

They quickly raced over to Chebron, who was bent over the body of the croc's victim.

"Why, she is just a girl!" Amuba shouted. "She's no older than your sister, Chebron."

"Do you think she passed away?" Chebron asked in a hushed voice.

"I think she has only fainted," Jethro answered. "Hey," he yelled to one of the villagers gathered around the crocodile, "one of you run down to the water and fetch a gourdful."

"I don't think she's dead," Amuba said. "It looked like the crocodile had grabbed her by the leg."

"We must carry her somewhere," Jethro said, "and find some woman to tend to her. I will check if there's a hut nearby." He leaped on top of some rising ground and looked around. "There's a cottage right nearby," he said as he returned. "I bet she's from there."

Asking two peasants to run and fetch female assistance, he lifted the delicate figure and brought her up the hill, with the two boys trailing behind. At the foot of a dune, they spotted a cottage nestled behind it. It was in better condition than the usual peasant huts. The baked clay walls had been painted white and partially covered with beautiful flowers. A patch of carefully tended land surrounded it. Jethro stepped into the cottage. Sitting on a bench at the far end was an elderly man. He appeared very old; his hair and long beard were snowy white.

"What is it?" he cried out as Jethro entered. "Has the God of our fathers again struck me in my old age and taken away my little lamb? I heard her crying, but my legs have lost strength, and I couldn't get up to go to her aid."

"I believe the child isn't hurt too badly," Jethro said. "We had just killed a hippo when we heard her screaming, and upon running up, found a huge crocodile trying to drag her to the river, but we managed to make him drop her. I hope she isn't too injured. He seemed to have taken her by the leg. We've sent out to get some women. Most likely, they'll arrive soon. Ah! Here's the water."

Jethro and the boys carefully laid the girl down on a couch in the corner of the room and sprinkled some water on her face, taking the gourd from the peasant who brought it while Amuba gently rubbed her hands. After a few minutes, the girl opened her eyes. Two women entered the hut, and Jethro left the girls in their care.

Amuba asked, "I trust the girl isn't hurt too badly? By the looks of her clothing, she's an Israelite, though we thought we had left their land behind us on the other side of the desert. I'm glad her garments are thicker than the usual Egyptian peasant women's, or else the crocodile's teeth would've torn her severely."

A few minutes later, one of the women came out and told them that the maid had recovered and that she was almost unharmed. "The crocodile seemed to have only grabbed her garments, not her skin," the woman said. "Her grandfather would like to thank you for your help."

They re-entered the cottage. The girl was sitting on the floor at her grandfather's feet with one of his hands in hers while he was caressing her head with his other. As soon as they entered, the ladies, understanding that their help was no longer required, left the cottage.

"Who are those to whom I owe the life of my grandchild?" the elderly man asked.

"I am Chebron, the son of Ameres, the high priest of the temple of Osiris at Thebes. My friends, Amuba and Jethro, two from the Rebu nation, were brought to Egypt and my father's home."

"We are his servants," Amuba stated, "though he is kind enough to call us his friends."

"It's strange," the elderly man said, "that the son of an Osiris priest should appear to gladden the remaining few hours of someone who has always fought against the Egyptian gods. If the crocodile had taken away my Ruth, it might have been better for her, given that she'll be all alone in the world by the time the sun has risen and set multiple times."

The girl gasped and, getting up on her knees, hugged the old man's neck.

"It must be this way, my Ruth. I have lived a hundred and ten years in this heathen land, and my journey is ending; without you, I'd be satisfied that it's so since my life has been sorrow and bitterness. I consider her my grandchild, but in truth, she is the daughter of my grandchild, and all who were in between us have gone away before me and left us together. But she has faith in the God of Abraham, and he'll find a protector for her."

Chebron, who had become familiar with some of the customs of the Israelites living in Egypt, could tell from the old man's words that Jethro's assumptions were accurate and that he was from the same race.

"You're an Israelite," he said kindly. "How come you're not living amongst your people rather than alone amongst strangers?"

"I left them thirty years ago when Ruth's mother was still a tiny child. They wouldn't let me stay in peace with them but instead sent me out because I spoke up against them."

"Because you spoke up against them?" Chebron asked in astonishment.

"Yes, my father had already aged when I was born. However, he was one of the few people that held tightly to our ancestors' faith. He taught me that there was only one God, the God of Abraham, Isaac, and Jacob, and that all other gods were merely sculptures of wood and stone. I stuck to that faith, although eventually, I was the only one of our people who still believed in it. The others had forgotten their God and were worshipping the gods of the Egyptians. They viewed my words as delusions when I spoke to them and felt I insulted the gods they served.

"My sons went with the rest, but my daughter learned the true faith from my lips and held on to it. She passed it on to her daughter after her, and ten years ago, when the time came for her to pass on, she sent Ruth to me through a messenger, praying that I would raise her in our ancestors' faith. She knew I was already quite old, but she didn't doubt that God would provide protectors for the child when I was no longer around. So for ten years, we have lived here together, working our land and living off its fruits and selling baskets woven by us, which we exchange for fish with our neighbors. The child worships the God of our fathers and has been thriving here for the past ten years, but I am saddened by the thought that my days are numbered and that I see no way after me but that Ruth will return to our people, who will draw her away from the true faith."

"Never, grandfather," the young lady stated firmly. "They may beat and persecute me, but I will never deny my God."

"The Israelites are a tough people," the elderly man said, shaking his head, "and they are obstinate and will likely prevail against someone so vulnerable. Still, all matters are in the hands of God, who will reveal himself at the right time to his people who have forgotten him."

Amuba, looking at the girl, thought she had greater strength and resilience than the old man gave her credit for. Her face was of the same style of beauty as some of the young women he had seen in the villages of the Israelites but of a more refined and better quality. Her face was almost oval, with soft black hair and exquisitely outlined eyebrows that almost ran in a straight line beneath her forehead. Her eyes were big and gentle, with long lashes hiding them, but a solidness about her lips and chin indicated a determined will and strengthened her declaration "Never."

There was a bit of a pause then, and then Chebron stated almost bashfully:

"My father, the high priest of Osiris, is knowledgeable and open-minded. He's aware of your religion, and I recall him mentioning that when the Israelites first arrived in this land, they only worshiped one God. My sister is the same age as Ruth and is kind and gentle. If I speak to my father, I'm sure he'll gladly take Ruth into his household, not only as a friend and companion to Mysa but also to allow her to worship as she sees fit."

Chebron gazed intently at the old man.

"Your words are delightful and compassionate, young man, and your voice is trustworthy. A few years ago, I would have said that I would rather have the maiden die than be a handmaid in the house of an Egyptian; however, as the end of my life draws near, I have a different perspective, and perhaps it would be better for her to be there than among those who used to know the true God, but have forgotten Him and embraced idolatry. Throughout my life, I have always prayed and believed that God would provide Ruth with a protector, and now it seems that the way you have been brought here in these last days of my life is a response to my prayer. Ruth, my child, you have heard the offer, and it is up to you to decide. Will you go with this young Egyptian gentleman and serve his sister as a handmaid, or will you go back to the villages of our people?"

Ruth had stood up by now and was looking intently at Chebron; her gaze shifted to the faces of Amuba and Jethro and slowly returned to Chebron.

"I'm sure God has chosen for me," she said eventually. "He sent these people here to save and watch over me. They seem kind and trustworthy. If the father of this young man accepts me, I'll be the handmaid of his daughter when you leave me."

"That's wonderful," the old man said, relieved. "Now I'm ready to go since my prayers have been answered. May God act towards you and yours, Egyptian, as you treat my child."

"May it be so," Chebron responded respectfully.

"I can tell you," Jethro said to the elderly grandfather, "that your daughter won't be as happy anywhere else in Egypt as in Ameres' household. He's the master of Amuba and me, but do you see how his son treats us? Not as servants but as friends. Ameres is an incredibly kind man, and Mysa, whose personal attendant I am, I'd give my life to protect her. Your grandchild couldn't possibly be in better hands. Ameres has often asked Amuba and me about our gods, but he's never asked us to give them up for the gods of Egypt."

"So now," Chebron declared, "we will be on our way; you are likely exhausted from the excitement, and Ruth needs some rest and a peaceful atmosphere after her scare. We've camped about a mile away by the lake and will come back and visit you tomorrow."

No one spoke for a while after they left the house, and then Chebron said:

"It almost seems like what that old man said was true and that his God had sent us there to find someone to protect his daughter. It was strange that we happened to be close enough to hear her scream when the crocodile seized her and that we managed to rescue her just in the nick of time. It took all three: us being there, the crocodile attacking her, and us arriving in time to prevent her from getting dragged into the river. A crocodile could have taken her away a million times without anyone being around to save her. The chances of the one who managed to save her being able to offer her a good home after her grandfather's passing was just astronomical."

"It is peculiar," Amuba mused. "You don't think your father will have any problem taking her in?"

"Oh no, he may say he doesn't want more servants in the house, but when he sees her, he'll be delighted to have such a companion for Mysa. If it were my mother, I don't know - she'd probably say no, but once she's aware it's been settled, she won't aruge one way or the other. I'll write my father a letter, give him all the details, and send off one of the slaves immediately. He should be back by tomorrow, and it will bring a smile to my father's face knowing it's all taken care of. I also want to tell my father of my distress."

"What distress?" Amuba gasped in shock. "You haven't said anything about being troubled."

"Don't you understand, Amuba? I'm in trouble because I hurt the crocodile; it's a sin, but what else could I do?"

Amuba had to fight the urge to grin.

"You had to do something, Chebron, as there was no time to think. He was going too fast for you to tell him that he was wrong for taking a girl, so you took the only means you could to stop him; also, the hit you gave him didn't hurt him. It was Jethro and the hunter who killed him."

"But they couldn't have done that if I hadn't slowed him down."

"That's true, Chebron, but if that weren't the case, he would have made it to the water with the girl and eaten her up. So, unless you think the crocodile's life is more important than hers, I don't think you should be blaming yourself."

"You don't understand me, Amuba," Chebron said crossly. "I think an animal's life is as significant as a human's; however, the crocodiles are sacred, and bad luck comes to those who harm them."

"Well, in that case, misfortune must hit those areas where the crocodile is killed no matter where it is. I haven't heard about those parts of Egypt being more vulnerable to plague and famine than places where the crocodile is revered."

Chebron didn't have a response. What Amuba said was most likely accurate, but on the other hand, he had always been told that the crocodile was sacred, so he couldn't explain why these creatures were killed freely in some regions of Egypt. It was another of the questions he kept coming across. Finally, after a long silence, he answered:

"It could appear to be as you say; however, Amuba, certain gods are venerated in one area and others in another. Therefore, the god of the region where the beast is considered sacred would likely be angry if the animals s after were killed. But, at the same time, he may not be particularly concerned with the affairs of a place where he is not venerated."

"In that situation, Chebron, you can be at ease. Let's agree that it is wrong to kill a crocodile in a place in which he is considered sacred. It's possible that there won't be a bad outcome from killing an animal where it isn't sacred."

"I trust that's the case, Amuba, and since the crocodile isn't a sacred creature here, no damage may come from my hitting one, even though I would give everything I hadn't been compelled to do as such. I trust that my father will similarly consider the issue."

"I do not doubt that he will do as such, Chebron, especially since we agreed that you didn't cause any genuine harm to the animal."

"Isn't it odd, Jethro," Amuba said when Chebron had entered the tent, "that brilliant and instructed individuals like the Egyptians should be so senseless concerning creatures?"

"It's odd, Amuba, and I almost laughed when I heard you and Chebron seriously discussing it. It's almost as if everyone held the same view, yet one would assume people could see how ridiculous it is. Different animals are worshipped in some parts of the country and slaughtered in others, and no one seems to have any negative repercussions. What should we do tomorrow?"

"I don't think that's been decided yet; we've done one of the activities already. Rabah said we could go out and try different fishing methods, join the fowlers and watch them catch birds with clap nets, or go out into the desert and hunt ibex. Chebron hasn't chosen yet, but we'll know what he plans to do once he writes his letter."

After Chebron finished his lengthy letter, he called Rabah and asked him to send it immediately with the swiftest of his slaves.

"He'll make it," he said confidently, "before my father goes to bed. If he doesn't reply immediately, he'll probably answer in the morning, and at the very least, the man should be back by lunchtime."

At dinner, Amuba asked Chebron what they should do the following day.

"We could go and watch the people with the clap nets," Chebron replied. "They have different types of nets, and they catch a lot of pigeons and other birds. I think that should be enough for tomorrow. We've had four days of tough work, and a relaxed day will be nice, and if we get bored, we can take a boat across the lake and look at the Great Sea beyond the sand dunes that divide the lake from it, plus; I'm expecting to get my father's response, and I'd like to talk some more with that old Israelite. It's intriguing to learn about the religion his ancestors believed in, and it appears that he and his grandchild are now the last people who still have faith."

"A quiet day would be perfect for me, Chebron; I'm not sure I'd be able to come with you anyway. The crocodile's tail left my ribs aching, and I'm not sure I'll be able to move tomorrow."

Sure enough, Amuba was so incapacitated from stiffness and pain the day after that he couldn't get out of bed.

Not long after breakfast, a messenger arrived with a letter from Ameres. It read:

"Chebron, Mysa could benefit from having a friend her age. Your story of this old Israelite and his daughter intrigues me, and I think she'd make a wonderful companion for Mysa. I would have liked to speak with the old man myself and learn more about the religion Joseph and his people brought to Egypt. I've questioned many Israelites before, but all profess to know nothing but the Egyptian faith. If you can, try to gain more insight from him."

"Assure him from me that his daughter will be treated kindly and with respect in my household, and no attempts will be made to change her religion. Regarding the encounter with the crocodile, I don't think you need to worry. The crocodile is not considered sacred in this area, and the people with you would have likely caught up and killed it anyway. As for the girl, when the old man dies, she should travel to Thebes by boat. She should have no trouble finding my house and will be welcomed upon arrival. I will write to Mysa and tell her you have discovered an Israelite handmaiden as her special attendant. She should assume this position when the girl arrives before my return.

"It wouldn't be a good idea for her to come here if her grandfather passes away before we head home. Firstly, she would be in the way, and secondly, her features and clothing would give away that she's an Israelite. Furthermore, people in the villages she travels through may detain her, or, if she arrives here, the fact that she's leaving with us could be a subject of complaint, and the Israelites probably wouldn't hesitate to say I took a young woman of their tribe as a slave. So that's why she should go up the river to Thebes.

"Since they're poor, it would be best to leave some money with them to cover the boat fare and her expenses during the trip. I'm now going ahead of schedule with the steward's tasks, and I'll be inspecting the canals and planning new ones in about three days. So, if you've had of sporting by then, you better start your journey back."

Chebron couldn't contain his joy as he finished the letter from his father. "My father has consented!" he exclaimed. "I felt he would, but it made me anxious until I read his response. I'm going to tell the grandfather right away. Jethro, I don't need you this morning. Why don't you stay with Amuba or take the boat out fishing or hunting?"

With that, Chebron was off to the cottage. He found Ruth gardening and asked what had happened with the crocodile. "I'm not sure," she replied. "I usually go down to the lake to get water for the garden many times a day, watching out for these creatures before I fill my jar. But yesterday, I turned a corner when I was hit with tremendous force, and the creature grabbed me. I screamed, but I knew no one could hear me since there are no close neighbors and Grandfather hasn't been able to walk for months. So I prayed for help with all my heart, and God answered. He sent you to save me."

"Do they go up so far from the river very often?"

"Not often. But yesterday, we had a portion of a goat from a neighbor and were cooking it, and maybe the smell attracted the crocodile; they're known for having a sharp sense of smell and even barging into homes to steal meat right off the stove."

"I see you're still walking with a limp."

"Yes. Grandfather wanted me to take it easy for a few days, but I'm sure I'll be as good as new once the bruises heal and the pain subsides. Plus, someone needs to take care of the garden, right? Grandfather's been shaken by yesterday's excitement, and he's not feeling his best this morning."

She beckoned him inside the cottage.

"Your granddaughter said you're not feeling well today," Chebron began.

"At my age," the elderly man uttered, "even the smallest thing can upset me, and yesterday's event was anything but small. I'm surprised I didn't pass away from the distress."

"I have some great news for you," Chebron responded. "I sent a message to my father yesterday, and I just got the response." And taking out the scroll, he read aloud the part where Ameres assured his willingness to accept Ruth in his home and that no one would make her change her faith.

"Praise be to the Lord!" the old man shouted. "The Lord even works through animals, and the crocodile that seemed to be threatening my granddaughter was the Lord's answer to my prayer. I thank you, my young lord; may the God of my fathers treat you like you care for my daughter. Can she stay with me until my last days?"

"Of course. We wouldn't even think of taking her now. Now, my father sends instructions on what she should do and money to cover the cost of her voyage up the Nile to Thebes. This is what my father is saying." He read the part of the scroll that's about the journey. "And now," he exclaimed, "let me read what my father says about your religion. He's always searching for truth and would love for me to hear from you and tell him all about the God you worship."

"I'll be glad to, my young master. The tale is straightforward, for it's uncomplicated, unlike your religion's many gods."

Chebron sat on a stack of rushes and was ready to listen to the elderly man's story of the God of the Israelites.

CHAPTER VIII

The Conspiracy in the Temple

The group stayed near the lake for two days, fishing and hunting. Afterward, they traveled back to the base camp of Ameres. He spent two months surveying canals, reinforcing the dikes, and ensuring the gates and channels were in excellent condition. Next, levels were taken to create new branches, which would expand the cultivation area. The Israelites were asked to help with the work, but they complained, even though Ameres promised to pay them for their labor. Eventually, after ensuring all was ready, he left with his son for Thebes.

Two weeks after coming home, he heard that a woman named Ruth sought an audience with him. He asked his servant to bring her to him and summoned Chebron from his studies. The boy arrived first and, when Ruth entered, presented her to his father.

"Welcome, child, to our home," the high priest said. "I heard the news of your grandfather's passing. Are you only just arriving?"

Ruth replied, "He passed away a month ago, my lord, and it took me two weeks to find passage here."

"Chebron, ask Mysa to join us," Ameres said, and the lad immediately fetched Mysa, who had heard about Ruth's arrival and was eager to learn more about her.

"This is Ruth, Mysa," Ameres said when she entered the room. "She's come to stay with us. She's been through a lot and is without family, so I'm counting on you to show her kindness and understanding. She may not be used to our ways yet, but I'm sure you'll make her feel welcome soon."

"I'll do my best to cheer her up," Mysa answered, gazing at her new companion.

Although the girls were about the same age, Ruth seemed the elder of the two. Mysa was still almost a child, full of joy and life. Her grandfather's passing had crushed Ruth, and she appeared more seasoned than Mysa, the distinction being in attitude as opposed to in face or figure. For quite some time, Ruth had numerous commitments on her shoulders. There was the consideration and medical care of the old man, the improvement of the greenery enclosure on which their endurance relied, the trading the produce for their needs, and making meals. Her grandfather had been treating her like a grown-up individual, and her eyes articulated alertness and gravity. Mysa, then again, was a cheerful girl who had never known the requirement for work or effort; her life had been like a late spring day, liberated from all care and stress. This way, when she gazed at Ruth, Mysa quickly understood that she was a more mature individual than anticipated.

"I feel we'll get along well," Mysa said when her survey was finished, "once we become more familiar with each other, and I'm hoping you'll like me as well; that's what my father said since we'll be together."

Ruth admired Mysa's cheerful countenance and said, "I'm certain we will. I haven't had the chance to interact with other girls my age yet, so I'm sure I'll be awkward at first, but I'll do my best to make you happy since your father and brother have been so kind to me."

"All right, take her away, Mysa. I've told your mother she's coming, and I have to get back to my reading," Ameres said. "Show her around your garden and animals, tell her where she'll sleep, and put her in the care of old Male; he'll make sure she has whatever she needs and get any clothes or other items she needs."

In no time, Ruth quickly settled into her new home. She was like a companion-attendant to Mysa, joining her in walks with Jethro, playing in the garden, helping her feed the animals, and amusing her when she wanted to stay indoors with stories of her life by the Great Sea. Ruth's spirits lifted in this new, wondrous, beautiful environment, and soon enough, the laughter of the two girls echoed through Mysa's garden.

Shortly after their trip to Lower Egypt, a special event came around - Chebron was initiated into the lowest rank of the priesthood. Initially, his duties were minimal, as applicants of higher rank, mostly the sons of superior priests, weren't expected to do any labor that pertained to the lower class. Progressing through the ranks was gradual, but their advancement was swift until they reached a point where study and knowledge alone were necessary for promotion. After that, they only had to partake in the services and ceremonies of the temple that were mandatory for all.

His duties allowed him plenty of time to pursue his studies and daily life, and he almost felt as if he were back home. He was now granted access to the temple at all times and could explore the inner chambers, the apartments with the sacred animals, and areas only priests were usually allowed to enter. Chebron loved to wander in the bright moonlight when no one was around, and the courts were quiet and peaceful. The majestic architecture and figures of the gods held an extraordinary influence over his imagination at night that he could not find during the daytime. The altars of the main gods were constantly lit with flames, which gave their faces an ethereal life-like expression. Occasionally, a priest in a white linen robe would pass by; but for the most part, Chebron had the grounds to himself and could reflect without disturbance. His mind was more inclined to reverence and devotion to the gods when the moonlight shone on the marble floor and the open courts.

During the day, no matter how hard he tried, he could not achieve the same spiritual connection.

Occasionally, a priest donning his white linen robes would wander through the empty courts, yet, mostly, Chebron had exclusive ownership of the area and could meditate without disturbance. He discovered that his mind was then prepared to an elevated level of respect and devotion to the gods that it could not reach when the sun radiated onto the marble floor and the courts were full of worshipers. But, no matter how hard he tried, he could not completely get into the feeling of the situation. Whenever he walked in the solemn parade bearing a sacred vessel or one of the holy symbols, questions regarding whether there could be anything in common between the carved image and the divinity it represented would cross his mind.

He would contemplate whether the god was genuinely satisfied with these processions, whether he felt genuine delight in the carrying around sacred vessels, symbols, and offerings of blossoms. He was appalled at his doubts and did his best to expel them from his intellect. Occasionally it felt to him as if some harsh punishment should be inflicted on him for permitting himself to reason on matters so far beyond his understanding, and he now rejoiced at what he previously was likely to bemoan, that his father had decided against his dedicating his entire life to the service of the temple.

Sometimes he contemplated speaking to his father and confessing that his mind was clouded with doubt, yet the possibility of the shock that such an admission would cause kept him from doing so. Even with Amuba, he stayed quiet, believing that Amuba would not understand him. His companion strongly believed in the deities of his country but acknowledged that the Egyptian gods were as efficient in providing aid to the Egyptians as his own were to the Rebu. Moreover, the truth that the Egyptians were so mighty and prosperous, and conquered other countries, was, he was inclined to believe, due to the superior power of their gods.

The temples' beauty, the processions' glory, and the reverence with which the people worshipped their gods captivated Chebron. Although the strangeness of the images stirred his curiosity, he accepted that the gods could take any shape they wished. Thus, Chebron did not expect to receive understanding from Amuba, so he stayed silent. However, he sometimes took Amuba with him to the temple. The doors were always open so they could enter and meet the priests unnoticed.

When they did wander through the temple, they were both deeply moved by its grandeur and eerie atmosphere in the moonlight. Amuba wondered if he ever returned home and introduced the worship of these powerful Egyptian gods, would they protect the Rebu?

Near the house of Ameres stood the home of Ptylus, a priest second in rank to the high priest in the Temple of Osiris.

There was not much warmth between the two priests, for they differed in character and outlook. Ptylus was narrow-minded and zealous in his faith and meticulous in the practice of rituals; haughty and proud in his attitude, and professing to scorn any knowledge outside of religion, but secretly burning with envy at the praise which the people held for Ameres, and his fame as one of the leading engineers, astronomers, and politicians in Egypt. He had been one of the fiercest opponents of the changes proposed by Ameres and had attempted to stir up such animosity against him that it would be necessary for him to resign his position in the temple.

His disappointment was huge when — due to the influence of the king himself, who held Ameres in too much trust and affection to allow himself to be swayed in his opinion even by what he viewed as the mistaken opinions of the high priest of Osiris — his conspiracies failed. Still, since then, he had kept a close watch on his colleague's actions without finding the slightest reason for complaint about him. For Ameres was a practical man, and having been unsuccessful in gaining approval for his views, he had not kept fighting against the current, knowing that by doing so, he would only bring himself and his family to ruin and shame without making any real progress.

He was meticulous in carrying out his duties in the temple, the only difference being that while others made offerings to Osiris, he devoted his offerings to the great God, whom Osiris was merely a representation of the real god.

The two families had a close relationship. Even though the wives didn't get along, they had similar personalities - they both enjoyed luxury and wanted to be noticed. They both had a laid-back, sophisticated attitude in public, but at home were quite different. The two households competed in entertaining and hosting feasts, with the high priest's wife feeling insulted that the wife of someone of lower status was challenging her. On the other hand, the wife of Ptylus was infuriated by her rival's air of superiority when visiting her. She knew her husband's animosity towards Ameres and did what she could to support him, shaking her head and pretending to know something sinister when his name was mentioned. She left her friends to believe she could tell some dark stories if she wished.

Ameres, on his part, had never talked about his views on religion or his differences of opinion with his colleagues at home. He and his wife had little in common. He allowed her the freedom to do whatever she liked, hosting frequent gatherings for her female friends and spending money as she pleased, as long as it didn't interfere with his lifestyle. He also maintained control of Chebron and Mysa's studies.

One day, when he was in his study, his wife entered. He looked up disapproving, as it was understood that he would not be disturbed while occupied with his books unless it was for something important.

"You must forgive me for interrupting you this once, Ameres; something important has happened. Nicotis, Ptylus' wife, was here this afternoon, and do you know what she had come for? A proposition from her and her husband that their son Plexo should marry our Mysa!"

Ameres exclaimed in surprise and anger. "She's still a child! This is ridiculous!"

"Ameres, Mysa isn't so much a youngster anymore. She's closer to fifteen than fourteen, and making arrangements a year ahead of time is common. I've considered discussing it with you for a while; it's time to think of her future."

Ameres was quiet. Everything his wife said was accurate, and Mysa had arrived at the age when Egyptian ladies were usually engaged. It was an unwelcome shock to him, however. He had seen Mysa as still a child, and his affections were focused on her and Chebron. He had little warmth or sympathy for his oldest child, who was like his mother in character.

"All right," he said in an unusual tone of annoyance, "if Mysa has achieved the age when we must begin to consider whom she is to wed, we will consider it. However, there is no requirement for urgency. As for Plexo, I have noticed him regularly when he has been here with Chebron, and I don't care for his disposition. He's egotistical and authoritarian and, at the same time, shallow and absurd. That isn't the sort of young man I will give Mysa to."

The response wasn't good enough for his wife. She agreed with him in opposing the suggested union, but for entirely different reasons. She had been looking forward to Mysa making a successful marriage, which would increase her own influence and status. On formal occasions, as the high priest's wife and a priestess of Osiris, she was present at all the royal banquets; however, due to Ameres's simple tastes and behaviors, she couldn't take the role she desired in other celebrations. She thought that if Mysa married a great military leader or even one of the royal family members, she would be able to take the place in society she was aiming for and thought she should have as the wife of Ameres, the high priest of Osiris and one of the most reliable advisors to the king.

This wouldn't be the outcome if Mysa married the son of someone with a lower title in the temple than her husband and considerably lower in the public's eyes. Therefore, even though she was content that her husband was objecting to the match for other causes, she refrained from pushing her own point of view, clearly aware that Ameres would not appreciate it.

Consequently, she only said:

"I'm pleased you disapprove of the engagement, Ameres, and I completely agree with you about Ptylus's son. But what excuse shall I give Nicotis for not going along with it?"

"Give the real one, of course!" Ameres said, astonished. "What other reason could there be? As far as rank and wealth, there's no problem. He's an only son, and although Ptylus may not have as much money as I do (what with my governmental appointments), he has the means to give his son at least as much as Mysa could hope for. Refusing the proposal without giving a reason would be a sure way to make Ptylus angry."

"I don't think, Amense, that he'd be happy with us pointing out any flaws in his son, but there's nothing we can do about that. Parents can't expect others to view their children as they do. If I were to offer a husband for Chebron and got turned down because of certain qualities the parents wanted in a son-in-law, I wouldn't be offended. I may think that Chebron has those qualities, but if they don't think so, why should I be angry?"

"Not everyone agrees with you, Ameres, and no one likes their children being disrespected. However, if you want me to pass on to Nicotis that you have a distaste for her son, I will do so."

"Don't phrase it like that, Amense. It's not that I have a personal problem with him. I certainly don't like him, but that has nothing to do with my decision. I might like him a lot but still think he wouldn't be a good husband for Mysa, or I might dislike him personally and still feel like I can trust him to make Mysa happy. You can tell Nicotis that from what I've seen of Plexo and what I know about him, I don't think a union between him and Mysa would lead to her being content. So I'm declining any attempts to start negotiations for their marriage."

Amense was delighted, as she thought this message coming from her husband's mouth would be a massive blow to her opponent, outweighing all the successes she had achieved against her by talking about all the lavish banquets and events she attended.

If Amense had been present when Nicotis told Ptylus that

the offer had been rejected, she might have realized that the satisfaction of getting revenge on a rival sometimes comes at a high price.

"You know the woman, Ptylus, and you can imagine the air of arrogance she had when she declined our proposal. I wanted at that moment to be a peasant's wife instead of a lady of quality, so I could have made her regret her insolence for a long time. I had to contain myself just to smile and say that maybe, the two weren't as compatible as we'd hoped and that we were only giving Plexo what he wanted, as we had a different match in mind that would be much more beneficial. Of course, she replied that she was glad to hear it, but she could tell I was lying since the lotus flower I was holding shook with my anger."

"So, this objection was made about Plexo specifically?" Ptylus said forlornly.

"That's what it seemed like. She didn't admit that she was determined that her daughter should marry one of the royal princes, although it's likely that's what she thought since she can be very determined and ambitious. Instead, she said, formally, that while it would be pleasant for both the families if they were joined, her husband thought that the two young people were too different and that he feared such a marriage wouldn't make either of them happy; and, as he had his unique ideas about a couple needing to agree on all matters, he thought it better to forget about it. I was tempted to tell her that Ameres didn't seem to have followed this idea in his case since everyone knows that he and Amense have no single opinion in common - that she goes her way and he goes his."

"Let them both be aware!" Ptylus exclaimed. "They will discover that we are not to be insulted without consequence. This Ameres, whom the people regard as so holy, is inwardly a nonbeliever of the gods. If he wasn't a favorite of Thotmes, he would have already been shamed and humiliated, and I would be the high priest in his place since his son, Neco, is too youthful for such a high role. Still, he is climbing in rank, and every year his father lives and holds office, he will be more and more seen as his rightful heir. A few more years and my prospect will be gone."

"So," Nicotis declared emphatically, "Ameres should not remain in power for many more years. We have discussed this issue extensively, and you have always promised me that I would eventually be married to the high priest and that Plexo would be next in line for the office. It is about time you fulfilled your promises."

"Enough is enough, Nicotis! We've put up with this man for too long while he has falsely served the gods. He refused our offer, and he must face the repercussions. I have been too lenient, and it's time to take action. I have a powerful following among the upper priesthood who believe Ameres is a dishonor to our faith and a risk to our religion. They will be by my side since they agree that his place as High Priest insults the gods. Don't question me, Nicotis, but trust that I'll keep my promises. I will be High Priest; Plexo can marry the girl he loves, strengthening my standing while making his succession more secure."

"That's great, Ptylus. I've been asking myself why you put up with Ameres' rule for so long. So if I can help you in any way, I'll do it. Oh, and Amense sent us an invite to a feast she's throwing next week. Should we go?"

"Definitely. We can't show we are in any way offended by what has already happened. For Ameres himself, it doesn't matter. He has such a good opinion of himself that nothing can convince him he has any enemies. But, in light of what I have decided, it wouldn't be right for anyone to think there is any bad blood between us."

Excellent preparations were made by Amense for the banquet the upcoming week, as she had determined that this would completely outshine the celebrations of Nicotis. Like usual, Ameres had left all the details to her, and she held back nothing in expenditure. A couple of days before the event, large quantities of food were shipped in from the farm and the city's markets; and on the morning of the party, a battalion of professional cooks showed up to ready the feast. The head cooks oversaw their labors. The main courses included beef and goose, ibex, gazelle, and oryx; though large flocks of sheep were kept for their wool, the Egyptians did not consume the flesh. In addition, there were plenty of ducks, quails, and other little birds. The head cooks managed to cut up the meat and select different portions for boiling or roasting. One servant worked a bellows with his feet, raising the fire to the desired heat; another skimmed the boiling pots with a spoon; and a third pounded salt, pepper, and other ingredients in a large mortar.

Bakers and confectioners made light bread and pastry; the bread was made in rolls sprinkled at the top with carraway and other seeds. The dessert was made of fruit and other ingredients mixed with dough, and a skillful workman formed this into various artistic shapes, such as oxen, vases, temples, and other forms. Besides the meats, all the most delicate fish were abundant.

When noon approached, Ameres and Amense took their seats on two chairs at the upper end of the chief apartment, and as the guests arrived, each came up to them to receive their welcome. Finally, when all had arrived, the women took their places on chairs at one side of the hall, the men on the other. Then servants brought in tables, piled up with dishes containing the viands, and in some cases filled with fruits and decorated with flowers, and placed them down the center of the room.

Cups of wine were handed to the guests, lotus flowers were given to them to hold in their hands, and garlands were placed around their necks. Stands, each containing several jars of wine, stoppered with heads of wheat and decked with garlands, were ranged about the room. Many small tables were now brought in, and around these, the guests took their seats upon low stools and chairs—the women occupying those on one side of the room, the men those on the other.

The servants placed the dishes on the small tables, male attendants waited on the men, while females served the women. Egyptians were unacquainted with the use of knives and forks, the meat being cut up by the attendants into small pieces, and the guests helping themselves from the dishes by using pieces of bread held between their fingers. Vegetables formed a large part of the meal, the meats being mixed with them to serve as flavoring; in a hot climate, a vegetable diet is far more healthy than one composed mainly of meat. While the meal proceeded, a party of female musicians played and sang on the ground in one corner of the room.

The banquet lasted for a long time, with many dishes presented. Then, when it was half over, the figure of a mummy about three feet in length was brought around and given to each guest one after another as a reminder of the uncertainty of existence. But as all present were accustomed to this ceremony, it didn't have much effect, and the sound of conversation and laughter, although quieter for a minute, broke out again as soon as the mummy was removed. Wine of many kinds was served during the dinner, the women and the men drinking it.

When everything was done, the servants brought golden basins with perfumed water and napkins, and the guests removed the gravy from their fingers. Then the tiny tables and stools were removed, and the guests took their places on the chairs along the sides of the room. Next, the parties of male and female dancers came in and performed. Female acrobats and tumblers then entered and went through various performances. Next, jugglers showed great skill, while the musicians of multiple nationalities played in turns upon the instruments used in their own countries. All this time, the attendants moved among the guests, serving them wine and keeping them supplied with fresh flowers. Finally, a bard recited an ode in honor of the glories of King Thotmes, and it was not until late in the evening that the entertainment ended.

"It was a great success!" Amense said to Ameres when everyone was gone and the last visitor had been assisted by his servants; many could not walk without help. "Nothing could have been better—it'll be the talk of the whole town, and I could see Nicotis was full of jealousy and agitation. I deserve much credit, Ameres, since you haven't done anything for the arrangements."

"I am happy for you to have all the credit, Amense," Ameres said wearily, "and I'm glad you're pleased. For me, the whole thing is tedious. All this abundance of food, this excessive use of wine, and the actors' and dancers' poses and antics are revolting. However, if everyone else was happy, of course, I'm satisfied."

"You are the most unsatisfactory husband a woman ever had," Amense retorted. "I believe you would be perfectly happy shut up in your study with your rolls of manuscript all your life without seeing another human being except for a slave to bring you bread, fruit, and water twice daily."

"I think I should, my dear," Ameres replied calmly. "At any rate, I should prefer it to a party like this."

CHAPTER IX

A Startling Event

Chebron and Amuba returned to the temple by moonlight some days later. It had been almost a month since they had been there; they avoided the place during the day when the darkness and gloom of the courts, lit only by the lamps of the altars, was so great. Amuba, free from the superstitions that influenced his companion, would have gone with him at night, although he felt the darkness and the dim, strange figures of the gods more strongly in the moonlight. Chebron, more imaginative and easily affected, found the night terrible and would only go into the silent courts when the moon was up.

When they entered one of the inner courts, they found a massive door in the wall standing open.

"Where does this lead to?"

Amuba asked. "I don't know. I have never seen it open before. I think it must have been left open by accident. Let's see where it leads to."

Opening it, they saw a flight of stairs in the thickness of the wall.

"It leads up to the roof," Chebron said in surprise. "I didn't know there were stairs to the roof, for when repairs are needed, the workmen go up by ladders."

"Let us go up, Chebron; looking down upon the courts will be interesting."

"Yes, but we must be careful, Amuba; if anyone below caught sight of us, they might sound an alarm."

"We need only stay there a minute or two," Amuba urged. "There are so few people around that we are not likely to be seen, for if we walk silently, no one is likely to look so far up."

Amuba led the way up the stairs, and Chebron reluctantly followed. They felt their way as they went and, after climbing for some distance, found that the stairs ended in a narrow passage. At the end of that passage was an opening just three feet high and wide enough for a man to pass through. That opened into the outer air as enough light passed through to let them see where they were standing. Amuba crawled out through the opening at the end. Beyond was a ledge a foot wide; beyond that rose a dome some six feet high and eight or ten feet along the ledge.

"Come on, Chebron; there is plenty of room for both of us," he said, looking backward. Chebron quickly joined him.

"Where are we?" Amuba asked. "There is the sky overhead. We are twenty feet from the top of the wall, and where this ledge ends, it seems to go straight down just before it gets to the sides of this stone."

Chebron looked around him.

"This must be the head of one of the statues," he said after a pause. "What a strange place! I wonder what it can have been made for. Look, there's a hole here!"

Just in front of them was an opening six inches in diameter in the stone.

Amuba pushed his hand down.

"It seems to go a long way down," he said, "but it is narrowing," and removing his arm, he looked down the hole.

"There's an opening at the other end," he said; " it looks like a small narrow slit. It must have been made so that anyone standing here could see down below, though I don't think they could see much through such a small hole. I should think, Chebron, if this is the top of the head of one of the great statues, that slit must be where his lips are. What do you think?" Chebron agreed that it was likely.

"In that case," Amuba went on, "I think this hole must be made to allow the priests to give answers through the mouth of the statue to the people asking for favors from it. I have heard that the statues sometimes gave answers to the worshipers. Perhaps this is the secret to it."

Chebron was silent. The idea was painful to him; for if this were so, it was evident the priests were practicing trickery.

"I think we had better go," he said at last. "We were wrong to come up here."

"Let me look over the side first," Amuba said. "It seems that I can hear voices below."

But the size of the head kept him from seeing anything beyond. Returning, he put his foot in the hole and raised himself enough to get on the top of the stone, which was flat enough here that there was no risk of falling off. Leaning forward, he looked over the edge. Just as Amuba had guessed, he found himself on the head of the principal idol in the temple. Around the altar at its foot were seven or eight men, all of whom he knew by the whiteness of their garment to be priests. Listening intently, he could hear their words. After waiting a minute, he crawled back.

"Come up here, Chebron; something important is going on."

Chebron joined him, and the two, lying close together, looked down at the court.

"I tell you, we have to get rid of him," one of the group below said in tones louder than had been used before. "You know as well as I do that his heart is not in the worship of the gods. He only talks about doing new things; unless we take matters into our hands, there is no saying what he might do. He might end the same worship of the gods. We can't overthrow him out in the open because he has the king's support. Anything we've done before hasn't made any difference. Because of this, I think he has to die. There are plenty of small chambers and recesses which we might trick him into entering, then be killed without difficulty, and his body taken away by night and thrown into some unused catacombs.

"There will be an uproar when he is missed, but no one will ever learn the truth of his disappearance. I am ready to kill him with my hands, and I will regard the deed as pleasing to the gods. Therefore, if you are ready to undertake the other arrangements, and two of you will join me in seeing that this happens without anyone noticing, I will take the matter in hand. I hate him, with his airs of holiness and his pretend love for the people. If we want our religion to succeed, he has to die."

There was a chorus of praise from the others.

"Leave me to decide the time and place," the speaker said, "and the excuse on which we will lead him to his doom. Those who will not be helping me in the act must be nearby and ensure that no one comes that way. We'll need to make some excuse or other if something is heard. Afterward, we'll have to spread rumors about what happened. We won't decide anything tonight, but we don't have to hurry. Let's meet here three nights from now."

Chebron touched Amuba, and the two crawled back to where they stood on the ledge.

"The villains are planning a murder in the very temple!" Chebron said. "I will give them a scare," and applying his mouth to the orifice, he cried: "Beware, evil villains! Your plans will fail, and ruin will fall upon you!"

"Come on, Chebron!" Amuba exclaimed, pulling his tunic. "Some of them might know the secret of this statue, and in that case, they will kill us without mercy if they find us here."

Passing through the opening, they groped to the top of the stairs. Then, they hurried down as fast as possible in the darkness and ran out of the door.

"I hear footsteps!" Amuba exclaimed as they did so. "Run for your life, Chebron!"

Just as they left the court, they heard the noise of angry voices and hurried footsteps close by. They ran at full speed through several courts and apartments.

"We had better hide, Amuba."

"It will be no use trying to do that. They will guard the entrance gates, give the alarm, and set all the priests on duty to search the temple. No, come along quickly. They can't be sure who spoke to them and will wait until someone comes down the stairs to see that no one is hiding. We are safe for now, but there are no good hiding places. I think you had better walk straight to the entrance, Chebron. Your presence here is natural enough; if someone sees you at the gates, they'll let you pass out without suspicion. I will try and find myself a hiding place."

"I certainly will not do that, Amuba. I will not run away and leave you in trouble, especially as my impulsiveness got us into it."

"Is there any place where workmen are engaged on the walls?" Amuba asked suddenly.

"Yes, in the third court right after you come in," Chebron replied. "They are repainting the figures on the upper part of the wall. I was watching them work yesterday."

"Then, in that case, there must be some ladders. With them, we might get away safely. Let us go to the court quickly, but walk silently, and if you hear a footstep approaching, hide in the shadow behind the statue. Listen! They are sounding the alarm. They know they don't have enough guards to scour this great temple."

Shouts were heard, and the lads went toward the court Chebron had spoken of. The temple now was echoing with sounds from the priests, who had been asleep as usual when not engaged in watching the lights, had now been woken by one of their number. He ran in and told them some unholy people had entered the temple.

"Here is the place," Chebron said, stopping at the foot of the wall.

Here stood two or three long light ladders. Some of these reached a part of the distance up the walls, but the top of one could be seen against the skyline.

"Get on, Chebron! There is no time to lose. They might be here at any moment."

Chebron stepped on, followed closely by his friend. Just as he got to the top of the wall, several men carrying torches ran into the court and began to search along the side. Just as Amuba joined Chebron, one of the searchers caught sight of them and ran toward the ladder with a shout.

"Pull, Chebron!" Amuba exclaimed as he tried to haul up the ladder.

Chebron at once assisted him, and the foot of the ladder was already many feet above the ground before the men reached it. The height of the wall was some fifty feet, and since the ladder was light, they could pull it up to the top. The wall was twelve feet thick, and as soon as the ladder was up, Amuba said: "Keep away from the edge, Chebron, or it is possible that in this bright moonlight, we might be recognized. We leave at once. They will tie the short ladders together and be after us quickly."

"Which way should we go?"

"Toward the outer wall, as far as possible from the gate. Bring the ladder along."

They put it on their shoulders and ran out. As nervous as he was, Amuba could not help noticing his surroundings. The massive walls were topped with white cement and stretched like broad ribbons, crossing and recrossing each other in regular parallelograms on a black ground. Five minutes' running took them to the outer wall, and the ladder was again lowered, and they descended and then stood at its foot for a moment to listen. Everything was still and silent.

"Luckily, they did not think of sending men to watch outside the walls when they first caught sight of us, or we would have been captured. I expect they thought of nothing but getting down the other ladders and fastening them together. Let's get away from the temple, and then we will return to your house at leisure. We had better get out of sight before our pursuers find the top of the ladder; then, since they will have no idea in which direction we have gone, they will give up the chase." Finally, after an hour's walking, they reached home. On the way, they had discussed whether or not Chebron should tell Ameres what had taken place and had agreed that it would be best to be silent.

"Your father would not like to know that you have discovered the secret of the image, Chebron. If it was not for that, I should say you should tell him. But I do not see that it would do any good now. Of course, we do not know who the men were who were plotting or whom they were plotting against. But one thing is pretty certain, they won't try to carry out their plans now, for they can't tell how much of their conversation was overheard, and their fear of discovery will end this scheme of theirs, at least for now."

Chebron agreed with Amuba and decided they would say nothing unless circumstances changed. They entered the house quietly and reached their apartment without disturbing any of the inhabitants.

One of the temple's priests arrived early the following morning and demanded to see Ameres. "I have bad news to give you, my lord," he said. "Your son Neco has been killed this morning."

"Neco killed?" Ameres repeated.

"It is, unfortunately, all too true, lord. He left the house where he lived with two other priests a short distance from the temple's entrance at his usual time. It was his turn to offer the sacrifices at dawn, and it must have been dark when he left the house. Since he did not arrive at the proper time, a messenger was sent to fetch him, and he found him lying dead but a few feet from his door, stabbed through the heart."

Ameres waved his hand to signify that he would be alone and sat down half-stunned by the sudden shock.

There wasn't much affection between himself and his eldest son Neco. Neco was cold and formal, and although Ameres would have gladly relaxed around him in his own house, as he had done with Chebron, Neco had never responded to his feelings. He had always been scrupulous in following the Egyptian custom of sons being respectful and obedient to their fathers. Unless commanded to do so, he had never taken a seat in his father's presence, had never addressed him unless spoken to, had only made appearances at stated times to pay respects, and when dismissed, had quickly hurried away to his tutor priest.

As he grew older, the gap between Ameres and Neco widened. Ameres sadly realized Neco's narrow-mindedness and lack of understanding. He saw that Neco's devotion to temple service and religious observances was driven by ambition, as he hoped to become the high priest one day. He guessed that Neco's eagerness to leave home and join two other young priests was a silent way of protesting against the more liberal views of his father.

Although living close by, it was rare that Neco would ever enter the house again after leaving it; usually picking a time when his father wasn't home and only visiting his mother. Hearing the news of his unexpected passing was hard to bear, and Ameres was still for a few minutes until a sudden outburst of wailing in the house showed that the messenger had given his message to the servants and that they had conveyed it to their mistress. Ameres quickly went to his wife's room and tried to comfort her but to no avail.

Amense was frantic with grief. Despite being fond of the indulgences of the world, she had great respect for religion, and Neco's enthusiasm in fulfilling his religious obligations gave her great pride and happiness. Not only was it good to hear her son spoken of as one of the most promising young priests, but she also saw that he would progress rapidly and soon become the designated heir to his father's position. Chebron and Mysa accepted their brother's death with much more composure. They had barely seen him for the prior three years, and nothing connected them, even when living at home. They were more astonished by his sudden death than sad at his loss.

Ameres immediately went to Neco's home to learn more about the situation. There he could not find anything that would provide a clue. Neco had been late at the temple and had not returned until long after the rest of the family had gone to bed, and no one had seen him before he left in the morning. No sound of a fight or cry for help had been heard. His death had been instantaneous. Someone stabbed him in the back, likely hiding close to the door in anticipation of his exit.

The general opinion in the temple and the vicinity was that one of the temple attendants, who had been previously reprimanded or punished by Neco for carelessness or negligence in his duties or the handling of the holy animals, must have been driven by a desire for revenge to committing the murder. However, as a large number of the attendants had been reported by Neco at one time or another, it was impossible to pinpoint the crime on a single individual due to his constant search for minor infractions.

The magistrates arrived shortly after Ameres to look into the case, called in all who might have had a motive of vengeance against Neco and asked them about their activities during the night. They staunchly declared that they had been in bed at the time of the murder, and there was no evidence to incriminate anyone more than the others. After the inquiry, Ameres instructed to bring the body to his home.

Covered in white sheets, it was put onto a kind of sled. Six of the temple's attendants pulled it, with Ameres and Chebron walking behind and a procession of priests after them. When it reached the house, Amense and Mysa, their hair down, received the body, crying out loud in grief, joined by all the house's women. It was taken to an inner room, and until the evening, loud wailing was kept up, many female relatives and friends joining in the lament. Later in the evening, the body was taken out, placed on another sled, and followed by the male relatives, friends, attendants, and slaves of the house; it was taken to Chigron, the embalmer. During the forty days of the procedure, the strictest mourning was observed in the house. No meat, wheat bread, or wine was consumed, nor were baths taken. All the males shaved their eyebrows, and the house echoed with the loud cries of the women.

At the end of that period, the mummy was returned with great ceremony and placed in the designated room of large Egyptian homes for their dead. The coffin was positioned upright against the wall. Similar services to those practiced at the temple were held. Ameres and a few of the leopard-skin-clad priests conducted the rituals. Incense and beverages were presented. Amense and Mysa were present at the observance and wept, their hair disheveled and dust on their heads. Oil was poured over the mummy's head, and after the event, Amense and Mysa hugged the mummified body, washing its feet with their tears and voicing sorrow for the departed.

In the evening, a feast in memory of the dead was held. On this occasion, the signs of sadness were abandoned, and the joyous aspect of the departed's journey to eternity remained. A vast number of friends and relatives were there. The visitors were anointed and decorated with blossoms, as was customary at these festivities. After the banquet, the mummy was pulled through the room as a symbol that their spirit was still among them. Amense wanted to keep the mummy in the house for a while, as was often the custom, but Ameres thought the funeral should occur immediately.

Three days later, the procession started from the house. Servants carrying tables loaded with fruits, cakes, blossoms, vases of ointment, wine, a few young geese in a crate for sacrifice, chairs, wooden tables, napkins, and other items went first. Then came others carrying small cupboards containing the images of the gods; they also had daggers, bows, sandals, and fans, and each had a napkin on their shoulder. Then came a table with offerings and a chariot pulled by a pair of horses, the charioteer walking behind the chariot. Then came the bearers of a sacred boat and the mysterious eye of Horus, the god of stability. Others carried small images of blue pottery depicting the deceased as Osiris and the bird signifying the soul. Then eight women in the class of paid mourners came along, beating their chests, flinging dust over their heads, and crying out loud lamentations.

Ameres, dressed in a leopard skin, and having in his hands the censer and vase of libation, accompanied by his attendants bearing the various implements used in the services, followed by several priests dressed in leopard skins, now came along. Immediately after, they followed the consecrated boat placed on a sled, containing the mummy case in a large external case adorned with paintings. Four oxen and seven men drew it. Amense and Mysa were seated in the boat. The sled was covered with flowers, and Chebron followed with other relatives and friends of the dead, beating their chests and wailing.

When they reached the holy lake, a considerable man-made body of water, the coffin was removed from the small vessel it had been transported in and put into the baris, the sacred boat of the dead. This was a beautiful boat with a high cabin. Amense, Mysa, and Chebron took their places here. It was towed by a large boat with sails and oars. The procession members then got on other splendidly decorated sailing boats and crossed the lake together. The procession was then put back together and went in the same order to the tomb. Here the mummy case was laid on the slab destined for it, and a ritual with libation and incense was performed. The tomb door was shut but not locked, as offerings would be made regularly for many years. The procession then walked back to the house.

During this time, no solid clues had been uncovered about the murderers. Upon visiting the temple on the day of Neco's death, Chebron heard all sorts of wild rumors. People had greatly exaggerated the previous night's events, believing that a large group of men had gone there to steal the sacred vessels, but they were startled before breaking into the underground area where the vessels were kept. They escaped by climbing ladders and leaping over the wall. It was assumed that this was connected to Neco's death. After returning with this news, Chebron and Amuba agreed they needed to tell Ameres immediately. That evening, Ameres asked Chebron to join him in his study.

"Have you heard any news in the temple, Chebron, about the incident that occurred there last night? I can't figure out how it has anything to do with your brother's demise; however, it is peculiar. Do you know who first found the burglars last night? Some are saying it was Ptylus, yet I have no idea what he was doing there at that time. Priests named four or five other men as having roused them, yet curiously, none are at the temple today. I got a letter from Ptylus claiming he was suddenly asked to visit some family members at the coast near the mouth of the Nile. The others sent similar excuses. I have been to their residences, yet all seem to have left early this morning. This is strange since none told me they had something to do elsewhere. What could be their reason for running away when ordinarily they would get praise and honor for having protected the temple's vessels? Have you heard anything that could help make sense of the situation?"

"I haven't heard anything, father, but I can tell you a lot. I would have spoken to you immediately if it weren't for the news about Neco." Chebron then told Ameres how he and Amuba had visited the temple the night before, climbing the stairs behind the image of the god and listening in on a plan to assassinate someone unknown.

"This is a remarkable story, Chebron," Ameres said after he finished his story. "You would have been killed if you had been discovered. How the door leading to the stairs opened is beyond me. The place is only rarely used when it is deemed necessary to influence an event in one way or another. I can only guess that when last used, which was some months ago, the door must have been left unsecured, and it only opened on its own now. But that's a minor detail, and luckily, you made the discovery. As for the conspiracy you heard, it's much more serious. Ptylus and the others' sudden disappearance would suggest they were guilty. It was strange for them to be in the temple so late, and, as you said, they couldn't know how much of their conversation was overheard. I have no idea whom the plot was aimed at. It must have been someone significant."

"Do you think, father, the plot could have been to murder Neco? This is what Amuba and I thought when we talked about it this afternoon."

"I don't think so," Ameres said, taking a moment to consider. "It's unlikely that four or five people would conspire to kill someone of Neco's stature. Everyone respected him in the temple."

Chebron glanced at his father. "Ptylus is a power-hungry man, and he might have had aspirations to be high priest. If Neco's eldest son were fit to take the role, he would've probably been chosen."

"Chebron, that may be true, but we have no reason to assume Ptylus is behind such a wicked plan. After all, why would he share it with others? And, since they know they were overheard last night, they would not have gone through with it. Plus, since no real plan was established, they wouldn't have had a chance to set up a new murder plot. If they killed Neco, it must have been because they thought he was one of the eavesdroppers. His figure is somewhat similar to yours, and they may have gotten a look at you on the walls with your priest's attire. He had been in the temple late and likely left before you were discovered. Thus, suspecting they were heard and that Neco was the listener, they removed him. Of course, it's only a guess that Ptylus had anything to do with what you overheard last night. His absence today is the only thing we can use against him, but it's not enough to make a move. This entire mystery is terrible, and I promise to do my best to solve it.

In any case, we can't do anything for now. Once Ptylus and the other four priests realize that no accusations are being made, they'll return. They'll assume that any listener was scared away by the commotion in the temple. They'll think that the person who heard them, whoever it was, is either too scared to come forward or heard only a few words and is unaware of the speaker's identity. It would take a brave person to accuse five priests of the temple. You can't be blamed for the events that have transpired because it was the gods' will that you'd discovered what you did — they may even intend to use you to bring the guilty to justice. As for the conspiracy, it will probably be abandoned since they can never be sure how much is known of their conversation and if the eavesdroppers are waiting for a royal commission to expose them. You must not visit or enter the temple unless your duties require it.

Mysa and her mother were overjoyed to receive a message from Bubastes the day after Neco's funeral. Months prior, the sacred cat in the great temple in Lower Egypt had fallen ill and, despite the care and attention they provided, had unfortunately passed away. Finding a successor was difficult and essential, and the cat must have specific markings to be eligible. To ensure they found the right cat to fill the vacancy, a group of priests set out from Bubastes to explore Egypt.

The whole nation was worked up about the question of the sacred cat, and at each town, they went to, the priests got records of all the cats that, dependent on size, shape, and color, could be viewed as potential competitors for the situation. When one of the gatherings of the priests had arrived at Thebes, Amense had sent them a depiction of Mysa's huge cat Paucis. Until this point, Amense had not indicated any enthusiasm for her little girl's pets, hardly ever venturing out into the garden except to sit in the shade of the trees close to the fountain briefly in the evening when the sun had lost its intensity.

In a few instances, she had taken a mild interest in the matter since it was fitting that the mistress of the house should take care of such a revered creature and also because everyone agreed that Paucis was a remarkable specimen in terms of size and beauty. As a result, she quickly sent a message to the priests, inviting them to come and evaluate the cat. Usually, the participants of the race to become Bubastes' sacred cat were presented in baskets for inspection, but the priests were more than happy to come in person to the house of the high priest of Osiris.

Amense gave the priests a warm welcome, introducing Mysa as the owner. They were amazed by the size and beauty of the cat, though its markings were not exact. They had seen no cat that compared to Paucis since they left Bubastes. After the parties of searchers returned to Bubastes, their reports would be compared. If none of the cats met all the requirements, the temple's high priest would visit the top contenders. If one cat proved worthy, it would be chosen for the honored position.

If none of them came up to the standard, the post would remain unfilled for a year or two, when it might be hoped that among the new generation of cats, they would find a worthy successor. For themselves, they had to continue their search in Thebes and surroundings, as all the cats must be examined; but they assured Amense that they thought it most improbable that a cat equal to Paucis would be found.

Time passed, and it was not until a week after the funeral of Neco that a message arrived saying that the report concerning Paucis by the priests who had visited Thebes was so much better than any other of the searchers' assertions that the high priest decided only Paucis was worthy of the honor.

The messenger declared that within two weeks, a delegation composed of the high priest and several prominent figures of the temple, along with a group of lower clergy members and attendants, would set out from Bubastes by boat to receive the sacred cat and ceremoniously escort her to the Bubastes shrine. Mysa was ecstatic about the honor bestowed upon her cat. In private, she wasn't as fond of Paucis as she was of some of the less distinguished cats; since Paucis, once it grew up, had none of the playfulness of the rest of the cats but instead carried itself with a tranquil dignity that would be good for its new position, yet made it less enjoyable for Mysa than its humbler yet more active companions.

Amense was overjoyed with the news. It was seen as the highest honor that could be bestowed on an Egyptian for one of their animals to be chosen to fill the top post in one of the temples, and only second to Apis himself was the sacred cat of the great goddess, known as Baste, Bubastes, or Pasht.

As soon as the news was out, all of Mysa's family and friends rushed in to offer their congratulations; the sheer number of visitors to her enclosure was enough to disrupt Paucis' peace, and Amense, wanting to ensure the animal was healthy when the priests came, allowed only those guests she wanted to honor to see it.

CHAPTER X

The Cat of Bubastes

Chebron and Mysa had noticed a strange shift in the behavior of their feathered and furry friends in the garden enclosure. Instead of coming over to say hello, the wildfowl stayed bunched up in the reeds, and the ibis was slow to respond to their greetings. Something unusual was undoubtedly going on.

"They were disturbed about something," Chebron declared on the third morning. "It must have been a bird of prey swooping down on them. Look at all the feathers lying here and there; some are stained with blood. Look at this beautiful drake that the Far East merchants brought us. Its partner is missing. It may have been a hawk or some creature from the weasel family. In any event, we need to do something about it. This is the third morning that we have noticed the birds behaving differently. Doubtless, three of them have been taken away. Amuba and I will keep a lookout tomorrow with our bows and arrows and see if we can put an end to the perpetrator. If this continues, we'll lose all our beloved pets."

Early the following day, Chebron and Amuba arrived at the enclosure just after dawn and hid in the shrubs to wait for the visitor. The ducks were happily playing in the pond, seemingly having forgotten their fear from the day before; and when the sun rose, the dogs came out of their house and lay in the sunshine while the cats groomed themselves on a ledge behind a fence; the cats were only allowed to run around the enclosure when someone was there to keep them from chasing the birds.

For an hour, nothing seemed out of place. Then, suddenly, one of the birds gave a loud warning cry. Instantly, all the birds took flight, trying to find refuge in the reeds nearby. Before the last one could make it, a hawk swooped in from above and grabbed one of the waterfowl. Amuba and Chebron sprang into action and shot their arrows at the hawk. Amuba's shot was on target, and the hawk dropped dead, still clutching its prey. Chebron's arrow flew wide, missing its mark after a branch deflected it.

Amuba gave a shout of triumph and jumped out from among the bushes. But he paused and turned as an exclamation of alarm came from Chebron. Then, to his astonishment, he saw a look of horror on Chebron's face. His bow was still outstretched, and he stood as if petrified.

"What's the matter, Chebron?" Amuba exclaimed. "What has happened? Has a deadly snake bit you? What is it, Chebron?"

"Don't you see?" Chebron said in a low voice.

"I don't see anything," Amuba replied, looking around and, at the same time, putting another arrow into his bowstring, ready to stop the attack of some dangerous creature. "Where is it? I can see nothing."

"My arrow; it glanced off a twig and entered there; I saw one of the cats fall. I must have killed it."

Two years before, Amuba would have laughed at the shock reflected on Chebron's face after shooting a cat. However, he had been in Egypt for a long time and knew how serious the consequences of such an act could be. It would have been better if Chebron's arrow had hit a human instead. In that scenario, an explanation of the accident, compensation to the deceased's family, and an offering to one of the temples would have been enough to absolve him of the transgression; but to kill a cat, even by accident, was an unforgivable sin in the eyes of the Egyptian people, and the perpetrator would be torn to pieces by an angry mob. Knowing this, he immediately understood the dire implications of Chebron's words.

For a moment, he felt almost as stunned as Chebron himself, but he quickly recovered his presence of mind.

"There is only one thing to be done, Chebron; we must dig a hole and bury it quickly. I will run and find a hoe."

Throwing down his bow and arrows, he ran to the little shed at the other end of the garden where the tools were kept, bidding a casual hello to the men already working there. He soon rejoined Chebron, who had not moved from where he had shot the unlucky arrow.

"Do you think this is acceptable, Amuba? Don't you think I had better go and tell my father?"

"I do not think so, Chebron. It would be right at once to confer with him upon any other matter, but as a high priest, it would be a terrible thing to place upon his shoulders. It would be his duty at once to denounce you, and if he kept it secret and the matter was found out, it would make him guilty too. So let's just keep it to ourselves."

"I can't even think about going in," Chebron said, awestruck. "This is too awful."

"That's something I can handle," Amuba replied casually. "For me, a cat is just a cat and nothing else, so I'd be just as happy to bury it as I would that hawk which caused all the trouble."

With that, he strode to an open area and, entering a thick bush beyond the cat house, dug a deep hole and went inside. Despite his lack of faith in the specialness of one animal over another, he had been around Egyptians for long enough to sense a feeling of reverence as he entered and observed it was the largest of the cats that Chebron killed.

After pulling out the arrow, he lifted the animal, and putting it under his cloak, he went out again, entering the bushes, and buried it in the hole he had dug. He smoothed the soil carefully over it and scattered a few dead leaves on the top.

"There, no one would notice that," he said to himself when he had finished, "but it's unlucky it's that cat of all others."

Then he went in, carefully erased the marks of blood upon the floor, brought out the shaft, took it down to the pond, carefully washed the blood from it, and then returned to Chebron.

"Is it—" Chebron asked as he approached. He did not say more, but Amuba understood him.

"I am sorry to say it is," he replied. "It is terrible, for one of the others might not have been missed. But, of course, there is no hoping that now."

Chebron seemed paralyzed at the news.

"Chebron, come on," Amuba encouraged, "we can't surrender to fear. I'll leave the cat house door open, and when they realize it's missing, they'll think it escaped and strayed away. In any case, we won't be suspect if we show a brave face. If it comes to the worst and someone is suspicious, we'll have to get out of the way. But we still have plenty of time to think about that; for now, you must act like nothing happened."

"But how can I?" Chebron uttered with a broken voice. "It's just a cat for you, but for me, it's a creature that I've tragically taken away. It's far worse than if I killed a person."

"A cat is just a cat," Amuba reiterated. "I understand what you feel about it, though it sounds ridiculous. There are plenty of cats in Thebes; they can choose another for the temple. But I realize the danger of what just happened, and I know that if anyone finds out, we're done for."

"You had nothing to do with this mess," Chebron said; "there's no reason why you should take the fall with me."

"We were both in this together, Chebron, and it could have been my arrow that killed the cat just as easily as yours. We set out to kill a hawk, but instead, we stumbled into a terrible situation - no matter how I look at it, the people of Thebes consider it a god. If we're discovered, it'll be certain death for us. So we must keep our wits about us to make it out alive. Unless you don't want to live anymore, you'd better straighten yourself up, or I'll have to run for it alone. So if you don't care about your life, just tell me now, and I'll get a good start running for my life."

"I will tell my father," Chebron said suddenly, "and abide by his words. If he thinks it his duty to make sure I'm punished, so be it; in that case, you will run no risk."

"But I don't mind running the risk, Chebron; I am ready to share the consequences with you."

"No; I must tell my father," Chebron asserted, "and accept whatever he decides. I know I can't handle this situation alone, and my expression will give us away. I have committed the most horrible sin an Egyptian can commit, and I'm not brave enough to keep this nightmare to myself."

"Very well, Chebron, I won't attempt to talk you out of it; I'll talk with Jethro. To both of us, shooting a cat is not worth a second thought; but he will understand the ramifications, and if we flee, he'll join us. Do you mind me speaking to him? You can trust him as much as you can trust me."

Chebron nodded and strode away towards the house.

"Chebron, please!" Amuba said, "Don't walk like that. If any workers spot you, they'll know something is wrong, and it'll be held against you when the animal goes missing."

Chebron tried to walk with as much confidence as he could muster. Amuba watched him for a moment and then shook his head with frustration.

"Chebron is smart and knowledgeable, and I know he's not short on bravery, but the Egyptians seem to lose their nerve under pressure. Chebron looks like he's going to collapse any second. I mean, he's in a real jam, and if he dared to face it, it could be easier for all of us. But I don't think it's the thought that he did something so irreverent that's crushing him. It's more the fear of death. It's almost comical that killing a cat could bring someone so low."

As soon as Chebron stepped into the house, he went to the room where his father was engrossed in study. He pulled the thick curtains closed behind him, walked a few steps forward, then got down on one knee and bowed his head to the floor.

"Chebron!" Ameres shouted, hastily setting down the papyrus he was working on and standing up. "What's wrong, my son? Why are you kneeling in front of me like this? Come on, get up and tell me what happened."

Chebron lifted his head but stayed on his knees. Ameres was alarmed by the look on his son's face. It had lost its healthy glow, and its color had drained away; beads of sweat were on his forehead, and his lips were dry and drawn.

"What is it, my son?" Ameres asked.

"I'm doomed! I've sinned against the gods beyond redemption! Amuba and I were hunting with our bows and arrows this morning, trying to kill a hawk that had been killing the waterfowl. It swooped down, and we both fired. Amuba brought the hawk down, but my arrow missed the mark and flew into the cats' den, killing Paucis, who had only been chosen two days before to serve as the sacred cat in the temple of Bubastes."

At the high priest's outcry of shock, he stepped back a foot from his son.

"This is terrible!" Ameres said, "your life is indeed gone. Even the king couldn't save his son from the people's anger if this happened."

"I'm not thinking of my own life, father, but of the horrible sin and that the shame will partly fall upon you and my mother and sister. Even if you're related to someone who's committed this crime is a terrible danger."

Ameres paced around the room several times before he spoke.

"Well, as to our share of the consequences, we'll have to endure. We have to think of you first. This is terrible, but it is an accident, and you are innocent of bad intentions. But your intention doesn't mean anything. Anyone who kills a cat must die, and the cat of Bubastes is the most sacred of all. So the question is, what should we do? First, you must leave instantly, but I'm afraid that won't help. As soon as it is known that the cat is dead, every man will be looking for you."

"Father, that's unlikely to happen. Amuba went and buried the cat among the shrubs and left the house door open so it looks like the cat was just out roaming. He asked me to run away with him right away. He insists he's ready to share my destiny since we were both involved in trying to take down the hawk. But he's wrong about that; I did this."

"Amuba did well," Ameres said. "We have time to think, at least."

"I don't want to run, father. What good will my life be if I have this stain on me? I can't believe you even want me in front of you since I am someone who has sinned against the gods."

Ameres just waved his hand in front of him.

"That doesn't bother me, I don't look at these things the same way as most men, and if you have to escape, I will tell you more. I don't blame you, and I am not ashamed of you. The most important thing now is to decide what to do. If you escaped now, you might even leave the country before they sounded the alarm. But then, your disappearance would be connected with the cat. If you stay here quietly, maybe no one will connect you with the fact that the cat is gone."

"It's clear that something has happened to the cat since it wouldn't wander too far from where it was raised. A cat of its size and look is quite special, so it would be easily noticed if it were nearby. Now go to your room and join Amuba like usual. I'll ensure your instructor knows you won't need him today as you don't feel well. I'll come to you shortly after I've figured out what to do. Stay strong, my boy; we may be able to avoid this danger."

Chebron was astonished to find his father talking to him with such compassion when he expected that his father would be so appalled by the awful crime of sacrilege that he would not have let him stay in the house after he had told him what happened. Instead, his father seemed to be mainly concerned about Chebron's life, and he was not affected by the most terrible event for Chebron himself - the religious aspect of it. When he entered the room for his studies, he saw Jethro and Amuba.

"My apologies for this, young master," Jethro declared as he entered the room. "I understand why you are so upset about the unfortunate death of the cat, even though I don't think it's worth making such a fuss about. I'm only here with Amuba to let you know that you can trust me and that I'm ready to go with you if you decide to flee."

"Thank you, Jethro," Chebron responded. "It would be a relief to have you and Amuba with me if I decide to run away; however, nothing is set in stone yet. I told my father everything so that he would make the final decision."

"So he won't report you," Amuba commented. "I thought he wouldn't."

"No, he's been surprisingly kind, which I find remarkable. I didn't think an Egyptian would be so understanding about something as tragic as this, even if their son did it. It's even more surprising coming from someone as respected as my father, a high priest to the gods." Jethro said,

"Your father is wise and knowledgeable, so he knows the gods won't be completely angry with a situation fate has put in motion. However, the real culprit behind the cat's death is the twig that caused your arrow to turn, and I don't think you're as much to blame as the hawk you shot."

However, this was useless to Chebron, who collapsed onto a couch in complete despair. Even if he could keep this awful thing a secret, he would have to confess and accept the punishment. How could he live knowing that the gods cursed him? His life would be nothing but misery. Physically, Chebron was not a coward, but he didn't have the strength of mind to allow some people to face difficult situations without crumbling. Amuba and Jethro's attempts to comfort him were also unsuccessful. He regarded Amuba like a brother and usually took his advice, but Amuba had no knowledge of the Egyptian gods, and could not understand the seriousness of his sacrilege, so his opinion didn't matter.

"Jethro," Amuba declared, "you said you'd take Mysa up to the pinnacle of the hills one of these days so that she could look out on the entire city. Make her want to go this morning or convince her to visit the town. Then, if she goes out to the garden, she'll instantly realize the cat is gone; if you can keep her away for the day, it'll give us much more time."

"But if Ameres decides you two should flee, I might come back to find you gone," Jethro replied.

"If he does, Jethro, he'll tell you the route we've taken and set up a meeting place for you to join us. Of course, he'd want you to come along, as he'd know that your expertise and physical power would be essential."

"I'm off then," Jethro conceded. "There have been a couple of trips she's wanted to take, and I can guarantee she'll go on one today. If she mentions wanting to visit her pets before leaving, I can tell her that you two have already been there this morning and checked on them."

"I don't plan to flee," Chebron replied, standing up, "unless my father orders me. I'd rather stay here and accept my destiny!"

Jethro was going to say something, but Amuba gestured for him to leave immediately and crossed the room, taking hold of Chebron's hot and sweaty hands.

"Let's not talk about it, Chebron," he said. "You've put the decision in your father's hands, and you can be sure he'll choose wisely, so the burden is off your shoulders for now. You couldn't find a better advisor anywhere in Egypt, and his holding such an important and holy office will add more weight to his words. If he thinks your mistake against the gods is so terrible that you don't have any hope of finding happiness in life, he'll tell you; if he thinks, as I do, that the gods can't punish an accident the same way as something done on purpose, and that by living a pious life you can hope to win their forgiveness, then he'll suggest that you run."

"He is knowledgeable in the core principles of your religion and will analyze the matter from a different perspective than the uneducated. Therefore, there is no need to worry. As far as any danger goes, I am willing to share it with you, take joint responsibility for this unfortunate incident, and admit that since we were both involved in the act that led to it, we are equally guilty of the crime."

"Alas, I cannot comprehend your distress – the feeling of fear at what you consider sacrilege; since we Rebu don't distinguish between the life of one creature and another, and we have no more qualms about shooting a cat than a deer. Your gods cannot be so influential in Egypt and powerless elsewhere, yet if they are as influential, why is it that their fury hasn't come down on other nations that kill without any reservation the animals that they so love is something I've often asked myself," Chebron remarked, quickly taking the bait since he and Amuba had had countless conversations on such topics. There were always questions he couldn't answer.

Later, when a servant informed Chebron and Amuba that Ameres wanted to speak to them, Chebron calmed from the initial jolt of excitement. The two boys bowed respectfully at the high priest and then waited respectfully for him to say something.

"I have summoned both of you," he said after a moment of silence. "I fear that since Amuba was with you during the uproar, the mob may be unable to distinguish between you." He regarded them attentively before continuing. "What do you think? Should I tell the truth, or should you flee?"

Amuba reacted promptly. "That's exactly what I've been telling Chebron. I believe I'm as guilty as him. It was only a matter of chance that my arrow missed the target instead of his. I'm ready to face the same consequence as him." Ameres lowered his head thoughtfully and then looked at his son.

"I, Father, though I'm willing to give in to your wishes, I'd like to ask you to let me accept the penalty for my actions. I'd rather die than face the guilt of this heinous crime."

"I knew you'd say that, Chebron, and I respect your decision," Ameres said solemnly.

Chebron's expression lightened while Amuba's became darker.

Ameres continued, "If I believed that the accidental killing of a cat was a mortal sin, I'd tell you to denounce yourself, but that's not my opinion."

Chebron looked at his father like he couldn't believe his hearing, and Amuba looked surprised.

"Chebron, you've asked me questions time and time again, but I have either avoided them or not answered. I saw that you had inherited the same inquisitive spirit as me, so I thought it best for you to stay away from the highest order of priesthood. If you had gone there, you would have acquired knowledge that could have made you as dissatisfied as me with the state of things around you. I would never have spoken to you if not for this unfortunate event. Nevertheless, I feel that I must tell you more.

"I have had a difficult internal struggle since you left, and I've thought long and hard about what I should do. On the one hand, I could tell you things nobody knows, but if anyone were to find out I whispered them to anyone, I'd be in deep trouble. However, if I stay silent, you will be doomed to a life of unhappiness. I have chosen the former option. I should tell you what you don't know yet: my beliefs go against those of the higher priesthood, as I think our knowledge should be shared with educated Egyptians who can appreciate it.

What I'm about to tell you is not, as a whole, fully understood by anyone. This is the result of my own contemplation, forming upon reflections I've gotten through my journey. Chebron, you asked me one day how we came to know about the gods – how did they initially disclose themselves, considering that they are not things that exist in this world? To which I responded to you at the time that these matters are mystifying – a convenient response we use to shut the mouths of the curious.

"Hear me out, and I'll explain how religion first came to be on Earth, not just in Egypt, but everywhere. People were aware of their limitations. Observing the cycles of nature—the movements of the stars, the processes of life, birth, and death—they rightly concluded that there was a divine power at work, but this power was too great for them to comprehend.

"He was everywhere and nowhere, living in everything yet invisible; he gave fertility and inflicted famine, gave life and dealt death, radiated light and heat, and sent storms and gales. His eternal and multifaceted nature was too complicated for the primitive intellect to understand, so they approached Him in parts. They venerated Him as the Sun, the giver of heat, life, and abundance; they adored Him as a destructive force, invoked

Him as a benevolent presence, and offered sacrifices to soothe His fury as a menacing one. As time passed, they regarded all His attributes – all the aspects and sides of Him – as distinct and separate, not as the qualities of a single God, but as the traits of numerous deities.

"Hence, a god of life and a god of death were born, one who provides fertility and one who brings famine. Various inanimate objects were thought to possess some made-up attribute, either for good or evil, and the all-powerful God became obscured and lost in the throng of minor deities. According to their intelligence, different nations imagined different gods. In some, serpents are sacred, likely due to their representation of a god's cunning and destructive power. Others revere trees. People in some countries venerate the sun; in others, it's the moon. Our ancestors in Egypt, being more intelligent than the barbarians in their midst, worshiped the qualities of gods under different names. Initially, eight significant gods were chosen to symbolize the primary characteristics of the Almighty. Chnoumis or Neuf represented the spirit of God—that spirit that permeates the entire universe. Ameura symbolized the intellect of God. Osiris was a symbol of the benevolence of God. Ptah embodied the working power and truthfulness of God. Khem exemplified the productive power—the god overseeing the multiplication of all creatures: human, animal, aquatic, and plant—and the other major gods and minor deities, which amount to too many to count."

"In the present day, certain animals, birds, and other creatures whose traits are seen to be similar to one or more of the gods are initially thought to be of them, then are considered to be holy to them, and eventually become intertwined with the gods and even begin to be perceived as the gods themselves. I believe this is the story of the religions of all nations. The learned and educated elite never wholly forget the original truths and acknowledge that the gods are just representations of the single omnipotent God. Unfortunately, the rest of the populace ignores the truth and venerates these various creatures as gods, which are only symbols and reflections.

"It is indeed necessary that it should be this way. People who are less educated and less aware find it simpler to revere things that they can see and understand, to make an effort to please those whose statues and religious structures they observe, to dread to bring upon themselves the indignation of those presented to them as destructive powers, than to venerate an incomprehensible God, with no visible shape, so powerful that the creative mind can't conceive him, so generous, so plentiful, so uniform and tranquil that the human brain can't even understand him. Humans are physical and must honor the physical in a way they believe they can fathom it. And thus, they make gods for themselves with forms, representations, emotions, and sensations comparable to those of the numerous creatures they find in their environment."

"The Israelite girl that we brought here and with whom I have talked often shares with me that her people, before arriving in this land, worshipped one God, similar to the one I have told you about, except that they looked at him as a special God of their own, providing for them more than any other people on Earth. However, otherwise, he corresponded to the Almighty One whom we worship in our hearts, who have had glimpses of the truth from before the time of the Pantheon of Egypt. Therefore, it appears that this small group of individuals who came to Egypt hundreds of years ago may have been the only people who maintained the unwavering worship of one God."

Chebron and Amuba stood in awe as the high priest spoke. Amuba's face beamed with pleasure and excitement as he heard words that seemed to alleviate all his doubts and worries. For Chebron, the news was both joyous and shocking. His curiosity had been growing for a while, but the sudden dismantling of his life-long beliefs and values was an immense surprise. Neither said anything after the priest's speech, and he continued after a moment of silence.

"Chebron, you should know that not everyone holds the same views I have expressed here. My ideas come from my studies of

Egyptian teachings and the traditions of other civilizations that have interacted with Egypt. Still, many of those who are most knowledgeable about our spiritual beliefs recognize that all of our gods are merely embodiments of a single higher power and do not exist as we depict them in our temples.

"When we offer sacrifices, we are not worshipping the images behind our altar, but instead paying homage to God, the creator, preserver, nurturer, ruler, and omnipotent being of good and evil. As a result, our services have no mockery, as they have a deeper meaning that is not understood by others. They worship a being with a moral code, whereas we worship the principles themselves. They interpret the mystical figure as a representation of a deity, whereas we interpret it as an attribute of a higher being."

"You might think that, in revealing all this, I am revealing secrets that should be told only to those who have been initiated into their religion. That I am being unfaithful to my vows. These are matters of my conscience. I have long thought that more people should be brought into the circle of initiates, and those educated and intelligent enough to appreciate the power of truth should no longer be kept in the dark. I was overruled and would not have spoken if this had not happened, but I see that your future happiness is in danger. If the secret were ever discovered, you would either be put to death, in despair and hopelessness, or have to flee and live in a foreign land in the same state. Ultimately, I felt that the balance of obligation lay in enlightening your mind by revealing what I know. It is not, as I said, only because of what I have been taught but because of my study and understanding of God's nature. So, my son, you can put aside the horror you felt because you thought you had offended the gods beyond forgiveness by accidentally killing a cat. The cat is only a representation of the qualities attributed to Bastet. Bastet herself is only a representation of one of the qualities of the One God."

"My father!" Chebron shouted, falling to his knees next to Ameres and grasping his hand. "You're a miracle! You've taken such a heavy burden off my mind! You've opened up such a great future for me if I can escape the danger I'm in now! Even if I pass away, I can do so feeling content about what comes after. If I make it, I won't be weighed down by the doubts and uncertainties hanging over me for so long. Though you haven't given me a glimpse of the great truth yet, I've felt that the answers you've given me haven't satisfied me. It's also seemed like you, with all your knowledge and wisdom, haven't been able to help me as you did with all the other questions I've asked you. But, father, you've given me life—more than just life. You've given me power over fate. Now, I'm ready to fly if you think that's best or to stay here and take on whatever comes my way."

"I don't think you should flee, Chebron. It would be an admission of guilt; I don't know where you could go. By tomorrow, they'll figure out the creature is missing, and a hunt will be launched. If you stick to heading towards the sea, you'll most likely be caught before you get there. Even if you reach a port ahead of your pursuers, you may have to wait days for a boat to sail."

"Then, again, if you were to hide in any kind of secluded spot, it would surely only be a matter of time before you were found - news of your whereabouts would spread across Egypt, and it would be everyone's duty to look for and denounce you. Messengers would be sent to all countries under the rule of Egypt's government, and even if you managed to pass the boundaries of Egypt by land or sea, the danger would still be just as great. Moreover, if you somehow managed to go beyond Egypt and reach a land beyond its control, you would be an exile for life. So I'm saying that running away should be your last resort, and it should only be done if someone were to discover you, but let's hope that luck won't be so unkind as to lead the searchers to the conclusion that the cat was killed here."

"When it's gone, everyone will search high and low for it. Ultimately, when it's determined to be irrecoverably lost, all kinds of theories will be proposed to explain it; some may guess that it wandered off to the hills and became the meal of hyenas or other wild animals; some will believe it was killed and stowed away; others will state that it made its way to the Nile and was taken away by a crocodile. Thus, there's no special reason why the finger should point at you more than anyone else, but you must carefully handle the situation."

CHAPTER XI

Dangers Thicken

When Chebron and Amuba returned to their study room, they didn't talk about the cat or the looming danger; they spoke of Ameres' incredible revelation. They couldn't doubt his words – they held him in such high regard that they accepted whatever he said. But it wasn't just that – they felt that what he said was true. His explanation filled them with joy, wiping out their confusion and doubt and dispelling the strange and confusing figures that had amused Amuba and confused Chebron.

"What Ruth said must be true," Amuba noted. "I remember that she told us how her forefathers who came down into Egypt believed in the existence of only one God, who couldn't be seen or depicted and was God of all the heavens and infinite. Everything she said about Him is right apart from the bias that he more favored her ancestors than others."

"It's incredible." Chebron reflected, pacing up and down the room. "Now that I know the truth, it's incredible that I did not doubt the existence of all the strange images in our temples. It had worried me so much, and now I see how foolish it was. It feels like the people of Egypt live in a delusion. How can those who know better let them stay in the dark?"

"I understood what your father said, Chebron, that he only

wants the more enlightened and educated people to get a glimpse of the truth. I can understand that. If all the lower class discovered that the gods they worshiped were merely reflections of a great God and not living gods, they would probably either attack and tear apart anybody who told them that as being blasphemous or, if they could be made to understand it, they would no longer adhere to any religion, and in their anger could tear down the temples, abolish the hierarchy of the clergy, cause chaos and destruction across the country, revolt against all authority, demolish with a single blow all the strength and grandeur of Egypt."

"That's true," Chebron said thoughtfully. "It's clear that ordinary people need something concrete to worship. They must believe in gods who will reprimand wrongdoers and reward the good. As they understand it, the religion of Egypt is more appropriate to their daily needs than venerating a deity so mighty, great, and good that their intellect isn't capable of comprehending him."

Ruth's entrance abruptly halted their conversation. "Paucis is missing. When we returned from our walk, we went to check on the animals, and the door of the house door was open, and the cat was gone. So Mysa says would you come and help us look for it? I was told to ask all the women who can be spared from the house to help with the search."

Work was immediately abandoned, for everyone knew that Paucis had been chosen to be the sacred cat at Bubastes; even if it had been one of the others, the news that it had gone missing would have caused a considerable stir. Moreover, cats were so highly valued that if one happened to die in a house, the inhabitants would grieve and shave their eyebrows in a sign of mourning; embalmers were then summoned, the dead cat was mummified, and then taken with great solemnity to the great catacombs set aside for the burial of the holy animals. Thus, the news that Paucis was lost was so significant that work was quickly put to one side, and the men and female slaves started to scour the garden, looking under every bush and tree and calling out for the missing pet. Naturally, Chebron and Amuba got involved in the search with just as much zeal as everyone else.

"Where could it have gone?" Mysa cried out in disbelief. "Why would it have wandered away? It never did before, even though the cat house door is usually left open all day. What do you think could have happened to it? Could it have jumped over the wall?"

"It could easily get over the wall," Chebron replied sorrowfully.

"It's a terrible calamity!" Mysa continued, tears streaming down her face. "Mother fainted when she heard the news, and her women are fanning her with feathers, smacking her hands, and sprinkling water on her face. What will be done if it doesn't come back before tomorrow? I hear a solemn procession is coming from Bubastes to take it away. Poor sweet Paucis! It seemed so content and happy, and it had everything it wanted! What could have made it wander off?"

"Cats can be unpredictable," Amuba noted. "Unlike dogs, who are always eager to obey their owners and will lay around for hours, waiting to be called."

"True, but Paucis wasn't a typical cat, Amuba. It didn't want to hunt for mice and birds. It had all the luxuries—plush beds to sleep on, fresh water and milk to drink, and plenty of food."

"But even with all that, cats can still follow their instinct to wander," Amuba said.

Ameres himself soon stepped out of the house and, on hearing that the cat was nowhere to be found in the garden or indoors, commanded the males of the household to go out searching, to inform all the neighbors what had happened and to urge them to look in their gardens. They were also to ask anyone they met if they had seen a cat that resembled Paucis.

"This is a dire situation," Ameres said. "Once the priest of Bubastes had chosen Paucis to be the holy cat of the temple of Bubastes, the utmost care and attention should have been taken when it comes to an animal that all of Egypt had their eyes on. For the past couple of weeks, the issue of which cat would take the coveted post has been discussed in every household. There has been great enthusiasm among families with cats that could even remotely be chosen. I shudder to think of the uproar if the cat isn't there when the procession arrives tomorrow from Bubastes to take her there. The commotion and stir will be tremendous, and the matter will be of national importance. All right then, don't just stand here, but go out and join in the search."

"I felt incredibly guilty when I talked to Mysa," Chebron said. "She is very proud that Paucis was chosen for the temple, but I know she has been struggling with losing her favorite. But of course, that was nothing compared to how she would feel when she finds out that no news of the creature can be found; and it was difficult to act like I didn't know anything about it when I knew all along it was lying dead and buried in the garden."

"Yes, I felt that too," Amuba agreed, "but there's nothing we can do about it. Mysa will likely have a much more painful sorrow to bear in her lifetime than the loss of a cat."

Throughout the day, the search continued, and by nightfall, numerous men with torches investigated every nook and cranny near Thebes. The news had spread far and wide, and many of the high priest's friends came to inquire about the incident and to express their condolences. Many theories were suggested about where the animal had gone, while the chances of its retrieval were discussed with excitement. It was generally assumed that it would quickly be found, as an animal of such remarkable features must have drawn attention wherever it went. But, on the other hand, if it didn't return of its own volition, as was commonly thought, it was sure that it would be recovered within hours.

Alarm spread through the household as, on the following morning, it was discovered that Mysa's beloved cat had not returned. For the first time, some hinted that something awful might have happened...a dog might have gotten it, or maybe it was carried off by a crocodile. However, no one dared suggest that a human was responsible for its disappearance; the thought was too monstrous.

Mysa wept herself to sleep, and her mother took the

misfortune so seriously that she stayed in bed. The slaves went about silently, speaking in hushed tones as if a death had occurred. Ameres and Chebron were anxious, and Amuba and Jethro went out to search and make inquiries in distant places - though they were secretly amused at the fuss over a missing cat.

Ameres' household was fortunate to have him in such a prestigious position. The escalating search for the missing cat would have quickly caused a public uproar if he had been a commoner. But the respect for the high priest of Osiris, his status, knowledge, and goodwill meant it was impossible to think the missing cat had been lost on his property. It was widely believed that after wandering off, as cats will do, it was either killed by a wild animal or eaten by a crocodile.

The penalty for killing a cat in Egypt was so severe, and the act was considered such a great sacrilege that it was almost unheard of. This was especially true for cats chosen for the temple of Bubastes, like the one owned by Ameres. After a week passed with no news of the cat, it was assumed that it was dead, and Ameres and his family mourned the loss by shaving their eyebrows, as was customary. It was almost inconceivable that human hands had killed the cat.

Although Ameres wasn't suspected of having anything to do with the cat's disappearance, the misfortune left a mark on his household. It was seen as a terrible stroke of misfortune that a cat, especially one so prized, could go missing on the eve of its installation as a sacred temple animal. Some people believed it was a sign of the gods' anger, and many friends and acquaintances kept their distance. But Ameres was unbothered by public opinion and carried on unperturbed, performing his temple duties and devoting the rest of his time to study.

Ameres' wife was deeply affected by the change in respect and status. She was displeased with the difference in the way their acquaintances treated them and the lack of invitations to entertainment. No matter how often Ameres attempted to calm her nerves with kind assurances that everything would be fine, she remained unconvinced. Her servants felt the full force of her frustrations; she continued pressuring Ameres to stand up for what was rightfully theirs.

But as the days went on, tensions only increased. Groups often gathered around the house, hurling angry words and insults when anyone came or left. Even as Ameres marched through the streets while bearing religious symbols, the crowd jeered and booed. Chebron was deeply affected by this hostility and begged his father to let him speak the truth and accept the consequences.

"I'm not afraid of dying, Father. Haven't you taught me to act like life is nothing? Isn't our feast a constant reminder that death is ever-present? You have Mysa and Mother. I fear death far less than the constant dread hovering over us."

Ameres refused to accept the sacrifice. "I initially thought the matter would die down, but I was wrong. The poor creature's selection as the temple's sacred cat has caused a huge uproar. I can't help but think someone is working behind the scenes to fan the flames. I believe Ptylus is involved somehow. Since his sudden absence and return after the night you heard a conversation, he has been putting on a show pretending he's our friend."

"I'm not sure if he was one of the people you overheard, but the fact that he suddenly disappeared supports that idea. Regardless, he likely has no reason to be cordial to me after I rejected his son as a husband for my daughter. When you initially told me what you heard, I thought they might be plotting against me. Now I'm sure of it.

"It's clear they didn't think anyone was listening, or else they would have done something to prevent their conversation from being overheard. And yet, his friendly attitude towards me has only made me more suspicious. I'm sure there's an enemy at work here. Even if you were to take the blame for the missing animal, it wouldn't only mean your death—it would mean destruction for all of us.

"The mob would instantly blame me if they found out about this, and even the king's favor cannot protect me if the public starts to turn against me. No, we must stick together on this one, son. Jethro suggested moving the cat elsewhere and hiding it, but the risk would be too great. The house is under surveillance - people have been roughly pushed and thrown around while going in and out at night. Some of them were even beaten and left almost naked. We can't take the chance that Jethro might be followed or attacked and the cat discovered. We have to keep things as they are."

Ameres didn't share with Chebron the full details of his conversation with Jethro. After turning down his offer to get rid of the cat's body, he said: "But, Jethro, even though you can't take on this risky endeavor, I trust you enough to give you a task that will show my confidence in your dedication to my family. If this storm comes, if the townspeople become aware that the sacred cat was killed here, a massive outburst of fanatical fury will sweep everything away."

"I'm ready to accept whatever fate awaits me, for I have done my best for the people. I have never shied away from hard work, and now I'm ready for a rest, but I would still like to save Chebron and Mysa from harm. Mysa may need a protector, but I can't do anything to help her. I'm counting on you, Jethro, to save Chebron and Amuba. I believe that Chebron has potential; he's intelligent and ki, kind-hearted, and on par with other boys his age. It's been my priority to ensure he's educated well. I'm calling on you, Jethro, to do whatever you can to help him and Amuba.

"If the slaves are questioned and possibly punished, it will be revealed that the two boys were present amongst the animals the day before the cat was missing. It's also been noticed that they had their bows and arrows with them. So it will be assumed that both of them committed the act. Chebron would have spoken the truth if given a chance. However, a frenzied mob does not wait to listen, and the boys will each face the same fate.

"You, an outsider to our customs, may find it difficult to understand the frenzy and anger in which the people of Egypt reacted when a cat was killed. I doubt that even the king would be safe if he were found guilty of such a crime, which is especially serious because the animal was supposed to be taken to the temple of Bubastes. But, of course, if there is an uprising, they have no choice but to flee. But where could they go?

"There's no safe place for them in Egypt. Going north and reaching the sea before the news spreads to the ports is impossible. Messengers will be sent to nearby cities, and even the provinces east of the Mediterranean Sea will be alerted. Leaving the country and crossing the desert is risky, as they could be sent back upon arrival. The routes to the Arabian Sea are also blocked. Their only hope seems to be reaching the remote area up the Nile and reaching Meroe, where Egypt's authority is merely symbolic. They could reach the Arabian Sea, cross it, and travel back up through the Mediterranean Sea to their homeland. Before they leave the tribal regions and embark on their journey, this news would have been forgotten, and the risk of arrest for involvement in this matter would have disappeared.

"I know that you would do all you can to ensure the safety and well-being of the son of your late king, and if it is possible to navigate the perils of such an undertaking, I am sure you will be able to guide him through them. Therefore, I ask you to extend the same protection to Chebron and provide him with the same support you will give to Amuba."

"I am more than happy to promise that, my lord," Jethro replied. "Chebron has been more like a brother to Amuba than a servant since we arrived here, and I will treat him as if he were his kin now that we face such danger. The journey will be lengthy and treacherous, but I agree it is the only path to freedom."

"I entrust my son to your care, Jethro, with complete faith that he'll make his journey safe and sound. I have already handed a generous sum of money to Chigron, the embalmer, one of the leading businessmen in Egypt. Thanks to my patronage, he has been successful in his profession and is renowned for embalming sacred animals of our temple and several others. He will keep the boys secure until your journey is ready to begin.

"When you're a few days south of Thebes, you'll be relatively safe from pursuit. They won't think of looking for you in that direction, so they'll assume you'll try to leave the country by sea, through the Eastern Desert, or you might try to reach some of the tribes in the west and make it to the Great Sea. At first, I thought that would be the best option, but the tribes are all under our control, so they would view any Egyptians among them as fugitives and turn them over to us.

"You can count on me to follow your instructions and do everything to help the two boys. I have no idea what the country we're passing through is or who the people are, but we'll do our best to get to the Arabian Sea, as you asked. Amuba's tough and strong, and Chebron is brave and skilled in battle, so we should travel in disguise. You also mentioned your daughter—how can I help her? I've been accompanying her on walks for months and would gladly give my life for her."

"I'm afraid there's nothing you can do," Ameres said hesitantly. "We have many friends, one of whom will surely take her in. I would like it if she could visit some of my relatives living at Amyla, fifty miles up the river. She stayed with them two years ago and would know the house, but I don't see how you could take her - the boys will be enough of a burden. She will have her mother with her, and though I'm afraid her mother has little real love for her, being too preoccupied with her desires and amusements, she should be able to find her a place among the many friends she has."

"I'm not just thinking about the present, but more importantly, the future. I want my little Mysa to get married happily. Unfortunately, she's a bit willful and has been spoiled, so even if I arrange a marriage for her, I won't let her marry someone she doesn't like. I'm worried she won't get the same consideration if something happens to me. Still, Jethro, I don't see any way you can help Mysa. We have to leave things to happen as they will."

"I hope your fears don't come true," Jethro said. "I can't believe a silly suspicion could make people forget how much they respected you." Ameres shook his head sadly.

"The people are always fickle and easily swayed, Jethro. Their deep reverence for the gods makes it easy for those who play on these emotions to whip them into a frenzy. All else pales in comparison to their religion in their eyes. It's an act of blind faith, though a sincere one. None of the people in the world are as devoted to their religion as the Egyptians. It's deeply entrenched in all aspects of their daily lives. From their feasts and processions to how they eat, drink, and dress, they consider the gods in all of it. They don't take even the tiniest action without consulting the gods. So while they usually follow the law, they become enraged at any perceived insult to their religion or deviation from its practices. I know we're in danger. My efforts to purify the people's religious beliefs have been used against me. I know from what I've heard that it's been whispered among them that despite my high rank, I have no respect for the gods."

"The claim is completely false, yet still immensely dangerous. It's hard to tackle a falsehood once it's left its mark, as it spreads like wildfire, and even the best evidence of its falsity may never reach a fraction of those who believe it. But let's not focus on that now. If any danger arises, you know exactly what to do—take the boys away and bring them to a safe place. If they're not at home, look for them and guide them there. Don't waste time trying to save me. If attacked, don't attempt to fight back unless necessary to make a getaway. Above all else, do not try to come to my aid. No matter how powerful, one person cannot stand up against a mob—your attempts to help me would be futile and could cost you your life, taking away the protector of Chebron and Amuba."

Jethro firmly promised to obey his instructions and do whatever was necessary to guarantee the boys' safety.

Two days later, Ameres sent Chebron and Amuba to the farm and told them to stay there until he called for them.

"You can't come and go here without creating a commotion," he said, "so it's best if you stay away. You're as likely to be suspected as I am. As for your mother and sister, the current situation is inconvenient for them, but that's all. They won't be in danger; no matter how ruthless a mob is, they won't bother the females."

"So why don't you leave until the trouble ends, father?"

"I can't just abandon my responsibilities, Chebron. And besides, it wouldn't do me any good. I'm convinced this outcry against me is just an excuse used by people who don't dare to face me head-on. If I left Thebes, they'd make up tales about me, and people would get even more worked up. So my only option is to endure this difficulty, trusting that my life has been free of any crime that would displease the almighty god I serve. I know my life is in his hands, and He'll call me home when it's time."

"Could you ask the king for some guards?"

"Yesterday, the king addressed me after the council," Ameres replied. "He was informed of the discontent of the people towards me. He said he knew my loyalty and high ranking as a priest of Osiris and understood that the accusations against me were false. However, in light of the people of Thebes's volatility and disquietude, he would be willing to send a battalion of soldiers to safeguard my residence. I declined. I argued that I was not guilty of wrongdoing; no one could accuse me of failing to perform my temple duties or saying anything to discredit our religion. Furthermore, I had nothing to do with the disappearance of the sacred cat, which is what people have been so worked up about. It must have been some kind of mishap. If I were to accept the armed protection, it would be an admission that I am guilty and have lost the gods' protection. It would also perpetuate the rumors and unrest, which I hope will eventually pass."

Chebron did not attempt to question the orders of Ameres, and an hour later, he and Amuba departed for the farm. However, before they left, Ameres had a lengthy discussion with Chebron, and he informed him that he had appointed him in charge of Jethro in the event of unrest.

"Bear in mind, Chebron," he said, "that whatever happens with this situation, you are not responsible for the mishap of killing the cat. Everything is in the control of the divine God, and your arrow would not have hit the twig and flown directly to that animal's heart if it were not His will. Additionally, you must always recall that the loss of this cat is only an excuse for the uproar."

"The general public thinks they are mad because of the sacred cat's death; however, they are tools my enemies use. I do not doubt that the plot you heard about in the temple was about me, and if the cat's death hadn't been so convenient and used to help them against me, the plot would have taken a different form. I sincerely hope that nothing happens to your sister before we see each other again and that she never has to marry the son of the person who plotted against me. But there's no use thinking about it now. If something does happen, remember that I have put you in Jethro's care and have given him my trust. He is wise, strong, and brave and can be counted on to do what is right. In Amuba, you will find a friend who will be like a brother to you. So goodbye, my son, and may the great one who rules over all keep you safe!"

CHAPTER XII

The Death of Ameres

The days went by slowly on the farm. The boys walked out absentmindedly to observe the cows walking in the field and the other operations on the lands, but they were too concerned with what was happening in the city to be moved by the work on the farm. On the second and fourth days after their arrival, Jethro had given them a brief visit to say there was no shift in the circumstances. The officer in control of some militia whom the king had sent down to near the house had come down to the mob as they were yelling outside the gate and warned them of the stern disapproval of the king unless they stopped their demonstrations, but had been answered with shouts, "The gods are above all kings, and not even kings can protect those who insult them." Amense, he said, had left the residence and stayed with some relatives in the city, proclaiming that the anxiety and humiliation were killing her. She had wanted to bring Mysa with her, but the girl had firmly refused to depart from her father, and as her mother seemed uninterested whether she went or stayed, she had had her way. Then, in a private chat with Amuba, Jethro said:

"We are all relieved that she left; even before you left, she was bad enough, but for the last three days, she has been doing nothing but sobbing and lamenting, making the home almost unbearable. Ameres keeps going back and forth between his house and the temple, walking unaffectedly through those crowded around his door, who are generally silent when he passes, intimidated by someone they have so highly respected. As for Mysa, she seems to think of nothing else but her father. The Hebrew girl is a great help to her because while their mistress' attitude and the public's outcry scare the other maids, causing them to walk around the house in terror, Ruth remains calm and composed as if she were back in her humble cottage with her grandpa. She supports and encourages Mysa a lot, and Ameres told me this morning that Mysa was lucky to have such a brave and resolute companion like Ruth at this time."

On the evening of the fifth day, Jethro came bursting into the house. The boys jumped to their feet, instantly recognizing the distress on his face. He had run the six miles from the farm to the city at a sprint, his face covered in blood, and his breath was short.

"Hurry, my lord!" he said urgently. "There's no time to lose. It's all been uncovered, and they'll be chasing you soon."

"What happened to my father?" Chebron asked in alarm.

"I will tell you all about it afterward, Chebron. There is no time for talking now; we must follow his orders immediately. Where are the fellows who are spying over you?"

"One of them is probably seated outside at the entrance to the farm. You must have passed him as you entered," Amuba replied. "I have not seen more than one at a time since they first came."

"Take up your arms and follow me," Jethro said, taking a heavy staff from the corner of the room, and, followed by the young men, he went outside the gate.

Darkness descended as a man approached them as if to see who they were. Without a word, Jethro launched forward and struck the man with his staff, and he dropped to the ground soundlessly.

"He won't be able to alert anyone," Jethro said sternly, sprinting towards the city faster than Chebron could keep up. At times, the boy asked about his father's safety, but Jethro seemed to ignore him and kept running at a consistent speed.

Abruptly, Jethro stopped and listened. A vague, disordered noise could be heard ahead of them, and Jethro stepped away from the road and made his way through the fields. Amuba listened to the sound growing louder and soon realized a group of people were moving along the road.

"I'm glad I managed to get away," Jethro said. "They would have trapped both of you had they arrived at the farm, and you were caught off guard."

Jethro didn't go back to the road. Instead, he kept going at an angle toward the base of the hills close to the city.

"Where are you headed, Jethro?" Amuba asked eventually.

"I'm going to Chigron, the embalmer. Ameres has arranged with him to keep you hidden there for now."

The boys recognized the place, as they had been there several times before to witness embalming the bodies and preparing them for the funeral. It was a state-of-the-art facility, for Chigron was one of the most renowned embalmers of the time; not only did he embalm, but his team was also responsible for additional tasks such as wrapping the body in mummy cloths, constructing large sarcophagi, and finally delivering the body to their bereaved families. Different personnel usually handled these tasks, with embalmers returning the bodies to the families after embalming. Specialists prepared the corpse for burial, while experienced embalmers created the ornate mummy cases or sarcophagi. Of the three professions, the embalmers held the highest reverence; their work was considered sacred and associated with the priests.

In Chigron's business, the men of the three professions worked independently and separately from each other. Although Chigron was in charge of all, he only directly managed the embalming, the men of the other professions being guided by their supervisors. It was as if the three businesses had been situated near each other purely for convenience.

When they arrived at Chigron's home, Jethro knocked on the door alone. An assistant appeared. "Give this ring to Chigron,"

Jethro said, "and tell him that the bearer of it would like to talk to him here."

Within a couple of minutes, Chigron himself came out.

"I've brought the boys here in compliance with Ameres's order," Jethro said. "He told me he had worked out the details with you."

"And Ameres himself?" Chigron asked.

"He's gone," Jethro said. "The people who wanted to bring him down have achieved their goal, and an angry mob broke into his house and killed him this afternoon. Chebron doesn't know yet, although I'm sure he can sense that something terrible has happened, as I refused to answer his questions, worried that he might collapse when he needed to be strong the most."

The Egyptian let out a cry of sorrow. "What a bunch of fools and lunatics!" he exclaimed. "No one in the whole country deserved respect more than Ameres. He was fair and kind, always willing to help those in need, wise in his decisions, and influential in his advice. It's like the gods are furious with Egypt for allowing such a remarkable person to die at the hands of a mob. But where are the boys? I'll take them to the place I already set up. The workers have all left, so we don't have to worry about going through the house."

At Jethro's request, the boys came in.

"Come with me, my lord," Chigron said to Chebron. "I've been ready for your coming for a while. It's a shame it's not for a happier situation."

The embalmer led the way through his part of the house; then, he entered a large room with sawdust covering the floor.

There were multiple bodies on the stone slabs in the first stages of preparation, while in the even bigger apartment behind were several stone baths, each long enough to fit a body. These were occupied by corpses already going through the first preparation step, lying under a strong salt and water solution. Then there were other chambers for bodies embalmed with methods other than salt.

The boys stepped out into the open air after passing through a door at the back. The hill towered above them, made of sheer rock. Chigron led the way along its foot until they reached a doorway carved into the rock wall. Throughout their journey, he held a lit lamp, even though the chambers housing the deceased were already illuminated with lamps hanging from the ceiling. Upon entering the doorway and closing it behind them, he took several other lamps from a nook in the wall, lit them, and gave one to each of his companions.

"This," he said, "was cut by a wealthy resident of Thebes centuries ago as a tomb for himself and his family. I do not know what became of him, but the place was never used beyond this chamber, which has been used for mummies of sacred animals. Everything in the main chamber is as it was left by those who created it. During the last ten days, I have privately stored up such items necessary for you, and I am sure you will not find yourself uncomfortable."

On entering the apartment, roughly twenty feet square, they discovered that the embalmer had not exaggerated his accomplishments. A table with several benches was in the middle; three couches filled with rushes were placed against the wall. Mats had been laid out to cover the floor and provide warmth to the feet, and lamps ready to be lit were on the table. In a corner, two jars of wine with drinking vessels were situated.

"Everything except the food is here," Chigron said. "I couldn't get that ready until I knew you were coming, but be certain you'll be served regularly. There's no chance of anyone from the business coming here. They don't have any reason to come to the rear of the house, and probably few even know of this tomb's existence. If I have any reason to feel there's danger, I'll take other measures to keep you safe. If you need anything, don't hesitate to say so. I owe my position to Lord Ameres' support, and I'll do whatever it takes to ensure his son is secure. Now, my lord, I'll leave, and shortly I'll send a trustworthy servant to bring you the food I'm sure you need."

Chebron said a few words of thanks, but he was too anxious and sad to say more. The moment Chigron had left, he turned to

Jethro.

"Jethro, tell me what happened - I'm ready to hear the worst. Is it true my father is no more?" Chebron asked anxiously.

"Unfortunately, it is, Chebron," Jethro replied solemnly. "Your honorable father was killed by a low and cowardly mob, fired up by some wrong-doers of the priesthood."

Chebron collapsed onto the couch, weeping, while Amuba was just as grief-stricken, for Ameres had always treated him like a father. It wasn't until the following day that Chebron regained enough composure to ask Jethro to explain the details of his father's passing.

"I was in the garden," Jethro started. "Mysa and Ruth were in a boat on the pond, and I was towing them when I heard a commotion by the gate. I pulled the boat ashore and quickly ushered them to the house, telling Mysa to stay put in her room, no matter the noise she might hear, per her father's orders. I then headed out to the gate. When I arrived, it fell in, and a mob stormed in. With only myself and two or three gardeners who had run up to the scene, there was no stopping them. As they reached the house, your father stepped out to the porch and said, 'Good people, what do you want?'

"The crowd grew quiet momentarily, taken aback by Ameres' presence and composed attitude. But soon, some behind him yelled, 'Where is the sacred cat? We will find it! Others called, 'Down with the impious priest!' Ameres replied, 'Go ahead and search the place if you must; you don't need my permission since you've already taken matters into your own hands. But I beg you, don't enter the house. There are the ladies of my family and other women in there, and I swear to you that the cat is not there, alive or dead.'

"The shout went up, 'Let's search the garden!' In all of this, I noticed that there were two sides to the mob, one being ignorant and prejudiced, really believing that a crime had been committed against their gods, and the other being the instigators, who kept to the shadows. I didn't like it when the crowd so quickly abandoned the notion of searching the house and scattered themselves in the garden because it seemed to me that they might have gotten some type of clue from one of the gardeners or someone else that would've put them on the right path. I saw that some of the mob had hunting dogs, which made me even more nervous. I told one of the people to rush off and call the police, and then I joined the crowd.

"I grew increasingly anxious as the troops rushed straight to the pen where the animals were kept. They immediately started searching, with their dogs at their heels. I jumped when I felt a hand on my shoulder; it was Ameres. "Remember what I told you, Jethro," he said quietly. "I entrust Chebron to you."

"My lord, why are you here? The troops aren't too far away. Why don't you put yourself under their protection?" I asked.

"'Jethro, I haven't done anything wrong,' he replied calmly. 'I haven't done anything to anger the gods or hurt any of my countrymen. So why would I run away?'

"At that moment, there was a furious yell from the crowd, and I knew one of the terrible dogs had discovered the dead cat and dug it up. Then I heard a voice above the others, 'See! Even now, the evidence is here. It's been pierced by an arrow, just like I said. The sacred cat has been killed!' Then the crowd turned. 'Go, Jethro,' Ameres said. 'This is my final order.'

"But then I still couldn't obey him. The people rushed toward him, yelling, "Down with the one who mocks the gods! Down with the killer of the sacred cat!" They had death in their eyes. I charged at them in response. After that, everything was chaotic. I had grabbed a staff from the portico as I passed and swung it at everything in sight. So many dropped, I'm sure, before they got close to me. A barrage of blows struck me, and the staff ultimately slipped from my hands. I was knocked down several times, but I kept getting back up. Then, it felt like a dream, as I heard your father's command, "I entrust Chebron to you," and I forced my way through them and lunged at a group further on, but it was clear that I couldn't do anything there.

"Your father lay on the ground, looking as peaceful as when he had spoken to me just minutes before, but his white garments were stained with blood, and a dagger stood over his heart. There was no time to take in more. He had given me his last command, and I shook off those who tried to hold me back, dodging the blows from their knives, and I ran. I saw the troops I had sent for coming toward the house, but it was too late. I had pursuers on my heels, so I took the path to the farm without hesitation. That's all I have to tell you."

Chebron was weeping profusely, and Amuba, similarly moved, walked over to him.

"Chebron, console yourself. I understand your feelings but don't blame yourself for this disaster. You know what your father said—that it was an accident and probably the will of the Almighty that your arrow should go where it did. He said he thought this was all a plot and, as we heard in the temple, some people were determined to take his life."

A few minutes later, the embalmer came in with food. He could see that Chebron had heard the news of his father's fate.

"Have you heard anything about what's happening in the city?" Amuba asked him.

"Yes," Chigron responded, "nothing else is being discussed. Many of those involved in the act got away either through the door before the troops arrived or over the walls, but many of them were captured and are now in prison for their blasphemous act of attacking the high priest of Osiris. There were disturbances in the city at night, with some people saying the act was justified, while others had a different opinion."

"Those taken prisoner all insisted that they had heard from a reliable source that the cat had been buried in the area and that you and my young lord here had killed it, as you had been spotted going to the area armed with bows and arrows for a while, after which the cat never showed up again. Generally, it's thought that the culprits will be punished - some with flogging, some with death - and that your lives are at risk too, even though your father's friendship with the king couldn't protect you; the law must be obeyed, and according to Egyptian law, anyone who takes the life of a cat must be put to death."

"I'm willing to accept whatever fate awaits me," Chebron said, "and my greatest regret now is that I didn't take responsibility for the cat's death the moment it happened. I would have taken the blame, and my father and everyone else would have been free."

"Your whole family would have felt the disgrace," the embalmer said, "for those close to one who committed such an act must also suffer. I'm not blaming you, Chebron; I know your father didn't blame you. When he arranged for me to provide you with a hiding place, he told me that even though you might need a refuge, it wouldn't be for something you did wrong. Given the serious guilt from unintentionally taking a cat's life, especially one sacred in the land, I don't know how he could have said that. Your father's wisdom was comparable to his goodness; I can't understand what he said, but I'm happy to accept it and will do whatever I can to help you. The search for you will be rigorous, but we must remain hopeful."

"I'm going to see what's happening," Jethro said. "It may be that it's safer to leave immediately than to stay here."

"If that's the case," the embalmer said, "you'll have to disguise yourself before you start. It's known that Ameres had two fair-skinned slaves and that one was involved with my young lord here; the other, after fighting fiercely in the garden and reportedly killing several of his master's enemies, managed to escape. Fortunately, I have the materials here. We use lots of paint and stains for the dry clothes of the dead and the decorations of their coffins, and I can easily make you as dark as any of our people. That, with one of my wigs and Egyptian garments, will change you so that, as long as you don't look anyone directly in the face, there's no chance of you being recognized, but you mustn't look up, or even with the blackened lashes, the lightness of your eyes will give you away."

In no time, Jethro was transformed into a middle-class citizen of Thebes and set out on his mission. Later that day, a few officials started asking questions about the missing boys. Not satisfied with the answers, they began to search every room of the establishment.

"We know they had visited here multiple times and that Ameres was your patron," they said to Chigron. "We must check anywhere they may have been hiding, even though we don't believe anyone here would harbor the perpetrators of such a sacrilegious act. We won't let them escape. We've sent messages all over Egypt, and since they don't have horses, they can't have gone far. You were the first place we looked since all the servants said the same – that the son of Ameres was a regular visitor here."

"He didn't come by very often," Chigron commented, "though he did drop in occasionally and seemed quite intrigued by the whole process."

Chebron had visited the embalmer's place several times. Amuba had accompanied him, despite his discomfort with the whole situation, which he found rather repulsive. Chebron, however, had a much different outlook on the matter. Death was considered a sacred event in Egypt, and all associated rituals and ceremonies had a religious context. Therefore, they did not dread death but saw it as a sleep lasting three thousand years. For this reason, the bodies of humans and divine animals were carefully preserved and placed either in grand tombs or carved out of rock.

They firmly believed that the carefully preserved remains would last and the body would return to its former shape when the spirit returned. Accordingly, the corpses of people from all backgrounds were embalmed. The process for the wealthier individuals was far more costly and lengthy than for the poorer classes. An official scribe would first mark the corpse's side to indicate where an aperture should be made, which would then be cut by a person. This person would be chased away with insults and pelted with stones as the operation was considered both dishonorable and sacred.

The embalmers removed the internal organs through the aperture, cleansing and embalming them in spices before depositing them in four vases to be placed in the tomb with the coffins. Each vase contained parts sacred to a separate deity. The body was then filled with aromatic resin and spices and rubbed for thirty days with a mixture of the same ingredients. The very wealthy had their entire body gilded; other cases only featured the face and certain portions of the body. The mummy's skin was an olive color, dry and flexible, while the features, teeth, hair of the head, and eyebrows were all well-preserved.

In some cases, instead of the aromatic resin, the bodies were filled with bitumen; in others, saltpeter was used, and the bodies were soaked in it for a prolonged period and eventually filled with resin and bitumen. For the second grade of mummies, those of middle-class individuals, the incision was omitted, but resin or bitumen was used, and the bodies were soaked in salt for an extended period. Finally, the bodies were dipped into a liquid pitch for the less affluent classes. However, Chigron's business did not use these practices, catering only to the wealthy.

After the preparation, the body was handed over to a different team of professionals who wrapped it in linen bandages. For the wealthy, these bandages could sometimes reach up to one thousand yards in length. The body was then enclosed in a close-fitting case and decorated with a pattern of beads and bangles. Next, the face was covered in a thick layer of gold leaf, and the eyes were made of enamel. Next, this case was placed into successive cases, sometimes up to four in total, similarly ornamented with painting and gilding. Finally, it was placed in a sarcophagus or coffin made from wood or stone and decorated with paintings and sculptures. The body was then handed over to the deceased's family, and a solemn procession, followed by mourning relatives, took the coffin across the sacred lake while they threw dust upon their heads.

Every Egyptian city had a lake, natural or man-made, that was used for funerals. Before the funeral, the judges and public were informed of the date and would gather at the lake's edge. Then the coffin was loaded onto the boat; anyone present could accuse the deceased of having led an evil life. If the accuser couldn't prove their charge, they were punished harshly. If there was no accuser, or the accusation couldn't be verified, the deceased was declared innocent, and their body was loaded onto the boat and carried across the lake. Finally, the body was taken to the family catacombs or a room specially prepared for reception in the deceased's house.

Those denied the right to burial felt the family's most tremendous grief and shame, for they believed that this would bar them from the heavenly afterlife and that the departed spirit could be condemned to inhabit the body of an unclean animal in the course of its journey. However, knowing that their actions would be judged in the afterlife ensured that even powerful kings were kept in check and encouraged them to be kind to their subjects.

Chebron's brain, while watching the embalming process, thus thought of the future of the spirit that had inhabited the body he was looking at. Had it already passed into the body of another animal? Was it still disconnected, searching for a new home? How many changes would it undergo, and how long would it be before it returned to this human form? The shortest transition time was believed to be three thousand years, but in other cases, the period was much longer.

Since Amuba was not gifted with a strong imagination and saw in the whole matter merely the preservation of a body, which in his opinion had much better have been either buried or placed on a funeral pile and destroyed by fire, these visits to the embalmers had constituted the most unpleasant part of his duties as Chebron's companion.

Jethro had anticipated when he left that his visit to the city would be of short duration and that he should return in an hour at the latest. However, as the day passed and night fell without his return, the lads became exceedingly anxious and feared that something serious had taken place to detain him. Either his disguise had been detected, and the people seized him, or another great misfortune must have happened.

Jethro was supposed to have made a list of supplies they needed for their journey, and Chigron had promised to buy them, but his nonappearance disrupted their plans. Chigron went into the city to see if he could find out what had happened to Jethro. His name had been connected with the boys accused of killing a cat. It wasn't believed that he had done it, but since he was close to them and disappeared around the time they left the farm, it was assumed he was working with them. Chigron came back and said he couldn't find out anything about Jethro.

No one was talking about anything else in the city but the previous day's events, and the people's anger was divided between the murderers of Ameres and the slayers of the sacred cat. The boys were full of grief and confusion. To Amuba, Jethro had taken the place of an older brother. He had cheered him up in the darkest moment of his life and had been his friend and companion ever since, and the thought that something might have happened to him filled him with sadness. Mixed with this was an intense worry about the future. Without Jethro's strong arm and advice, how was this terrible journey supposed to be accomplished?

Chebron was in no state to act or plan. A deep depression had seized him; he didn't care whether he escaped and would have welcomed detection and death as a relief. So you can imagine how relieved Amuba was when, late in the evening, they heard footsteps in the outer chamber, and Jethro walked in. He sprang to his feet with a cry of happiness.

"Oh, Jethro! I'm glad you're back. I've been worried sick without you. What happened to you that made you so late in coming home?"

"There's a new trouble," Jethro replied sternly.

"New trouble, Jethro? In what way?" Even Chebron, who had barely lifted his head when Jethro came in, looked interested now, waiting for Jethro to continue.

"Mysa's been kidnapped," he replied grimly.

Chebron jumped to his feet. He was devoted to his sister, and for a moment, this new calamity pushed the others out of his mind.

"Mysa's been abducted!" both Amuba and he exclaimed

simultaneously. "Who did it? When did it happen? How did you find out?" The boys launched into a flurry of questions.

"After leaving here, I went downtown as planned," Jethro replied. "It was easy to find out what happened since no one was doing any business, and the streets were full of people discussing yesterday's events. Everyone in the city is rattled by the fact that two such heinous acts of blasphemy—the killing of the revered cat of Bubastes and the murder of a high priest of Osiris—occurred so close together. People are prophesying that a disastrous consequence will befall the land and that the gods will seek retribution.

"A royal decree has been issued to hunt down every person involved in Ameres's murder, and they will be met with the harshest punishments. The same decree that orders your capture wherever found and orders all officials throughout the kingdom to keep a strict watch in the towns and villages, inspect any strangers who may arrive, and send all young men bound in chains that may not provide a satisfactory explanation. In addition, sacrifices will be made at all the temples throughout the land to mollify the wrath of the gods. Messengers have been dispatched in all directions in the provinces, and all appeared to think our refuge would be discovered in a few hours. However, all were sure that we had made either for the seacoast or the desert on one side or the other, and as the messengers would reach the coast before we could do so, it was considered impossible to get through unnoticed.

"I approached the house, not intending to go in and just wanting to know what was happening. The gates were open, and many people went in and out to satisfy their curiosity. I blended in with the rest and managed to slip inside the house. Guards were on duty, and nobody was allowed to enter, so I went to the back. Suddenly, Lyptis, the old servant, came out to get some water. I addressed her using my disguise, and she showed no reaction. I then trusted that she was loyal to the family and decided to reveal my true identity. She immediately recognized me, and I signaled her to stay quiet. We stepped away together to a secluded spot, and she was crying.

"Oh, Jethro!" she exclaimed, have the gods ever thrown misfortune like this on a family? My master is dead; his son Chebron is hunted like a wild animal, and my mistress Mysa is gone!"

"Gone!" I exclaimed. "What do you mean?"

"Didn't you hear?" she said.

"I haven't heard anything! Tell me everything!"

"Just after the gates were knocked down and the crowd rushed into the garden, four men ran into the house and searched the rooms until they came to my young mistress's. We heard a scream, and a moment later, they came out carrying a figure wrapped up. We tried to stop them, but only women were in the house. They knocked two of us to the ground and ran out. Some of us ran into the garden screaming for help, but we saw a terrible scene. A big fight was going on, and then you broke free, covered in blood and wounds, and ran past us. No one paid any attention to us or our screams."

"'When the soldiers arrived, we told the officer what had happened, but it was too late then, and nothing could be done. If a guard had been over the house, all these things would never have happened.'

"I asked her if she could describe the appearance of the men to me. She said that they were attired as respectable citizens but that from their language and manner, she believed they were criminals of the lowest class.

"For a time, I was so overwhelmed with this news that I could think of nothing, but I went out and roamed the streets. Then, finally, I thought of the girl Ruth. She was with Mysa then and might, if questioned, be able to tell me more than the old woman had done. I therefore returned, but I had to wait for three hours before old Lyptis came out again.

"I want to talk to Ruth," I said. Send her out to me."

"Ruth is gone," she said.

"Gone!" I repeated. 'Where and when?"

"We don't know. It wasn't until hours after Mysa was carried off that anyone thought of her. We were too overwhelmed with grief at the death of our dear lord and the loss of Mysa to give a thought to the young Israelite. Then one asked, where was she? No one had noticed her. So we went to Mysa's chamber, thinking that the villains who carried our young mistress off might have killed her, but there were no signs of her there."

"But she was with Mysa, wasn't she," I asked, "when was the attack made? Didn't she pass in with her when she came in from the garden?"

"Yes," she replied, "they came in together and passed through us; we gathered in the front room, being very scared at the noise at the door. As they passed us, our young mistress said, 'Be quiet; what's the point of screaming and crying?'" I asked if she was sure Ruth was not carried off as well as Mysa. "She said, 'I am quite sure. One held a person, and the other three made a path.'"

"'And that was the last time,' I asked, 'that any of you saw the Israelite?'

"'It was,' she answered. 'She must have passed out by the door at the end of the passage, which she might have done without being observed by any of us.'

"This was a new mystery. I could not guess why Ruth would flee because as soon as the soldiers appeared, there was no more danger in remaining. Besides, I did not think Ruth was one to shrink from danger. Finally, however, no more was to be learned, and I went out into the streets again."

CHAPTER XIII

The Search for Mysa

"It's possible Ruth went to tell my mother that Mysa was gone," Chebron guessed when Jethro had gotten this far in his story.

"That couldn't have been," Jethro replied, "because your mother returned early this morning to the house with many relatives, and they were all weeping and mourning around your father's body. So if Ruth had gone to her, she would've either returned with her, or Lyptis would've heard where she was."

"Did you hear how my mother took her misfortunes, Jethro?"

"She was overwhelmed with grief, Lyptis said, at your father's death-so overwhelmed that she seemed to have no thought for anything else. She had been told the night before that Mysa was missing, but it seemed to make no impression. She only said that friends must have carried her off to save her from the danger that Chebron's wickedness had brought upon us. This morning she made some further inquiries but did not seem in any severe distress, but the magistrates, when they came last night to inquire into the whole matter, took note of Mysa having been carried off, and when on their coming again this morning they found that nothing had been heard of her, gave orders that a search should be done for her. Moreover, a proclamation was issued this afternoon denouncing punishment on those who carried her off and demanding anyone who could give any information on the subject to present themselves immediately.

"Since I left the house, I have been wandering around, trying to think of what to do. I hope something will come to me to help me find the villains who took Mysa."

"You're not thinking of going ahead with our plans for tomorrow, Jethro?" Chebron asked anxiously. "We could never leave here not knowing what happened to her."

"Absolutely not, Chebron. I feel it's my responsibility and duty to remain here until she's located. Your father spoke to me about her and you, but he didn't see how we could help, so he said she'd have to take her chances - meaning she'd have to rely on your mother to find a husband eventually. But this current situation has changed everything. She needs us to help her out actively, and whatever risk that brings, we need to postpone our departure.

"We don't know if we can stay here for long. Every day without news of your capture increases the risk of being discovered. Still, we may be safe here for the next day or two. After that, however, Chigron is taking a massive risk by hiding us here, and if the danger becomes too great for him, we need to escape to the hills. There are some secluded areas where we could hide for a while. But, for now, our only focus should be to search and rescue Mysa.

"The villain Ptylus had a few reasons to direct this evil plan. Primarily, he was enraged by the rejection of his son's marriage proposal. Secondly, upon the death of Ameres, he would have become the High Priest. Lastly, Ptylus assumed that if he kidnapped Mysa and married her to his son, she would bring a considerable portion of her father's land as a dowry. With his influence as High Priest, he was confident that Mysa would get a share of the estate, especially after taking out Chebron and his father.

"He only needs to keep Mysa confined until his position as High Priest is secure, and then if he gets the King's approval of the match, Mysa couldn't turn it down."

"I think you accurately understand the entire situation, Amuba, and we can see the whole conspiracy. The question is, what should we do?"

Chebron enthused, pacing the room, "That cannot be allowed, Jethro!" "Mysa cannot stand Plexo. She spoke of him with horror when Ptylus proposed the match. I don't like him either. He's sly, crafty, and cruel. It'd be better for Mysa to die than marry him."

"I can assure you, Chebron," Jethro declared, "this marriage will never happen. We may not find Mysa, who could be hidden either in Ptylus' home, one of the many chambers of the temple, or in the nearby caves; however, I can still locate Plexo, and before we leave Egypt, I will take out him and his father, whom I perceive as Ameres' killer. Of course, I might not achieve this and escape, and in that case, you will have to travel by yourself; nonetheless, I will not depart from Egypt and let them benefit from their crime." As he finished talking, Chigron appeared.

"I was coming to see if Jethro had returned."

He was told the reasons for his long absence—Mysa's kidnapping and their determination to remain and search for her hiding place. He shook his head.

"It is a hasty decision. Even if you could come and go as you please, your chances of finding her hiding place would be pretty slim - and since you are being hunted, the quest seems to be a total loss. On the other hand, staying here for a long time would be reckless.

"I'm saying this for my own sake and yours too. First, there are so many people here that your coming and going would be noticed by someone; second, the cave would be searched again and again. If it wasn't for my workers, I could hide you in the house; if I saw anyone looking for you, I could put you in one of the inner chambers of the mummies and put another few cases on top. Then, you would lie among several dead bodies in a similar condition, so no one would think to open the cases.

"It would be too risky to try and hide here with so many people around. But there are plenty of caves and burial places higher up on the hillside where you can easily find a place to hide. Some of these caves have a few sarcophagi with mummies inside. If we choose one of them, I can move the mummies to another cave, and you can take their place in the sarcophagus. Close the lid, and you'll be safe from any searchers if they come close."

"It would be a sin to move the dead!" Chebron said with a shudder.

"It would be a crime for anyone else," Chigron responded, "but not for us, for whom it's our job and responsibility to care for the deceased. After you have left, I can put the mummies back in their slots, and they won't be any worse off because of their brief movement. Of course, there must be no signs of occupation in the cave—nothing to make them suspicious that it has been disrupted. "

"I believe that is a great idea," Jethro said. "We can make places to sleep in the outdoors nearby. We'll be sleeping outdoors while on our journey, and it wouldn't be a problem to start right away. However, I think moving into one of these caves would be best. You never know when the searchers might be back here, so if you agree, Chigron, I'll wake up early tomorrow and come with you, pick a cave, and make our plans."

"I think that's the best plan," the embalmer said in agreement. "I'll bring you provisions every night. Now, let's get some rest."

It took a while for the group to calm down to sleep. First, they spoke of Mysa and discussed possible ways to find out where she was. Then they thought about Ruth, who would be alone in the vast city and might not have enough money to buy food.

"She had her jewelry," Jethro mentioned, "a silver bracelet given to her by Mysa that she always wore. In addition, she had two silver necklaces and earrings of her own. I'm sure they were given to her by her mother; they were very nice and would make good money. Ruth is a smart young lady; even though she was only fifteen, she had been in charge of a home and caring for her grandfather for a long time. I can't figure out why she would have run away unless she feared that everybody would be killed in all the noise and chaos. But even then, she would likely have been back this morning if not earlier."

"I can't help but think," Chebron said, "that she may have gone after Mysa. I know Ruth was very fond of her."

"She was," Jethro commented. "I often thought while walking behind them that seeing them together was beautiful. Of course, Mysa had a greater knowledge of all things, yet, it was Ruth who expressed her opinion most firmly, and Mysa listened to her as she spoke in that solemn manner of hers, like an older sister. Do you think she may have gone with her? I truly hope it was the case. But in that situation, the women must have noticed her."

"The women were out of their minds with fear," Chebron said, "and, I'm sure, were shrieking and wailing and paying no attention to anything else. If only I could be certain that Ruth is with Mysa, I'd feel less anxious, as I'm sure she'd be a source of comfort and support for her."

"No doubt she would," Jethro concurred. "Moreover, I'd have more hope of locating where they were hidden; for if Ruth were able to escape and spread the news, she'd likely take the first chance as soon as possible."

Not long after they lay down, Chigron arrived, announcing that dawn was close. At once, they got up and followed him. He guided them around the foot of the hill for a while and then, turning, started to climb a spot where it sloped slowly. As they went on, they came across many tombs, partially built with masonry and partly carved out of the rock behind; and it was not until they had walked for half an hour that he stopped in front of the entrance to one of these.

"This is the one that I considered would work best," he stated. "It is very isolated, and there is very little chance of anyone coming by. I know the stone door that blocks the entrance has not been sealed. I even know to whom the tomb belongs. The last mummy was put there not long ago, and the son of the man buried there told me that he did not want it to be sealed because his wife was very ill and feared she would soon follow his father. So, we won't have any problem getting in. Furthermore, there is a small tomb close by begun in the rock but was then abandoned--the owners changed their plans and had a bigger tomb made lower down the hill. Since nothing was built beyond the chamber and the narrow entrance, we can put the mummies from this chamber and cover the entrance with stones and dirt so that nobody would ever suspect it was there."

"That would be perfect," Jethro said. "Let's get started and make it ready right away."

The stone block that barred the entrance to the tomb was only three feet high and wide, but with a bit of effort, it was soon pushed back. Inside the tomb, four wooden sarcophagi stood in a row. Jethro and Chigron worked together to open three coffins, carefully removing the mummies and their outer cases. The inner cases were then carried to the unfinished tomb fifty yards away and stowed away. Finally, to hide their tracks, they piled the stones back in the entrance and returned to the tombs. "You'll be safe here," Chigron said. "You can keep the stone rolled back unless you see anyone coming. You'll make out any large group of searchers and see them coming up the hill before they get to you. If you see them, just close the door, get into one of the coffins, stay inside the inner case, and put the lid and the inner case over you. It's doubtful anyone will search for you, or if they do, they'll only search empty tombs. The fact that the stone hasn't been cemented is a lucky coincidence that only I and the owner know about. You don't have to hide unless it's necessary. But if passers-by see you, they might send someone to see if it's you they've been searching for. So, try to stay hidden during the day. You can come out and spend the night wherever you want as soon as it gets dark."

"We'll certainly take your advice," Jethro replied. "The plan you suggest is the safest. I don't think there's much chance of a thorough search of the tombs, but they may check those open and empty; as you point out, they would never dream of looking at the occupied tombs since they'd assume they're all securely sealed. In the worst case, we can always take refuge in the coffins; I'm sure no one would think of searching those."

"Come down when it gets dark," Chigron said, "and I'll get you everything you need for your journey: the peasant clothing I've prepared and the money Ameres gave me to keep for you. Then, if you need to leave soon, everything will be ready. I'll come an hour after the sun sets tomorrow night to check in on you. I'm telling you the exact hour so you can be here to meet me if you're not close by. Now, I leave you in the hands of the gods. This evening, I'll remove the room you've been using and clear away all signs that someone was living here."

Chebron thanked the embalmer for his kindness, effort, and the risk he took for them.

"I would have done more if I could," Chigron said. "Ameres' son has the highest claims upon me, and were it to cost me half my fortune, I would spend it to fulfill the last wishes he asked of me."

After the embalmer left them, the three friends sat inside the tomb, gazing over the peaceful city below.

"I wish we had our peasant dresses," Chebron said, "so we could join you and help in the search for Mysa."

"It would be way too risky," Jethro declared resolutely. "Too many people have spotted you participating in the services and the parade, so you have little hope of going undetected. Amuba has a lower chance of detection than you do. If he stained his skin, darkened his eyebrows, and shaved his head, he might be able to pass by as long as he kept his eyes glued to the ground; however, this wouldn't give him much of a chance of discovering any clues about Mysa."

"Any search you carry out must take place at night. I'm going to station myself near Ptylus' house today. I don't anticipate gaining any information by looking at the big wall surrounding it. Still, I'll be able to observe, as discreetly as I can without being noticed, all the slaves or servants who leave the house, especially if two of them go out together; then I may be able to overhear a couple of sentences of their conversation, and perhaps obtain some kind of clue to the puzzle. I admit the probability is low, and you shouldn't expect me to return with news."

"I wish, Jethro," Chebron said eagerly, "if it's at all possible, that you would go back to our house, visit the old woman, and get her to give you a set of my priest's robes; with those, I could sneak into the temple during the night and roam through the rooms and courtyards without being questioned. It's dark now, so nobody will recognize me if I don't get too close to a lamp. We heard a significant conversation there, so maybe I can eavesdrop on another."

"It would be risky to try it," Jethro said uncertainly.

"That doesn't matter at all!" Chebron exclaimed passionately. "All this mess happened because of me, and I'm willing to take any risks that come with it. But I don't think there's any chance someone will recognize me. Amuba and I went there together many times. Despite it always being a moonlit night, no one ever noticed that Amuba wasn't a regular temple attendant who had permission to go further."

"All right then," Jethro declared. "You will explore the temple, Amuba, and I will check every cave in the hills. Behind the temple are many grand tombs, probably Ptylus has chosen one of those as a refuge for Mysa. Many tombs were built by kings, nobles, and affluent priests who intend to use them as a resting place after death, and they could be adapted into a comfortable home. After we have tried there, if we don't find anything, we must move on and look farther out. No doubt Ptylus, like Ameres, owns farms and manors in the country, and Mysa may be hidden in one of these."

"I'm confident," Amuba proclaimed, "that a better idea would be for us to watch over Plexo. Ptylus has his obligations and is probably busy ensuring he gets elected to the high priesthood, but it's likely Plexo visits Mysa in her hiding place from time to time. He'll be desperate to persuade or frighten her into agreeing to marry him as soon as possible. He'll eventually lead us to her if we watch him closely enough."

"That will most certainly be the best course of action, Amuba. I hadn't considered it before, but it is, without a doubt, the plan that provides the best chance of success. We could search the country for years without finding her; although I want to keep your hopes alive, I had truly given up hope. But, as you say, if we follow Plexo, it is bound to lead us to her at some point. However, to do that, we'll need many disguises. I'll think it through as I walk today, and when I meet Chigron this evening, I'll ask him to get the disguises that he thinks are the best for us to use."

"As for me, Jethro," Chebron said, "I'll go to the temple in the evenings. It'll be peaceful by midnight, giving me time for sleep. During the day, I'll work with you. Get me a peasant woman's clothes. A female head covering and a disguise will keep me hidden even from people who know me well. Many women are taller than me so that it will work. But the disguise would be hard for Amuba, who's almost as tall as you."

"Yes, you could easily pass as a woman," Jethro agreed, "and the more of us there are to stake out this villain, the better. But I think we'll have better luck doing this at night. Plexo has temple duties and would likely pay his visits in the dark. So it'd just come down to who's faster on foot, and Amuba and I used to be runners. Only a swift horse will outrun us. I'm heading down to the city now. I feel more positive than before, and I'm starting to believe we can find out where they took Mysa."

The day crawled for Chebron and Amuba. They were not willing to show themselves outside the tomb, as Chigron had begged them not to do so; in any case, there were frequent people around the hillside since many people went to offer daily prayers at the tombs of their friends and family. They had much to discuss—the chances of discovering Mysa, the inquiry concerning where she should be put on the off chance that she was recovered, and the potential outcomes of the long and exciting journey before them. Amuba energized talk on all these points and started the discussion again whenever it died down since he saw that simply discussing Mysa lifted Chebron's attitude. It had pulled his thoughts far from his father's death and the events after the cat's death. It had given him a new purpose and had revived his spirits and enthusiasm for life. Both young men were happy when, late in the evening, they saw Jethro coming up the hill.

"No luck," he informed them as he arrived. "I've been hiding around Ptylus' house all day, observing everyone coming and going. Everyone's been gossiping about Ameres' death and the failed search for all of you. They mentioned Mysa being taken more than once, but they had no clue their master was involved, and they had no idea of her being in the house."

"It is possible she might be there without the slaves noticing. However, you know how news travels quickly in a household, and anything done by the master or mistress soon becomes common knowledge. Had anyone heard something unusual, it would have spread to all the servants. I doubt Ptylus would have risked bringing her home, as he might think her mother would suspect him just as we have. Furthermore, too many servants are there for the secret to be kept. If we want a clue, we should look in the temple or follow Plexo."

When the sun had set, Chebron and Jethro headed down the hill together. Chebron wore the garments of the priesthood that Jethro had brought with him, getting them from Lyptis. As they reached the house of the embalmer, Jethro went on and returned in thirty minutes with the disguises that Chigron had gathered. All of them, except the plain clothing of two peasants, were hidden in nearby bushes. They applied a liquid Chigron had given them to put on their skin before putting on the peasants' garments. After that, they made their way toward Ptylus' house.

While Chebron headed towards the temple, a short distance from the house, Jethro and Amuba sat by the wall close to the gate, ensuring nobody could leave without their knowledge. However, no one emerged beside the servants and visitors. They heard the gates being bolted at ten o'clock, yet they stayed until midnight when Chebron reunited with them. He had used his time strolling from court to court of the temple, but other than a solitary priest moving here and there to refresh the lamps of the altars, he had not seen anyone and had gone unnoticed. Amuba and Chebron were both inclined to be disheartened due to the lack of success in their surveillance, but Jethro scolded them for their restlessness.

"You shouldn't expect," he said, "that you'll be able to uncover a secret so well hidden in only a few hours. It could be weeks before we're successful. Let's begin our watch a couple of hours before sundown tomorrow. I'm more familiar with the help at Ptylus' house than you are since I've delivered messages there before. Plus, in this costume, I can't wander around without drawing attention to myself as you can. So, I'll watch him on the northern road from the city while you, dressed as peasants, can watch the house. Chebron, you should sit by the wall fifty yards from the house on the north side, and Amuba, you should stay on the other side of the road and a bit to the south of the gate. That way, you'll be able to see each other but not be together. An individual is less likely to draw attention than a pair of people since people will be looking for two boys. Since I can hardly recognize you now that your skin is dark, there's not much chance someone else will see through your disguise."

The following day at three in the afternoon, Amuba and Chebron, masquerading as villagers, descended to Ptylus' house and took their spots as planned. Later in the day, Amuba observed that one of the slaves from Ptylus' house abruptly halted his steps as he passed Chebron and stared intently at him. Amuba abandoned the place he was standing and ran over there. The slave talked to Chebron, who stood up. A moment later, the slave seized him. As they were battling, Amuba rushed up.

"What a find!" the slave yelled. "This is the murderer of the sacred cat. Help me to drag him into my master's house."

But to his astonishment, Amuba attacked him and struck him such a massive blow in the face that he let go of Chebron and reeled backward.

"Run for your life!" Amuba yelled at Chebron. "I will find another way."

The slave, after recovering from Amuba's blow, started rushing at Amuba and yelling at the top of his lungs, "Death to the insulters of the gods! Death to the one who slayed the sacred cat!"

But Amuba was both more powerful and agile than the slave,

who had grown weak from his comfortable life in the priest's home and wasn't ready for this challenge. Amuba evaded his attacker's grasp and struck him with all his might in the face, and as he stumbled back, Amuba struck him again, and the man collapsed. But, as more people heard the shouting and came to investigate, Amuba ran at full speed. As he had assumed, those who were nearby paused to help the man on the ground and to figure out what started the fight, and by the time they began to chase him, he was almost two hundred yards away. He could still hear the angry cry, "Death to the slayer of the sacred cat!"

By this time, he was at Chebron's side. "Run off to the side, Chebron, hide, and then go up the hill. I will go straight for a while. I can outrun and last longer than these slaves, and I will go straight. Do as I tell you," he said almost angrily when he saw that Chebron was hesitating. "If we stay together, they'll catch us both."

Chebron wasted no time and took the turn that Amuba had shown him. Amuba slowed his pace, sensing that if his pursuers saw they were gaining on him, they would ignore his companion, whose identity they weren't sure of. When Chebron looked back and saw everyone had followed the same route, he sped up again. He wasn't worried about the people behind him, but he was concerned he'd run into someone who'd misinterpret the situation, think he was a criminal, and try to stop him. A few people made feeble attempts to do that, but they hesitated to deal with a strong, determined young man they knew nothing about.

When he felt sure that Chebron was safe, he turned off the road and headed across the countryside. After fifteen minutes of running, he had passed through Thebes and its surrounding villas and detached houses. This area was carefully cultivated, with many channels running across to ensure the crops were sufficiently watered. The plots of land were tiny, each with a hut in the center.

Many of these were occupied, but usually, the farmers lived in the towns, just utilizing the huts when it was vital to frighten away the birds and keep a close watch on their produce. In some of these plots, the fruit trees were dense, and Amuba used the cover to veer off at a right angle to the path he had been following and then, designing his route to remain sheltered in the trees, ran until he arrived at a hut whose door was open. A peek inside revealed that the owner was not using it. He entered, closed the door behind him, went up the ladder, and flung himself onto some boards that lay on the rafters for storing fruit, taking the ladder up after him.

His last glance told him his pursuers were about four hundred yards behind him as he veered from his path. He would've kept running, confident that his speed and stamina would help him outrun them, but he knew that many of the farmers he had passed during his flight would join the pursuit once they learned of his crime. As a result, fresh pursuers would be added to the chase, and eventually, he would be overtaken. To avoid this, he decided to hide until nightfall.

He had scarcely flung himself down when he heard loud cries rise close by and had no doubt that some worker he hadn't noticed had seen him enter the hut. He jumped down from the loft again and, grabbing a stake from a bunch in the corner, he re-emerged. As he did that, he was abruptly seized. Wriggling free, he saw a burly Nubian wielding a hoe. Without hesitation, Amuba lunged forward with his stake. The Nubian blocked the strike with his hoe and delivered a forceful strike to Amuba.

Amuba sprang back quickly and dealt him a powerful blow to the wrist with his stake before the Nubian could protect himself. The Nubian dropped his hoe, screaming in pain and fury. Amuba followed up the blow on the wrist with one on the ankle and jumped away again as the man crumpled. But the Nubian's shouts had been heard, and the pursuers were now only fifty yards away. Amuba saw that their numbers had increased significantly, and for the first time, doubt about his ability to get away from them crossed his mind.

They were too close to try and hide anymore, and he now had only his speed to rely on. But he had already run nearly three miles while many of those behind him had just started, and he soon found that he could not widen the space between them. He kept on for another two miles, at first leaping the ditches lightly and without stopping, but at the end, he had a harder time climbing out. He was becoming completely exhausted. Those who had at first taken up the chase had long since abandoned it, but, as he had feared, fresh men constantly joined the ranks of his pursuers. They were only a few yards behind him when he found himself again on the high road.

He fell but struggled to his feet again; he was losing consciousness when a chariot drew up beside him, scattering his followers right and left. He heard loud voices raised in tones of indignant reproach and a renewal of the cries of hatred. Then, he felt strong arms around him, and after he was lifted, he fell unconscious.

CHAPTER XIV

A Prince of Egypt

Amuba was sprawled in a heap at the bottom of the chariot when he regained consciousness. Two men were in the vehicle with him; one he assumed to be the driver and the other the chariot owner.

In a few moments, the chariot veered off through a grand entrance. The driver hopped down and shut the gates, then steered the horses to the steps of an opulent mansion. The man beside him shouted, and two or three servants hurried down the stairs. Amuba was lifted out, brought into the house, and placed on a couch. A cup of wine was offered to his lips, and after he had taken a sip, a slave bathed his head with cold water and wrapped up the deep cuts from which blood was oozing.

The refreshing drink revitalized Amuba, and he propped himself up with his arm. A command was given, and the slaves left the room. Amuba looked up and saw a tall, regal figure standing before him. He immediately recognized this person, seeing him following the king in one of Egypt's processions. "Who are you? Is it true what those men said - that you were the one who killed the Cat of Bubastes?"

"My name is Amuba, my lord," the lad said, trying to stand up, but his questioner told him to remain seated. "I am a Rebu taken prisoner of war and handed as a slave to Ameres, high priest of

Osiris. I did not kill the cat, but it is true that I was there at its death and that it might just as well have been my arrow that accidentally pierced it as that of him who did so."

"Then it was an accident?" the noble said. "It was wholly an accident, my lord. We fired at a hawk that had been thinning the pet birds of my master's daughter. One of the arrows struck a tree and, glancing off, entered the cat's house and caused its death. We regretted it, knowing important the cat is to the Egyptians."

"And yet not to you, young man? You don't follow the gods of the Egyptians?"

"I don't, my lord," Amuba answered, "but at the same time, I wouldn't do anything to offend another's religion, although I don't value a cat's life over other animals."

"Then you worship the gods of your people?"

Amuba was silent for a moment.

"I will answer frankly, my lord, and I hope you will not be displeased. Since I came to Egypt, I have come to think that neither the gods of the Egyptians nor the gods my fathers worshiped are the true gods. Therefore, I believe that there is one great God over all and that the others are only his attributes, which men worship under the name of gods."

The Egyptian uttered an exclamation of surprise.

"Where did you get these beliefs?" he asked.

Amuba was silent.

"It must have been from Ameres himself," the noble went on, seeing that the lad was reluctant to answer. "I also knew him well and that he carried his beliefs intently. But how did he talk about this to a slave?"

"Ameres was good enough to make me a companion and friend to his son rather than a servant to him," Amuba replied, "partly because he thought I would give him a more active life, which he needed, for he was too studious. Also, partly because I had a high rank in my own country, of which my father was the king. But he never spoke of this matter until after the cat's accident. My friend Chebron was overwhelmed with guilt after the cat's death, preferring his own death to living with such a burden upon his mind. Then his father, seeing that his whole life would be stained and that he would probably be forced to run from Egypt and dwell in some other land, told him the belief that he held. I believed this even more because I had heard the same belief from an Israelite girl who served Ameres's daughter."

Again, Amuba's listener uttered an exclamation of surprise.

"I didn't know," he said, after a pause, "that there was an Israelite who still followed the religion of their ancestors."

"The maiden told me that they mostly worship the same as the Egyptians, and as far as she knew, she was the last who still held the old belief. She had been brought up by a great-grandfather who had been driven from his people and forced to dwell apart because he scolded his people for having forsaken their God. Nevertheless, he instructed her in his faith that there was but one God over all the earth."

"Do you know who I am?" the noble asked abruptly.

"I know you are one of the Egypt's princes, for I have seen you in a procession following closely behind the king with his sons and other princes."

"I am an Israelite," Amuba heard from the prince of Egypt, a sentence that left him astonished.

"It sounds strange, I know. But many years ago, during a great persecution against the Israelites, my parents, worried for my safety, placed me in a little cradle and set it floating on the water. It turns out this might have been the will of God because the water took me to the princess of Egypt, Thermuthis, as she bathed with her maidens. She adopted me, granting me all the rights and privileges of her son. I was given the name of Moses, written on a piece of papyrus found with me in the cradle. I was educated in all the learning of the Egyptians and lived my life as one of them. I had almost forgotten my true identity." Here, Moses paused and began to pace thoughtfully around the room.

"What has become of the girl you spoke of?" he asked suddenly, stopping before Amuba.

"I don't know, my lord. When Ameres was murdered, the

daughter was carried off, and Ruth, the Israelite, has been missing ever since. That's why we stayed here. Otherwise, we would have fled at once."

"You and the son of Ameres?"

"Yes, my lord, and another Rebu, one of my father's warriors and Ameres' slaves. Ameres trusted him completely and tasked him with helping Chebron escape and bringing us back to our land. When we found out that the girl was missing, we stayed to search for her."

"What will you do when you find her?"

"If we can rescue her, we'll give her to her mother and flee this land as planned. Unless you could get a pardon for Chebron for the accident."

"I could never do that," Moses said. "That's beyond my power; even the king couldn't escape death for this act. Until recently, I might have helped you, but now I am disfavored in the court."

After pacing the room for a while, Moses went on:

"If you find the Israelite girl, tell her she isn't the last of the Israelites who believe in the God of Abraham; I do too. You look surprised; this might make sense since I've been raised as an Egyptian.

"But our priests keep meticulous records of all matters related to the people's countries and religions we come into contact with. As such, it was quite easy for me, who has access to limitless knowledge, to look through the records of my people's first arrival, the rule of Joseph, the great governor, his family's arrival, and their establishment in this country. I learned that they believed in one God, whom they thought of as the only one in existence. I have had a great interest in the priesthood's teachings and noticed that this central concept seemed to be hidden beneath all the forms and mysteries of the Egyptian religion. No one I've spoken to has been willing to admit this openly; however, I heard reports that Ameres was brave enough to entertain the idea that there is only one God and that our earliest ancestors, who first worshiped Him under the different characteristics ascribed to Him, eventually lost the truth entirely and began to take the shadows for the real thing. Therefore, I said to myself, I will also believe in the one God worshipped by my forefathers in the hope that I may eventually learn more about Him."

"For years, I was happy to live as an Egyptian prince. But my heart has been with my people, and I'm determined to do whatever I can to help them. I've even spoken up in court on their behalf, which has caused some tension with the royal family. Strangely, I almost wish I could forget my past and focus on my current rank, but something draws me to them. Anyway, we've talked enough - I can see you're feeling better. Do you think you're able to walk?"

"Definitely," Amuba replied, getting up and walking across the room. "I haven't lost much blood, and I think I was only dizzy from the attack."

"It's best that you leave immediately; news of your presence has likely spread quickly to the city, and officials will arrive soon, demanding that you be handed over. Have some more wine and a piece of bread before you go. I'll assign you a trusted slave who will lead you through the garden, out of a small back door, and guide you to your desired destination. No doubt, the house is being watched from the front. When the officials arrive, I'll tell them the truth - I was driving by when I saw you being attacked and murdered by several peasants, so I brought you in my chariot. As for the claims that you killed the Cat of Bubastes, I assumed it was a lie to stop me from defending you. When I questioned you and found you innocent, I urged you to leave immediately, so you could escape your aggressors by going through the garden gate. As you're not an Israelite, they can't accuse me of shielding you from punishment. No need to thank me, time is of the essence, and you must hurry to get away before anyone notices your absence. May the God we both worship, though we don't yet know Him, protect and guide you and your family."

Moses pulled the curtains aside to the chamber entrance, clapped his hands, and summoned Mephres. The elderly slave came quickly, and Moses directed him to guide Amuba back to the city via an obscure route. Not wanting to linger and risk the arrival of the city officials, Moses quickly thanked Amuba for his visit and sent him away.

It was fortunate that Amuba had been given a guide because, when he stepped out into the night - the night had started to fall - he found it hard to find his way; his head was pounding from the blows he had been dealt, and his entire body ached. The old slave noticed he was stumbling, gave him his staff to carry, and then took his arm to support him. It seemed to Amuba that he was walking all night, but it was only a short time later that his guide saw that he could go no further and could not answer his questions about where he wanted to be led. He decided to stay with him until he could go on. He led Amuba to a nearby orchard and put him under a tree, covering him with his cloak.

He sighed with relief as he watched Amuba take heavy breaths—everyone in the house had heard about the lad's rescue from the angry peasants' hands.

"He was so close to death when he was saved," he thought. "Maxis said they were shouting that he had killed the Cat of Bubastes. My lord did the right thing by helping him escape, but I don't care if it's true. In my hometown in Libya, we don't worship the Egyptian gods anyway."

Several times during the night, the old man got up and picked large handfuls of wet grass and placed them on Amuba's head, and when he perceived the first rays of sun in the sky, he woke Amuba.

Amuba sat up and looked around with an air of astonishment. "Where am I?" he exclaimed.

"Welcome to the orchard, my friend," he said. "When I saw you couldn't continue your journey, I thought it best to bring you here and let you rest. I hope it did you some good."

"I remember now," Amuba said. "It felt like I was walking forever, with you supporting me."

"It was only an hour," the slave reassured him. "We're still not even two miles from my master's house."

"And you were watching me all night," Amuba said. "It was an hour after sunset when we left, correct? I can't thank you enough for your kindness."

"Don't mention it," the old man replied. "My lord put you in my care, and I can't go back until I'm sure you're safe. But if you can walk, we must get going. People may start looking for you when the sun rises."

"I'm good enough to go on," Amuba said. "The wet grass you put around me must have done its job. The heat has gone away, and the pain is gone." Amuba was now able to walk at a brisk pace.

Amuba was now able to walk quickly.

"Where do you want to go?" the slave asked shortly. "It's bright enough now for me to see your face, and it won't be good for others to see you. Your head is still swollen, and there is evidence of bruises and cuts on your scalp. People will notice you at once, and if anyone recognizes you from last night's doings, you will be immediately suspected."

"I'll go straight to the hills," Amuba said. "They're not too far away, and I can easily hide among the rocks until sundown."

"Let's go quickly then," the slave said; "it's only a half-hour away. But just in case we meet some peasants heading to work, I'll go ahead, and you follow a hundred yards behind. Then, if I see someone coming, I'll wave my hand above my head, and you should immediately move off the path into the orchard or vineyard and stay there until they pass."

Amuba followed these instructions, and it took him over an hour as he had to veer off the road multiple times to avoid groups of peasants. Eventually, he reached the base of the hill. He thanked his guide for his assistance and kind gesture and gave a message of gratitude to his lord. Then Amuba climbed the hill briefly and rested between a few boulders.

Although he had a good rest, he was still weak and shaken and didn't feel confident enough to hike the four miles between the hills and the tomb above the city. He dozed off again, and the sun was already setting when he woke up. He waited until it was out of sight and then climbed higher. As the hillside was in shadow, he didn't have to worry about anyone noticing him. By the time the darkness had set in, he was at the tomb they used as a hideout. A figure was standing there. He cried with joy when Jethro ran up and hugged him.

"My dear Amuba, I thought I wouldn't live to see you again!"

A few moments later, Chebron dashed out and embraced Amuba. "I can never forgive you or myself," he said reproachfully. "What right did you have to put yourself at risk for me? It was wrong, Amuba, and I have suffered terribly. Even though we are like brothers, why should you sacrifice yourself for me, particularly when my life is at stake and not yours? I kept telling myself a thousand times last night that I was cowardly and weak for letting you and Jethro risk your lives for me when if I just gave myself up, the people's anger would be pacified, and you could escape from this land safely. It's bad enough that you shared my risk, but when you take it all on, and I escape free, I won't accept that sacrifice anymore; tomorrow, I will surrender myself."

Amuba was about to argue, but Jethro silenced him with a touch. The Rebu knew how hard Chebron had suffered and how he had spent the night crying and blaming himself, so he decided it was better to let him have his say and let the upset pass before engaging him in debate.

"Amuba, are you hungry?" Jethro asked.

"Starving, Jethro. I haven't had anything except a mouthful of bread since we had a meal here yesterday, and you won't get any news out of me until I have eaten and had a drink." A meal of bread, cooked fish, and a glass of wine was consumed. Then Amuba said, "Now I will tell you all about it."

"We know the first part," Jethro said. "When I came here yesterday evening, I found Chebron beside himself with worry. He told me how Ptylus's slave had discovered him, and you leaped to rescue him. You both fled, but the pursuers followed your trail, leaving him to return unharmed. He'd been waiting anxiously for two hours when I arrived. I tried to convince him to stay put, assuming you'd come back, and I headed off to get updates.

"The whole town was in the streets - they'd heard that the slayers of the cat had been captured. One had escaped, but the other had been overtaken after a long chase and would have been slain if not for a prince who had arrived and taken him away in his chariot. Everyone was surprised and outraged, and two officers had gone to the prince's mansion, six miles away, to retrieve the fugitive and deliver them to the people.

"As soon as I heard the news, I rushed along the road to where you had been taken and hurried past the people gathered there. I had my sword with me and planned to leap onto the chariot, surprise and slay the drivers, and take you away with me; I knew you wouldn't be able to help escape since I heard you were already unconscious when they took you. People were standing along the road with torches, but I thought a surprise attack would be successful. Some said that even if the boy's story was true, he deserved punishment for attacking the slave who arrested Chebron. Others thought he'd been punished enough since he'd been beaten almost to death. Everyone thought the whole thing needed to be investigated.

"I rushed back with the news, and we stayed up all night keeping watch for you. When morning came, and you still hadn't arrived, we got worried again, wondering if you were too injured to return to us and that you'd be recaptured that day. We knew the search for Chebron would be relentless, so I insisted he stay put while I went to the city to get updates. But all I could get was the assurance that you hadn't been caught - although they had searched for you and Chebron. Now, Amuba, I don't want you to have to talk too much - tell us how you convinced the Egyptian prince that you weren't guilty."

"It's quite a long tale, Jethro, but now that I've had a bite to eat, I've got the strength to talk for hours. First, Chebron needs to know that when I diverted the pursuers from my trail, there was no way I expected to have to sacrifice myself - I was sure I would be able to outrun them. I certainly would have, had it not been for new pursuers constantly joining the chase and eventually wearing me out."

Amuba then recounted the entire story of his escape, attack by the peasants, and rescue. He also relayed his whole conversation with his rescuer and his ordeals after leaving his house. "So you can see," he added, "that it was the teachings of your father, Chebron, and the story which Ruth shared with us - a tale that her grandfather had told you regarding the God of their ancestors - that ended up saving my life. Had it not been for this prince of Israelite descent, who also believed in one God, he would unlikely have been so willing to protect me from the people's wrath. He most likely would not have risked a further backlash from the king had it not been for our shared faith in a single, great God."

"That's an incredible tale," Jethro said after Amuba finished his narrative, "and you have had a miraculous escape. Without the arrival of this prince with the heart and compassion to intervene on your behalf, you would have been killed. You were also incredibly fortunate due to the kindness of your guide; had it not been for the long rest and the steps he took to reduce your wounds, you would have been captured by the searchers this morning. Most importantly, I find it extraordinary that you were saved by probably the only person in Egypt with the courage and will to save you."

The following morning, Jethro and Amuba, after much convincing, eventually talked Chebron out of his decision to give himself up. The argument that had the most impact was that he would disobey his father's final orders if he did so. It was then decided that he should disguise himself as a woman for a more effective disguise and that the watch on Ptylus' house should be restarted from a distance. It was thought that the search in that area would be less intensive than in the other regions, as the officials wouldn't think it possible for him to return to the same place. Amuba's disguise was changed entirely to look like a very elderly peasant.

They had a lengthy discussion about the plan they should

adopt, with Amuba and Jethro wanting Chebron to leave the surveillance to them. But he refused to listen to this, saying that he was sure nobody would know him in his disguise as a woman.

"First, we have to find out which way he goes," he said. "After that, none of us need to go near the house. I will buy a basket and some flowers from one of the rural women who bring them in, and I will take my seat close to the gate. By 3 o'clock, Plexo will have finished his job at the temple and may start half an hour later. I will at least observe which road he takes. Then, when you meet me at dusk, you can stroll a mile down the road, the other twice as far. We will then see when he returns whether he has stayed on the road a long way or has turned off at any crossroads and can station ourselves the following day to find out more."

"The plan is excellent, Chebron, and we will go by it. Once we are on his track, I guarantee it will not be long before we locate him at his destination."

Subsequently, that afternoon Chebron, disguised as a peasant woman, took a seat with a basket of flowers fifty yards away from the entrance of Ptylus' house. Around the time he was expecting Plexo and his father to arrive from the temple, a light chariot with two horses left the gate. Plexo was the one driving, and an attendant was accompanying him. Chebron was sure that if Plexo planned to visit Mysa, he would take the road to the countryside. The post he took gave him a view of the intersection where the road branched into three - one going straight north along the middle of the valley. Two went to the right and left until one of them merged into the major road near the river, the other one into the road located on the side of the valley close to the hills. It was this last one that Plexo took, and even though he might have been going to visit someone living in one of the numerous villas spread across miles along the roadside, Chebron was still optimistic that he was headed to Mysa's concealed abode. As soon as it became dark, he was joined by Jethro and Amuba.

"He left at three o'clock!" Chebron exclaimed when they had reached him, "and he took the road leading to the foot of the hills."

"Let's go right away," Jethro said. "He may be back soon, and we must hurry. Chebron, you tiptoe ahead and wait at the point where the road up ahead connects with the main road. Then, Amuba, stop two miles further; I'll go two miles beyond that. We'll start here tomorrow if he passes me on this road."

Jethro had just reached the spot he had picked when he heard the sound of wheels in the distance. The night was still bright and clear as the moon had not come out yet. He advanced towards the chariot and easily identified Plexo. The latter angrily shouted when he saw Jethro and lashed his horses with the whip. A moment later, the chariot disappeared, and Jethro returned to the city, picking up Amuba and Chebron.

The next night, Amuba took his position a mile beyond where Jethro had seen the chariot, Jethro another mile ahead, and Chebron watched the crossroads near the city. Unfortunately, the chariot didn't pass them again, even though Chebron saw him leave the city at the same time as before.

"I was not expecting to find him here tonight," Jethro said as he joined the others after waiting three hours with no luck. "He probably won't come here two days in a row. He's more likely to leave her for a week, so she can mull over the impossibility of not buying her freedom by agreeing to marry him. He probably just went to visit friends today."

It wasn't until the fourth night of waiting that Plexo went by. This time he didn't even pass Jethro, so it was certain he had turned either right or left somewhere between Jethro's post and Amuba's. After discussing this, they decided not to return to their hiding spots near Thebes that night but to rest beneath some trees until morning and then look over the road carefully. It wasn't likely another chariot would go past before morning so they could follow the tracks on the hard road.

In this way, they discovered the road he had turned off, yet the tracks couldn't be seen anymore since it was hard and barely had any dust. It went towards the hills, as expected, but there were so many country mansions of the wealthy and so many crossroads leading to these and the farmhouses of the farmers that they felt they were still distant from their goal.

After talking about it, they decided that at dawn, they'd go up the hills and stay there during the day, and Jethro would go back to town once it was dark to get enough provisions for a week. This is what they did, and the following day they separated and went to the hills at a distance of around a mile apart, choosing spots where they could oversee the valley and plan to meet at a central point after dark.

CHAPTER XV

Ameres is Revenged

Six days had gone by without any sign of the watch being rewarded. Then, Chebron, standing opposite the road where they had noticed the wheels, saw a chariot turn from the main road into it. He wasn't sure at first, but as it came closer, he realized it was the vehicle he was looking for. The horses matched in color with the ones Plexo had, and even from a distance, he could tell the color of his clothes. However, he was not accompanied by a servant but a figure wearing a white garment, whom he assumed to be Ptylus, the one who killed his father. "That must be Ptylus," he said to himself, "my father's murderer. If I were by the road's edge with a bow and arrow, I would put an arrow right through his heart!"

The chariot veered away from the path they had been taking from Thebes and drew near the hills so that Chebron could no longer see from his post. Immediately, he jumped up and ran to join Amuba, stationed next to him. By the time he got there, Amuba had already gone on, so Chebron had to run with all his might to reach Jethro, who had been joined by Amuba a few minutes before.

"Did you see them?" he cried out.

"I caught sight of them and noted it down," Jethro answered. "Do you see that roof among the trees at the base of the hill, half a mile ahead? They turned off the road and got into those woods. Our search is finally over."

"What do you think we ought to do, Jethro? Wait until they set off again and then go down?"

"No," Jethro declared firmly. "We have two tasks: to save Mysa and punish the one who murdered Ameres. Even if we decide to delay our vengeance, we still have to press on. You saw Ptylus and his son. They must be here for some purpose, probably to threaten her into taking an oath to marry Plexo. What can a girl that age do against such evil characters? Maybe Plexo has been trying to woo her, but seeing that it didn't work, he called in Ptylus, who can threaten her with the wrath of the gods, not to mention imprisonment and harsh treatment. So, let's hurry up. Amuba and I have our strong peasant staves while you, Chebron, have a dagger hidden under your female clothing. We have the advantage of surprise. There probably won't be more than two people with a female servant. Ptylus doesn't want more than necessary to know about this. Of course, there's a chance that the four men who took her away are all on guard there, but even if that is the case, we can handle it without difficulty. Even if there were twenty, I wouldn't be afraid: honest people should never be scared."

"Especially," Amuba said, "when the honest man has biceps like yours, Jethro, and a heavy club in his hands!"

Jethro smiled but was so earnest that he didn't have time to answer, so he guided them along the hillside until they were directly behind the house, among the trees. Then they descended, climbing with difficulty over the wall enclosing the wood, and entered the compound. Taking care to be as quiet as possible, Jethro and his companions made their way through the wood and up to the house. It was modest in size but nicely built and was adorned with a colonnade supported by carved pillars. The garden around it was meticulously looked after, and the house, due to its hidden location, was well suited as a place of refuge for a wealthy priest or noble who wanted a few days of rest and respite from the hustle and bustle of the great city.

As they were all barefoot, they silently crossed the garden to the colonnade. Once they arrived, Jethro raised his hand for them to stop, for the voices of Ptylus and two others could be heard from the wide doorway of a room that opened to the colonnade. Both Chebron and Amuba immediately recognized Ptylus's voice.

"I will no longer tolerate this foolishness, Mysa. Considering your family's situation, you should be grateful for my son's offer. I demand an answer immediately. You can either swear to the gods that you accept Plexo as your future husband, declare that you chose to stay here willingly, and insist that you were only hiding due to the terrible desecration your brother committed. Or else you will be put in a tomb and remain there, alone and without sunlight, until you agree to my demands. Don't you realize, you foolish girl, that I, Ptylus, high priest of Osiris, cannot be defied by someone like you?"

A voice that the three listeners recognized as Ruth suddenly spoke up: "Do not listen to him, Mysa. Never lie to God, like this wicked man is forcing you to, no matter the consequences. You call yourself a high priest, sir. What kind of gods do you claim to serve if someone like you can minister to them? They would strike you dead at the altar if they were true gods, not mere stone statues."

Ptylus uttered a furious shout and grabbed the Hebrew girl by the shoulder. But his expression quickly changed to shock when Ruth struck him.

"Drag her here, Plexo!" he shouted. At that very moment, the three listeners rushed into the room.

Ptylus had the bravery that set him apart from the rest of his people, and while he was briefly taken aback by their sudden entrance, he didn't step back. Instead, he pulled out a sword from his belt and declared haughtily:

"Who are you, and what is the reason behind this intrusion?"

"We are the ones you have been hunting down, Ptylus; we have come here to avenge the death of Ameres. Just like you instigated the murder of Ameres, you must die - not to mention your wrongdoings for kidnapping the daughter of the man you killed."

Without saying a word, Ptylus lunged at Jethro with his sword, hoping to finish off this audacious peasant quickly. But, as he did so, Jethro spun his hefty club around his head and blocked the attack with it, shattering the sword into pieces.

Ptylus dropped his arm and looked straight at his opponent, saying:

"Scoundrel, do you have the audacity to murder the high priest of Osiris?"

"No," Jethro answered, "but I do have the courage to execute him," and he brought his strong club down with all of his strength onto the head of the priest.

At that very moment, Plexo, who had managed to steal away unnoticed, re-entered the room with three armed men in tow. Chebron and Amuba were so preoccupied with the fight between Jethro and the priest that they completely overlooked Plexo, who, with a menacing knife in hand, lunged at Chebron.

Ruth let out a desperate warning as she swiftly leaped forward and pushed Plexo out of the way. The force of the shove caused them both to stumble and fall. Ruth sprang back up, but Plexo lay unconscious on the ground. The three armed men were momentarily stunned by the fall of their two employers until they noticed two men and a woman before them and quickly rushed forward to attack. Jethro swung his staff, and the first assailant to come at him was sent to the ground in one fell swoop. The others hesitated uncertainly. "Drop your weapons, or you are dead men!" Jethro declared. "You're outnumbered, and if you move, you die!"

Chebron discarded his female robe, took out his dagger, and took his spot at the door; while Jethro and Amuba were advancing towards them, both men laid down their arms. "Hold out your hands," Jethro said. "My son, stay over them with your club, and shatter the skull of anyone who tries to move."

The men obeyed the order. Jethro cut pieces of cloth from their garments, twisted them into ropes, and tightly bound their wrists together. The serious tone in which Jethro had called

Amuba his son was not missed by either Amuba or Chebron, who noticed that Jethro was attempting to hide their identities. Mysa, who had shouted with joy when Jethro initially spoke, had collapsed in fear upon a couch and had hidden her face in her hands during the swift encounter. At the same time, Ruth remained still and alert nearby her, only shifting when Plexo lunged at Chebron and then retreating to Mysa's side again once she had regained her balance. Finally, she, too, understood Jethro's intentions in calling Amuba his son, and leaning towards Mysa, she declared:

"It's over now, Mysa, but be quiet. Don't talk until they tell us what they will do."

No sooner had the men been tied up than Jethro ensured the individual knocked out from his hit was tied similarly. He then turned to Plexo, who hadn't moved since he had dropped. He pivoted him to some degree and murmured a low exclamation of shock.

"Gastrion," he said to Chebron, "go with the young lady into the garden and stay there until we meet up with you."

Chebron walked out to the colonnade after Mysa and Ruth. When they were out of sight, Mysa threw her arms around him and wept with joy.

"Chebron!" she said, "you have come just in time. I thought we'd never get away from that awful man; I don't know what I would have done without Ruth. What's more, they have been telling me such horrendous things—yet they can't be true—that our adored father had been killed; and that it was you, Chebron, who killed poor Paucis; however, I didn't accept them—I realized it was all their wickedness."

"Don't worry about that," Chebron stated; "we will talk about all this later. The primary thing to do is to get you out of here. Jethro and Amuba will soon determine the best course of action. Are there any other people in the house?"

"There is one other man," Ruth answered, "and an old woman; I believe the other man is outside with the chariot."

"I should tell Jethro," Chebron said, and he returned to the room and told Jethro what he had learned.

"We should apprehend the woman first," Jethro declared, "and then go around the house and sneak up on the chariot from the other side. The man must have heard the commotion; if we stepped out of the door, he may jump into the chariot and drive away before we could catch him. But if we approach it from the back, we will take him into custody."

"But you forgot to tie up Plexo," Chebron said.

"Plexo is dead," Jethro declared. "He had the knife in his hand, and it pierced his heart when he fell. I'm thankful you paid attention to me when I spoke to Amuba. It was so important that his name was not uttered. This will cause quite a stir. There's nothing to tie us to Ptylus, and it could be assumed to have been perpetrated by criminals from the hills looking for something to take. It's not definitive that we played a role just because Mysa and Ruth got abducted. Plexo only got a glance at us, so it's probable that he shouted for help for his father. In any case, let's not mention any names. Now, let's finish up here."

The maidservant was soon discovered and bound. Then the four prisoners were placed in different rooms and firmly fastened to the walls or columns. "Never lock two prisoners up together," Jethro advised. "Keep that in mind. Lock up one, and they can't get away. Lock two up, and they'll surely escape. They can break each other's ropes with their teeth, loosen the knot, or even untie it with their fingers."

"What's next?" Amuba asked.

"We need to talk. You join the girls in the garden, Chebron. Amuba and I will take care of the other man."

As soon as Jethro and Amuba left, Chebron rejoined the girls.

"You saved my life, Ruth. I'll never forget it."

"You saved me from the crocodile. It was just a push and he fell. I barely know how it was done."

"Your quickness saved my life, all the same, Ruth. I hadn't noticed him until you cried out. We were worried about you too, Ruth. We hoped you might be with Mysa, but no one saw you leave with her."

"My place was with my mistress," Ruth said quietly. "She was more than a mistress to me. She was like a friend."

"But how did you get here, Chebron," Mysa asked again, "and why are you dressed up like a peasant woman? It's not appropriate for any man, let alone a priest. And Amuba and Jethro, too, they're dressed like peasants. Their faces seem changed too. They look darker. I wouldn't have recognized them without hearing Jethro's voice."

"It's a long story, and I'll tell you all about it soon. But first, we want to hear your story too. Oh! Here come the others. You owe your rescue to them just as much as to me. I might know more about our people's learning, but I don't have any of the readiness or coolness that Amuba does. And Jethro is as prudent as he is brave. I wouldn't have fared well if it hadn't been for these good friends of ours."

Mysa walked up to them as they approached.

"Oh, Jethro! I know how much I owe you and to you, Amuba. My courage was about to give way, even though Ruth tried hard to give me hope. I don't think I could've withstood that man's threats for much longer. You have no idea how happy I was when I recognized your voice."

"We were just as happy to find you as you were to see us," Jethro replied. "Amuba and I would've gladly given our lives for you. But now, let's have a consultation; there's a lot that we need to decide and figure out. First, let's go to the garden on the other side of the house. We can talk and keep watch for other intruders. This place is so hidden that others will unlikely come, but we still need to watch out."

They went to some seats placed beneath trees on the other side of the house. A fountain worked by the water of a little stream on the hillside played in front of them, and a few tame waterfowl swam in a shallow basin around it. Everything was still and peaceful, and to Chebron, it seemed as if the events of the last three weeks had been a hideous dream, and they were again sitting in the garden of their house at Thebes.

"Now, first of all," Mysa said, "I must have my questions

answered. How are my father and mother and everyone?"

Jethro took Amuba's arm and turned away. "We will leave you, Chebron, to tell Mysa what has happened. It will be better for you to do so alone."

Ruth also rose from her seat to leave, but Mysa put her hand on her arm. "I am frightened, Ruth; stay with me."

"You told me, Mysa," Chebron began, "that they had told you tales that our father was dead and I killed Paucis."

"No, I didn't believe them. It's not possible you could have done something like that. But when I thought about those men at the gate, the noise we heard, and the people rushing in shouting, I thought—I was afraid—that maybe it could be true about our father. But, Chebron, surely it's not so?"

"It is true, Mysa. They killed our father. I wish I had been there to have died by his side. Jethro fought to the end and would have died with him if our father hadn't commanded that if anything happened to him, he was to take charge of me and leave the land."

Mysa was crying bitterly now. Presently, she looked up. "But why would you want to leave the land, Chebron? Surely—surely it's not true that you——" The thing seemed too terrible for her to put into words.

"That I killed poor Paucis? That's true too, Mysa."

Mysa cried out in horror.

"Ruth!" she sobbed, "this is too awful!"

Ruth put her arms around the crying girl. "You can be sure, Mysa, that your brother didn't do it on purpose."

"But it doesn't matter," Mysa sobbed. "It was the sacred cat—the Cat of Bubastes."

"It was, Mysa, and at first I thought, like you, that even though it was an accident, the gods' anger would be poured out against me, that I was cursed, and my life was forfeit in this world, and my spirit was destined to dwell in unclean beasts after death. But when I told my father everything, he reassured me and told me not to fear the gods' wrath in any way."

He then related to his sister how the cat had been killed,

the steps he and Amuba had taken to conceal the body, and his confession to his father of his fault.

"I see it wasn't your fault, Chebron. But you know the laws of Egypt and the punishment for even accidentally killing a common cat. How could our father say that the gods wouldn't be angry?"

"I wish I could tell you everything he said, Mysa. I might have if I had stayed with you a little longer. But he did say it, and you know how wise and good he was. So I want you to remember what he said so you won't always think of me as cursed after I'm gone."

"Oh! I would never do that!" Mysa exclaimed, jumping up and throwing her arms around her brother's neck. "How could you think so? But why are you talking about leaving, and where would you go?"

"I have to leave, Mysa, because the people of Egypt don't see this the same way as our father. They're hunting us down to kill us, Amuba and me. They don't know the truth and think we're both guilty. So we have to flee. Our father gave Jethro clear instructions, and by now, we would have been long gone if we hadn't stopped to find and rescue you."

"So if the other things they told me are true, Chebron, it may also be true that the letter they showed me ordering me to agree to marry Plexo was from my mother. How could she tell me that when she knew I hated him, and she has repeatedly spoken scornfully of his family before me?"

"What did she say?" Chebron asked.

"She said that now disgrace had fallen on the family; I might think myself very fortunate in obtaining such an offer."

Chebron was silent. He knew that his mother had never shown any genuine love for Mysa or himself, that her thoughts were entirely devoted to dress and entertainment, and that any love she had to give had been bestowed upon his brother.

"I fear it is true, Mysa."

"But I will never marry Plexo!" Mysa exclaimed passionately. "My father always said I should never marry a man I disliked."

"You will never marry Plexo, Mysa—he is dead."

Ruth gasped.

"He killed himself, Ruth—that is, by accident. His dagger pierced his heart as he fell, and when Jethro went to look at him, he was dead."

"God punished him for his evil," Ruth said firmly. "Everything is in God's hands. Since I didn't mean to kill him, I'm not upset about his death. Also, he tried to take your life; if I had had a dagger in my hand, I would have used it."

"What will happen to me?" Mysa asked.

"You have to go back to your mother, Mysa. There's nothing else for you to do."

"I won't!" Mysa exclaimed. "She never loved me. She would have married me against my will to Plexo, even though she knew he was evil and that I hated him. She would make me marry someone else who was rich, regardless of my wishes. No, Chebron, nothing will make me go back to her."

Chebron looked perplexed.

"Here comes Jethro and Amuba. You should talk it over with them. I see nothing else for you to do."

As Jethro came up, Mysa walked to meet him.

"I will not return to my mother, Jethro!" she exclaimed impetuously. "She wanted me to marry Plexo. She would give me to someone else, and my father always said I should only marry someone I liked. You can never be so cruel as to give me up to her?"

"I know that your father's wishes were strong upon that point," Jethro said, "for he spoke to me of you when he gave me his commands respecting Chebron. He said that he wished I could watch over you as over him, and it was because of what he had said that I disregarded his orders as to us leaving quickly, and we lingered here hoping to free you. Still, I don't see anything else that could be done. Your mother doubtless wrote while still overpowered by grief at your father's loss and thought she acted for your welfare in securing you an advantageous marriage despite the cloud under which your family was resting."

"I will not go to her!" Mysa repeated. "She thought of herself, as she always did, and not of me in any way. You know it was so, Chebron—you cannot deny it!"

Chebron was silent. He was very close with his father but didn't have much affection for his mother. As a child, he was seldom allowed in her room. She said that his noise was too much, his talking gave her headaches, and his fidgeting was too much to bear. Nor had he been much with her since then. His father had seen to his welfare and that of Mysa. He would put aside his studies to walk and talk with them. He was always indulgent and always anxious to please them. So he could understand Mysa's feelings but saw no other option for her.

"But where could you go, Mysa?" Jethro asked. "Where could you be placed? Your mother would eventually hear of it wherever you were and reclaim you."

"I will go with Chebron, you, and Amuba," Mysa said positively.

"Impossible!" Jethro replied. "We embark on a huge journey full of dangers and exhaustion. We are going among unknown and savage peoples; the odds are a hundred to one against ever making it to the end of our journey. If that's the case for myself and young men like Chebron and Amuba—who are now past eighteen and will soon be men—what chance would there be of success with you with us?"

"I can walk just as well as Chebron," Mysa said. "You know that, Chebron. And I could endure hardship just as well. At any rate, I would rather suffer anything and be with him and all of you than stay here. The people murdered my father. My mother would sell me to the highest bidder. If the odds are so great that you will never get through your journey safely, my being with you cannot make them so much greater. I only have Chebron in the world, and I will go where he goes and die where he dies. The gods can protect me just as well on a journey as they can here. Haven't they protected you now, and Chebron, too, based on what he's saying? You will take me with you, won't you, dear

Jethro?" she begged pleadingly. "You say my father wished you to watch over me...don't forget me now. Ruth will come with us too, won't you, Ruth? Ruth isn't afraid of the journey more than me."

"I will go if you go, Mysa. The God of Israel can take us safely through all dangers if that's what he wants."

Jethro was silent. Such an addition to his responsibility would make the journey much more difficult. Still, on the other hand, he remembered how worried Ameres was about Mysa, and he asked himself what his late master would have wanted if he'd known how things stood. He glanced at Amuba and Chebron and saw they wanted the same thing as Mysa. He abruptly turned away and paced up and down the garden for some minutes. Then he returned to the group, who hadn't said a word since he left them.

"Mysa," he said gravely, "this is a big deal that you're asking; your presence will make our difficulties worse, increase our dangers, and may make it impossible for me to carry out your father's wishes and take Chebron to a place where he'll be safe from Egypt's persecution. Such an enterprise must be undertaken with great seriousness. If you go, you must be prepared to face death in all forms--from hunger and thirst and the weapons of the native people. It's even possible that you'll end up as a slave among them. It's a terrible journey for men, even more terrible for women. Still, if you're determined-- determined with the strength and mind of a woman, not a child--that after you've turned your back on Egypt, you'll never regret the step you've taken or want to go back, and you'll be able to handle all the trials that may come our way, then I say you can share our fate."

Mysa shouted with joy.

"I swear, Jethro, no matter what happens—difficulty, danger, or death—you will never hear a word of complaint from me. Aren't you glad, Ruth?"

"I think it's right," Ruth said seriously. "It's a big undertaking, but God's hand is in it. I also want to leave this land of idols;

except for people here, I don't have anyone who cares for me."

"And now, Jethro," Amuba said, "what should we do? It's already almost dark, so we could leave right away. Could we use the chariot?"

Jethro thought for a short time.

"Except for carrying any things we may want for our first start, I do not see that we can do so," he said, "for wherever we leave the chariot tomorrow, it will be found, and when it is known that Ptylus' chariot was missing it would soon be recognized as his, and therefore a clue to the fact that we had fled south. It would be out of the question to travel in it beyond tonight. Besides, it will only hold three at the most. No, if we use it, it must be to drive north and throw them off the scent. I think it will be worth doing that."

"I will undertake that part of the business," Amuba said. "There will be much for you to do tomorrow, Jethro, which only you can arrange. There's the boat to be hired, stores laid in, and everything to be made ready. I think the best plan is for you both to start with the girls for Thebes at once. You and Chebron can occupy your hiding place on the hill, and Chigron will gladly take the girls into his house. There is no danger of an immediate search being made for them.

"Tonight, when the priest and his son don't return, their servants will think they slept here. It won't be until late tomorrow afternoon that anyone will be alarmed or think to send a messenger over here; by then, the confusion and panic caused will be so great that probably no one will think to carry the news to the officials until the next morning. Besides, until the story of Mysa's visit and subsequent disappearance is more widely known, there's no reason to think that what happened was our fault; therefore, for the next forty-eight hours, I think they would be perfectly safe at the embalmer's. I'll drive the chariot thirty or forty miles north, then let the horses loose where they're sure to be found soon, and return on foot to join you in your hiding place tomorrow night."

"I believe that your plan, Amuba, is an outstanding one.

Before we start, I'm going to search the house. We don't want to take anything with us, and even if the house were full of treasures, we wouldn't touch any of them; but if I move some of the things around, it will look like we're robbers. The captives cannot know the actual state of affairs. Plexo, when he ran out to get help, didn't have much time to do anything other than order them to get their weapons and follow him; he probably didn't even have an idea that we were something else than what we looked like. Therefore, the initial impression will be that we are the worst kind of criminals, escaped slaves, and people without respect for the gods; because no Egyptians, even the most heinous ones, would have calmly laid hands on the high priest of Osiris without any other intentions than pure malice."

"They did it to my father!" Chebron said bitterly.

"Yes, but not in cold blood. Rumors had been spread among them that he was unfaithful to the gods, and then they were driven mad by fanaticism and fear of the death of that sacred cat. But no Egyptian, no matter how immoral and criminal, would lift a hand against a priest. You may as well accompany me, Amuba; it would be strange if only one of us participated in the search."

In ten minutes, Jethro and Amuba had tossed the place into chaos by trying to open chests and cabinets and spraying the floor with garments; then, taking a few of the most precious vases and jewels, they threw them into the pond around the fountain, where they would be concealed from sight by the water lilies that floated on its surface.

They reexamined the bindings of the captives and felt sure that by no means could they extricate themselves.

"They will doubtless be liberated by tomorrow night," Amuba said, "otherwise I wouldn't feel right leaving them here to starve and thirst."

"I am delighted to think there is a chance they will be here forty hours rather than just twenty," Jethro said. "No doubt this is not the first mission they have undertaken for their evil master, and they should be grateful we are not taking the most secure and suitable course, which would be to run them through with a sword and silence them for good. If I thought they had anything useful to tell, I would do it now; but I doubt they know anything that would help us. Of course, the priest's wife knows that Mysa is hidden here, and she will likely announce her disappearance, as she would consider it could provide a clue for capturing those who attacked the house and killed her husband and son; so I can't see much good would come from silencing them. But if you think otherwise, I will take care of them immediately."

Amuba shook his head, for although human life was considered of little value back in those days, except by the Egyptians, he could not bear the idea of killing prisoners in cold blood.

"No, they can't say anything, Jethro. It's probably best to move on; nothing is left to discuss. I think our plans had been organized long ago, except that you will need to get a bigger boat than you had originally planned, together with clothes for the girls. Of course, it would be better for Chebron to disguise himself as a female, but we can decide tomorrow night. There is a great selection of dresses for us at Chigron's."

Amuba took the horses to a stone water trough and let them drink their fill. Then he got up in the chariot and drove away while the rest of the group set off on foot for Thebes. However, it was too late when they arrived at Chigron's house that they thought it would be best not to wake anybody up, as people would be surprised by the arrival of women at such a late hour and not expected by the master; therefore, the girls spent the night in the rock chamber behind the building, while Jethro and Chebron lay down outside.

The moment the sun was up, they moved a bit away. Jethro went to the house as soon as there was any indication that someone was awake and told Chigron that they had found and rescued Mysa. Chigron was very disturbed when he heard about the death of the high priest and his son.

"I can't deny that these men have done wrong, Jethro, but that two high priests should be killed in such a short time is enough to draw the wrath of all the gods on Egypt. Nevertheless, the poor girls are not at fault, and I'll be more than happy to shelter them for the night, but I must confess that I'll be greatly relieved when you are on your way."

"I can easily understand that," Jethro said, "and trust me, the gratitude of those you have sheltered, which will remain with them for the rest of their lives, could compensate for any doubts that may arise about you assisting those who are victims to the superstitions of your countrymen."

Chigron called for his servants, informed them that some acquaintances had just arrived from the country, and asked them to ready a room. He went out and returned an hour later with the two girls. He took them into the house and to the room prepared for them so that any of the servants didn't spot them.

Then he summoned an old faithful servant, instructing her to attend to the guests throughout the day and not to let anyone else enter the room. He told her to make the other servants believe that the visitors were older women and that they were only staying for a few hours until some friends they would remain with were sent in a wagon to bring them to their home in the countryside. The old woman immediately prepared baths for the girls and then gave them something to eat, after which they lay down on couches and quickly drifted off to sleep; for the excitement of the previous night and the strangeness of their situation in the bare stone chamber had stopped them from getting any sleep during the night. They had spent the time talking about the devastating loss Mysa had suffered and the journey ahead of them.

CHAPTER XVI

Up the Nile

Late in the evening, Jethro returned to the concealed spot on the hill. Chigron had just come back from another journey to the city. He said:

"The whole town is in a state of frenzy. The news that Ptylus and his son had been found murdered has been made public, and the agitation is immense. The death of two prominent priests of Osiris in such a short time is regarded as an omen of some terrible national calamity. That one should have been killed was almost unheard of - a severe insult to the gods, but this second act of desecration nearly drove the people mad. Some consider it to be a punishment of Osiris and believe that it confirms what a few dared to suggest before - that the assassination of Ameres was engineered by a group of priests headed by Ptylus. Others perceive it as another demonstration of the god's wrath against Egypt.

"It is rumored that the king will participate in sacrifice services at the Temple of Osiris tomorrow. Sacrifices are supposed to be held in all the temples. A solemn fast will be declared tomorrow, and all the high and low people will have their eyebrows shaved and display the typical signs of mourning. As of yet, I have not heard of the two missing girls from the household, but I'm sure that when the authorities question those who were there, it will come to light, and they will admit that they took Mysa away at the orders of Ptylus when they attacked the house.

"At the moment, however, we don't need to worry about women; Chigron and I can take the girls down to the boat without fear. But it would be better if you didn't come with us; someone may notice that our number matches the three people present when Ptylus was killed and the two missing girls. That's why Chigron thinks it would be safer if you start walking to Mita, a village twenty miles upriver. The boat will stay there overnight; you can join us when it's dark. I'll tell the boatmen you've gone there to take care of some business for me."

"That sounds like the best plan," Amuba agreed. "Too many people know Chebron's face, so it wouldn't be safe for him to board the boat here in broad daylight. I'll take a two-hour nap before I start; I haven't slept since I left the chariot this morning and have already walked forty miles, so I need rest. I should've napped earlier today, but I was too occupied with my thoughts, especially since I thought we'd rest here overnight."

"I will wake you up," Chebron said. "I have been asleep most of the day because I had nothing to do since we arrived yesterday morning."

Chebron sat watching the stars until he noticed they had traveled two hours through the sky, then he woke up Amuba. They removed their peasant attire and put on the clothing prepared for them as the sons of a small trader. Amuba reluctantly agreed to shave his head the night after Ameres' death and was pleased to put on a wig since he was used to observing the bare heads of the peasants and felt strange and uncomfortable going outside in the same manner.

Once dressed, they set off and went down to the riverbank just above the town. They strolled along the broad causeway beside the river for a few miles before veering away towards a group of trees visible in the first light of dawn at a quarter of a mile away. They rested in the trees for hours before returning to the river and wandering along, admiring the boats. Those in the middle of the river were coasting down with the current lightly and quickly, their crew often singing joyously, rejoicing in the prospect of reuniting with their friends after a long absence. The boats heading upstream were close to the bank, their crew walking along the causeway and tugging at the towropes, as there wasn't enough wind to make the sails of any use in going against the stream. The vessels were of various shapes and sizes. They were used in bringing corn from the higher country down to Thebes, at this point, returned empty. Others were intricately painted boats from wealthy people with large rooms on board and beautiful, richly decorated sails. These carried their owners up and down the river between their mansions and the city.

Half an hour after sunset, the two friends showed up in Mita. The darkness came fast in Egypt after the sun had set, and it would have been difficult to recognize them if they had run into someone familiar with them on the streets. But, instead, the streets of the small village were bustling. Its distance from Thebes made it a popular overnight stop for boats that had left the major city early, and a lot of them were already moored off the bank, with more boats arriving successively. The boatmen and passengers were busy buying supplies from the stores; fishermen with baskets overflowing were loudly advertising their catch; fowlers, with strings of ducks and geese draped on poles from their shoulders, were also clamoring to make a sale.

The shops of the fruit sellers and bakers, as well as the sellers of vegetables that were a significant part of the Egyptian diet, were all filled to the brim, and the wine stores were thriving.

Chebron and Amuba made their progress through the bustling atmosphere, keeping a sharp eye out for Jethro, as they were sure that the boat would have arrived there several hours prior due to the early launch and that he would be watching out for them. In a few minutes, they spotted him examining one of the stores. He flinched as they moved toward and touched him, for he had not noticed them before.

"Everything okay?" Amuba asked.

"Everything has gone off excellently. We departed without

the tiniest difficulty. But get on board straight away; the girls are worried about you, even though I guaranteed them there was no possibility of you being uncovered en route to here."

Jethro headed to the boat, which was moored by the riverbank one hundred yards above the town, "so that," Jethro said, "they could make a quick start in the morning and be away before the rest of the vessels were underway."

"Here are your brothers," Jethro said loudly as he boarded the ship. "I found them loitering in the street, wasting time and chatting away, completely oblivious that you were waiting for dinner until they arrived."

Both entered the cabin, about eight feet wide and twelve feet long, but not tall enough for them to stand upright. The floor was covered with a thick carpet; comfortable cushions and pillows were arranged along each side, and thick matting hung from the top. During the day, the matting was rolled up and secured, allowing air to circulate through the cabin and those within to look out onto the river; however, it now blocked the openings, keeping out the evening breeze and the eyes of passers-by. At the far end of the cabin was a door that led to the smaller section allocated for the girls. A lamp hung from the beams above. Mysa was about to leap to her feet in delight when they entered, but Jethro abruptly exclaimed:

"Be careful of your head, child! You're not used to being in such low-ceilinged quarters yet."

"Thank heavens we're back together again!" Mysa said as Chebron, after embracing her, took a seat on the cushion beside her. "I'm almost delighted now, despite the horrible times that have passed."

"It does feel like home here," Chebron said, looking around, "especially after sleeping in the open air on the hard ground, as we've been doing for the past month."

"I hardly would have recognized you, Amuba," Mysa said. "You look so different in your wig and with your skin darkened."

"I must look pretty awful," Amuba replied a bit sadly.

"You don't look all that great," Mysa responded honestly. "At first, I used to think that your short, wavy golden hair was strange and that you would appear better in a wig like everyone else; but now I'm sorry it is gone."

"Here is our meal," Jethro declared as the curtains that served as a door were pulled aside, and one of the men entered carrying a plate of fried fish and another of stewed ducks, which he placed on the floor.

Jethro produced some cups and a jug of wine from a locker in the cabin, and then the men, as per his orders, brought in a jar of water for the use of the girls. Then sitting around the dishes, they began their meal, Jethro cutting up the food with his dagger and everyone helping themselves with the help of their fingers and pieces of bread, which served them as forks. Mysa had always been accustomed to using a table, but these were only found in the dwellings of the rich, and the people generally sat on the ground for their meals.

"We have not experienced any hardship yet," Mysa said, smiling. "I wouldn't mind if this went on for a while. I think this is much better than living in a house, don't you agree, Ruth?"

"This is more natural to me than your big house," Ruth replied, "and it is certainly a lot more like home and comfortable. The other servants were jealous of your kindness to me, so I don't think I was very popular with them."

"I wanted to suggest something," Jethro said. "It is better that we don't use our real names when talking to each other. The boatmen don't seem to suspect us, but they might find out our names after all the commotion a month ago. So we should probably change our names for now. You should call me father since that is the relationship we are supposed to have. Amuba can become Amnis, and Chebron can be Chefu."

"And I'll become Mytis," Mysa said. "What name will you take, Ruth? There isn't an Egyptian name quite like yours."

"It doesn't make a difference what you call me," Ruth said.

"We'll call you Nite," Mysa said. "I had an incredible friend with that name. However, she passed away."

"And there is one thing, Nite," Chebron said, "that I want you to comprehend. Right now, you talked to me as my lord Chebron. That sort of thing must not occur anymore. We are all runaways, and Mysa and I no longer have any rank. Jethro and Amuba are of high rank in their own country, and if we ever safely make it to their people, they will be nobles in the land, while we will be outsiders, as he was when he and Jethro came into Egypt. Thus any discussion of rank among us is only foolishness. We are runaways, and my life is forfeited if I am found in my own country. Jethro is our leader and guardian, both by our father's will and because he is older and more astute than us. Amuba is like my elder brother, being stronger, bolder, and more acquainted with danger than I; you and Mysa are sisters since you are both refugees."

"I'm delighted to hear that, brother," Mysa said. "I spoke with her last night, for she kept trying to treat me as though she was my servant; it is absurd when she is accompanying us to face our dangers only because she loves me. It's me who should look up to her, for I'm completely helpless, and I don't know anything about work or reality, while she's able to do all kinds of things; furthermore, when we were captives, it was she who was always courageous and hopeful, and kept my morale up when, I do think, if it hadn't been for her I would have passed away from sadness and fear."

"By the way," Jethro said, "we still haven't heard how it was that you were together. We heard of your abduction, but old Lyptis informed me that no one had observed anything of you."

"They were all petrified with fear," Ruth snorted disdainfully. "The men abruptly entered the room, grabbed Mysa, and immediately tied a shawl around her head before she could cry for help. I shrieked, and one struck me with a blow that knocked me to the ground. Then they took her away. I think I was dazed for a moment. When I regained consciousness, I saw they had left. I got up and ran down the corridor and through the hall, where the women were screaming and sobbing, and then out of the house through the garden and out of the gate. Then I noticed four men a short distance away carrying Mysa to a wagon parked a hundred yards away. I ran up just as they placed her inside it. One of them stepped towards me with a dagger. I said:

"'Let me go with her, and I will remain quiet. If not, I will shriek; if you kill me, it will only alert the people to your whereabouts.'

"The men were uncertain, so I rushed past them and jumped into the wagon and threw myself down beside Mysa, and then they drove away."

"It was courageous and kind of you, Ruth," Jethro stated, placing his hand on the girl's shoulder, "but why didn't you yell when you initially came out of the gate? It could have brought help and prevented Mysa from being abducted."

"I considered that," Ruth answered, "but there were a lot of rough men still entering through the gate; and knowing how the people had been aroused to anger against us, I didn't know what might occur if I raised the alarm. Additionally, I wasn't certain at first that these men, who seemed so rough and aggressive, were not allies, who were taking Mysa away to protect her from the raging crowd."

"Yes, that could have been the case," Jethro agreed. "In any case, child, you demonstrated courage and good sense. We had hoped you had been with Mysa, for we knew you would be a great comfort for her. However, since the women said you didn't leave with her, we saw no way it could be. And now, Mytis and Nite, it would be best for you to go to your cabin to get some rest; even though you have both journeyed well, all this has put a huge strain on you, and you are both looking tired and bleary-eyed. However, tonight you can sleep with peace of mind; for, for the moment, I believe there is no cause for the slightest anxiety."

It took some time before Jethro and his companions lay down to rest. They spoke long and seriously about the journey that was ahead of them, and when they had discussed this issue thoroughly, Chebron said:

"Until now, Jethro, I haven't asked you about my father's funeral. When is it going to be? I have thought about it often, but since you didn't mention it, I figured it would be better not to ask."

"I'm glad you didn't," Jethro replied. "It'll be ready in around ten days. I could tell you were guessing Chigron is embalming him; the process won't be finished for another four days, and, as you know, the relatives don't see the body after it's been with the embalmer until it's wrapped and in the coffin. Chigron has done so much that he must have had to go against his conscience; he holds that process in such high regard that I didn't want him to break that custom for you. Plus, my dear lad, I thought it would be better for your own sake not to relive your grief by looking at a now lifeless face.

"In the past month, you've been lucky enough to have plenty of things to keep your mind busy and haven't had time to dwell on the loss. You've been using all your strength and energy to find your sister, and I'm sure your father, as sensible and wise as he was, would rather have seen you being active and energetic in that search and planning for this new life we're about to begin than mourning for him. So with that in mind, I chose to stay quiet on the topic. But it may be of some comfort to you to know that everything will be done to give him a proper sendoff."

"The king and all the important people of Egypt will be present, and Thebes will gather its thousands to demonstrate its distress for the deed done by a portion of its inhabitants. Had it not been for the explicit commands of your father, I should have thought that it may have been advantageous for you to show up on that occasion, and it is possible that, for once, even the extremists would have been ready to pardon the offense of the offspring because of the wrong done to the parent. Nevertheless, this matter of Ptylus takes that out of the equation, for when it is broadly known that Mysa was abducted when Ptylus was killed, public sentiment will arrive at the reality and say that the escapees of whom they were in pursuit, the slayers of the sacred cat, were the protectors of the girl of Ameres and the executors of the high priest."

"You are correct, Jethro; it will be more beneficial for me not to have seen my father; I can consistently remember him now as I saw him last, which is a thousand times superior to if he lived in my memory as he rests in the funeral clothes in the embalming room of Chigron. Regarding what you say about my showing up at the memorial service, I would in no case have done it; I would a thousand times rather live as a pariah or meet my death at the hands of savages than request leniency at the hands of the mob of Thebes, and live to be pointed at all my life as the man who had committed the terrible offense of killing the sacred cat."

The conversation in the cabin had all been carried out in hushed tones; for even though they could see the crew enjoying their meal from the light of a torch made from resinous wood and were now wrapped in thick garments to keep away the night dew, they talked cautiously so that no word could be overheard. The boatmen were merry; they called a distant place near the edges of Upper Egypt their home and rarely had a job that enabled them to visit their loved ones. Thus the engagement was highly pleasing to them, for even though their leader had haggled over the terms, he and they would have been delighted to accept half the pay rate rather than miss such a golden chance. As Chebron concluded speaking, they were preparing for the night by laying down some mats on the boards of the fore deck. Then they huddled close to each other, covered themselves with a couple of mats, snuffed out the torch, and got ready to be asleep.

"Let's follow in their footsteps; however, under better conditions, I presume," Jethro said.

The cushions and pillows were nicely arranged, the lamp was turned low, and the boat's occupants were soundly asleep in no time. Not even a ray of light had managed to enter the cabin when Amuba was awoken by a boat movement caused by some commotion among the crew. He felt his way to the door, threw back the curtains, and looked outside; the sky had a faint greenish-yellow hue, but the stars were still radiantly shining.

"Good morning, young master!" the captain said. "I hope you slept well."

"So peaceful that I had difficulty believing it was already morning," Amuba responded. "How long before you set off?"

"We shall sail in ten minutes; there still isn't enough light to make out the shore."

"Chefu, are you awake?"

"Yes," Chebron answered groggily, "I am awake, thanks to your loud talking. Had you been quiet, we might have been able to sleep for another hour or more."

"You have had plenty of sleep over the last day," Amuba retorted. "Grab a cloth and let us disembark and jog along the riverbank for a mile and have a swim before the vessel comes by."

"It's much too cold for that," Chebron said.

"Rubbish! the water will invigorate you."

"Let's go, Chefu," Jethro said, "your brother is correct; a dip will reinvigorate us for the day."

The Egyptians were very particular when it came to bathing and washing. The heat and dust of the climate made cleanliness a must, and all classes took their daily bath—the wealthy in baths attached to their homes, the poor in the water of the lakes or canals. Jethro and the two boys leaped out of the boat and ran briskly along the bank for about a mile, stripped and took a dive into the river, and were dressed again just as the boat arrived with the four men towing it, and the captain steering with an oar at the rear. It was bright enough now for him to make out the faces of his passengers, and he brought the boat straight alongside the bank. The girls emerged from their cabin in a few minutes, looking invigorated and rosy.

"So you've had your baths?" Mysa said. "We heard what you were saying and took a bath."

"How did you manage that?" Chebron queried.

"We went out through the other door of our cabin in our woolen robes, over to the little platform where the person is steering, and we poured buckets of water on each other."

"And you both slept well?"

"Yes, definitely, and without waking up once until we heard Amnis call you to get up."

"You woke up everyone, Amnis," Chebron commented.

"And it was a good thing, too," Amuba laughed. "If we hadn't had our bath when we did, we wouldn't have had the chance all day. Now we all feel rejuvenated."

"I'm ready for something to eat," Mysa interjected.

"What would you like, Mytis?" Ruth asked. "I can cook, and I don't think the men will be ready to make breakfast for a while yet."

"I believe that will be an excellent idea, Mytis," Jethro said; "however, we should split up the work between us. The two boys should get the fire going on the flat stone hearth in front; I will get and prepare some fish; Nite will cook them, while Mytis will, following her guidance, make some cakes and put them into the hot ashes to bake. Then, we will have to take care of ourselves later. There's nothing like getting used to it. Of course, the men will cook the main meals, but we can make small meals in between. It's amazing how many times you can eat during the day when you're outdoors."

The meal, consisting of the fish, light dough cakes prepared with much amusement under Ruth's directions, and fruit, was ready in half an hour. The latter consisted of grapes and melons. The meal was savored, and the sun was already rising in the sky when it was finished. For an hour, the party sat on the deck forward, taking in the sight of boats moving down the stream and the villages on the opposite shore. Then, as the sun grew more intense, they welcomed the shelter of the cabin. The mats were rolled up to allow a free passage of air, and from their cushioned seats, they could see out from both sides.

Day after day passed peacefully and smoothly. The men would tow the boat from sunrise until eleven o'clock in the morning; then, they would moor her to the bank, make a meal, and if there were trees to offer shade, they would go ashore. If not, they would suspend some mats on poles over the boat and rest in their shade until three o'clock. Then they would tow until sunset, moor her for the night, cook their second meal, talk and sing for an hour or two, and then sleep. On occasions when the wind blew strongly enough, the boat could move upstream with assistance from the sail. This pleased the boatmen greatly, allowing them to fill their days with alternating eating and sleeping. Generally, the passengers would disembark and walk alongside the boat for an hour or two after their early breakfast and again when the day's heat was over. It made a routine and, at the same time, kept their muscles active.

"We may need to travel long distances on foot," Jethro stated, "and the more we prepare ourselves for walking, the better." The hours passed so calmly and agreeably that both Mysa and Chebron occasionally faulted themselves for feeling as content as they did, yet when the latter once said as much to Jethro, he replied:

"Don't be concerned about that. Remember that, above all else, it is a comfort to us that you and your sister are cheerful companions. It makes the trip less difficult for us. Moreover, a good mood and good health go hand in hand, and although, right now, our life is not difficult, there will be the need for health and strength shortly. Therefore, this escape and banishment are blessings instead of misfortunes to you. Just like Amuba's captivity following so closely the death of his father and mother was for him."

"I still can't believe," Mysa said, "that we are headed out on this risky mission. Everything is so peaceful and tranquil. We coast day by day without any worries or anxieties. I find it hard to imagine that the time is fast approaching when we must traverse deserts, possibly encounter wild beasts and uncivilized people, and be in peril of our lives."

"It will be a while before that, Mytis. It will be months of travel until we reach Meroe, the capital of the neighboring kingdom, which lies at the meeting of these two great arms of the river. I don't think there will be any danger up to that point, even though there may be some hardship since I hear there are some intense rapids to pass. It's only recently that the king conquered Meroe, defeated its armies, and demanded tribute, but since there is much trading between the two countries, I don't think there's any risk of being attacked. However, when we leave Meroe, our troubles will start; as I'm told, the route from there to the east through the city of Axoum, the capital of Abyssinia, goes through an untamed land rife with wild animals. Then again, beyond Axoum, the terrain is broken and hard to traverse to the sea.

"Chigron told me, however, that he had heard from a native of Meroe who had worked for him that there is a much shorter road to the sea from a spot at which the river makes a large turn many hundreds of miles beneath the capital. So, once we get further up, we should be able to look into this. I hope it's true, for if it is, it will save us time and effort."

As their journey went on, they passed several large towns. Hermonthis, which was on the western bank of the river they were following, was the first. Then came Esneh, with grand temples dedicated to Kneph and Neith, located five miles wide in a part of the Nile Valley. After that was Eilithya, on the eastern bank, with many temples towering above it and the sandstone rock behind it dotted with tombs.

A few miles further up the river, they arrived at Edfu. The hills closed around the river until they seemed to rise almost straight from the water's edge. This was a sacred place to the Egyptians, where they built temples to the Nile and its symbol, the crocodile. Also in this area were vast quarries used to supply the stone used to construct most of the temples of Upper Egypt.

Sixteen miles upriver, they passed by Ombi, which had a great temple dedicated to the crocodile-headed god Sebak. This part of Egypt was relatively barren, and the villages were scattered and small. The river's current was so strong in some places that it was necessary to hire several locals to help the boatmen pull the boat against the stream, and the progress was slow.

Four days after setting off from Ombi, they made it to Syene, which was by far the largest city they had come to since they left Thebes. This marked the end of the first stage of their journey. Up to that point, they had been traveling down a quiet river, which sometimes had a strong current but was generally steady and even. Ahead of them lay a series of cataracts and rapids to pass and a country to traverse, which often rose in revolt against the power of Egypt despite having been subdued many times.

They stayed for three days at Syene. They would have liked to continue without stopping, as the Egyptian rule stretched further up the river. Moreover, Syene was the last place where the governor would take an interest in the affairs of Egypt or where fugitives from justice could expect to be pursued. However, Jethro thought it wise to show no signs of haste, as it was customary to give boatmen a few days of rest before facing the more difficult work that awaited them.

There was a lot for them to see at Syene that was new. Trading with Meroe was a significant activity here. Most merchants engaging in this were based in Syene, buying the products of Upper and Lower Egypt and shipping them up the river. Additionally, they were buying and sending products from Meroe to Thebes. The streets were swamped with a variety of different people. Egyptians, wearing their perfect clothing and expressionless faces, merchants deep in their business, officers and soldiers since Syene was an important military post, and officials from the nearby quarries together with gangs of enslaved people from many different nations, all working under the orders of the officials.

Amidst the crowds were wild-looking figures wearing their clothes loosely, which made an incredible contrast with the clean garments of the Egyptians. Additionally, their messy hair was in stark contrast to the neat wigs of the middle-class Egyptians and the bald heads of the lower class. Their skins were much darker, though there was a difference. Among them were a few men of a different type, darker black with thicker lips and flatter features. These were Ethiopians from a place beyond Meroe who had also experienced the power of Egyptian arms.

"These people of Meroe," Amuba stated, "are quite alike in appearance to the Egyptians, Chebron. Their language is similar to yours; I can comprehend their conversation. Our oldest books mention that we are related to people of Asian descent rather than African. The people of Meroe claim that their distant ancestors came from Arabia and, in the beginning, spread along the western coast of the Red Sea, moved up to the highlands, and forced out the dark-skinned people who lived there."

"The origin of our people is unclear, but according to those well-versed in ancient learning, we may have come from Arabia. We have not always been one people; it was only in recent years, although an immense amount of time in human lives, that the people of Thebaid, or Upper Egypt, extended their rule over Lower Egypt and united the entire country. Even now, you know, the king wears two crowns - one of Upper Egypt and the other of the lower country. Along the shores of the Great Sea to the west are Libyans and others similar in race to ourselves. My father believed that the tribes that came from Asia initially pushed to the west, displacing or eliminating the black people. Then, with each new wave from the east, the others were driven further and further back until the ancestors of the people of Lower Egypt finally arrived and settled there.

"In Meroe, temples and religions are similar to what we have. I'm not sure whether they brought that religion from Arabia or we planted it during our various conquests of the country. Still, Upper Egypt and Meroe certainly have very little difference now."

"Are the people beyond Meroe all black like the ones we see here?"

"As far as I know, Amuba. Our merchants venture deep into the south to exchange our goods for gold and ivory. They find the area inhabited by black people living in poor villages without government, law, or order. They fight with each other and make slaves, which they also sell to our merchants. They are so different from us that it is certain that we are not of the same ancestry. However, they are strong and agile, making them great slaves. Between Meroe and the sea is a country called Abyssinia, populated by people of Arab descent, but more different from us than the ones from Meroe."

"They have excellent cities, but I don't believe their religion is the same as ours; our merchants say that their language can be comprehended, though it's more primitive. I have heard my father say that all the land situated east of the Nile and of its eastern branch that originates in Abyssinia and is called the Tacazze belongs to Asia instead of Africa."

The group noticed that the death by force of two consecutive leading priests of Osiris was one of the main subjects of discussion in Syene, but no one seemed to think that there was the slightest chance of anyone involved in those events making for the south. Nevertheless, Jethro considered it wise that the whole group should not disembark together; therefore, Amuba and Chebron usually went one direction, and he with the girls another. They visited the sacred island of Ebo opposite the town and the quarries of Phile, four miles away. Here they beheld the gangs of slaves cutting giant statues, obelisks, and shrines from the unyielding rock.

The outline of the rock was first traced, then the adjoining stones were eliminated with chisels and wedges, and eventually, the statue or obelisk was separated from the rock. After that, it was chipped and sculpted by the masons, placed on rollers, and dragged by hundreds of people down to the landing site beneath the rapids, and then put on rafts to be sailed down the river to its ultimate destination. They noticed many of these blocks of stone in various stages of manufacture. The multitude of slaves required was massive, and they inhabited huge buildings constructed close to the quarries, where the soldiers were also billeted to keep them under control.

As they watched the slaves labor away under harsh conditions, Jethro and Amuba were highly grateful for their good luck in being placed with Ameres instead of being consigned to a lifetime of such unceasing and repetitive labor. Among the slaves, they could identify several who, based on their skin color and appearance, were believed to be Rebu. However, since all those brought to Egypt were distributed initially amongst the priests and high-ranking officials, they assumed that due to stubbornness, misconduct, or from attempting to escape, they had incurred the wrath of their masters and were then assigned to government service.

Had the slaves been in the hands of private masters, Jethro and Amuba, who were deeply saddened by the state of their fellow countrymen, would have attempted to purchase them and take them with them on their journey. However, this was not an option now, nor was it possible to speak to them or even offer them some money to improve their circumstances without raising suspicion. Therefore, everyone was greatly relieved when the boat was pushed away from the shore on the morning of the fourth day after their arrival, and their journey through the rapids began.

CHAPTER XVII

Out of Egypt

When they left Thebes, the river had started to swell; though it hadn't yet peaked, a large quantity of water was flowing downstream. The boatmen assured Jethro that they could ascend the rapids with no issues, yet when the Nile was low, navigating it was often quite hazardous and sometimes impossible. So ten more men were hired in addition to the crew to take the boats across the rapids.

Although confident that there was no danger, the girls preferred to walk along the bank as the powerful current, sometimes rising in strong, abrupt waves, was a bit unnerving. Jethro and the boys joined them and, at times, had to grab hold of the rope and help pull as the water threatened to overpower the men hauling the boat. Eventually, they reached the top of the rapids and were glad to be back in their vessels as they sailed on the tranquil river. This went on for a month, with the wind propelling them forward at times, other times pulling them along the shallow waters close to the shore, and occasionally having to brave the wild rapids. When they moved further up, they realized that the cataract they had previously crossed was nothing compared to the ones they encountered later. To cross this rough patch, they had to unload the cargo and carry it up the rapids, and it took around forty men to drag the empty boat through the turbulent waters. If the helmsman made the slightest error, this would cause the boat to crash against the rocks rising in the middle of the channel. But before arriving at the second change, they waited several days at Ibsciak, where their crew belonged.

As they journeyed the hundred and eighty miles between Syene and this place, they encountered many temples and towns but none as grand as this. Here, two immense grotto temples were erected; the first, dedicated to Amun and Phre and funded by Rameses himself, the other dedicated to Athor by Queen Lofreai. These temples were engraved with the records of Rameses' victories over various African and Asian nations.

Jethro offered to charter another boat for them if they wished to stay longer at this location, but they chose to remain only for a week out of satisfaction with the boat and their arrangement. After passing the second cataract, they arrived at Behni, a vast city with many temples and public buildings, the largest dedicated to Thoth. Along the river, a belt of cultivated land stretched for several miles with numerous villages, providing all kinds of food with ease.

They finally reached Semneh, the destination the boatmen had agreed to take them to. At that time, this was the farthest boundary of Egyptian power. The river here made a considerable curve eastwards, then flowed southwards and westwards, forming a large loop. This could be bypassed by traversing the desert to Merawe. This prosperous town marked the northern boundary of the Meroe power, with the desert providing a suitable neutral ground between the two kingdoms. On occasion, when under the control of a powerful king, Egypt would expand its borders far down south, and at other times a warlike monarch of Meroe would push the Egyptian border almost to Syene. Yet, the Nile as far south as Semneh was usually considered part of Egypt.

The merchants who arrived at Semneh usually waited until there were enough of them to form a strong caravan for mutual defense against the inhabitants of the desert, who were independent of both Egypt and Meroe. They attacked and robbed groups crossing the desert unless powerful and armed enough to stand up to them. They pitched two tents and unloaded their cargo and products, and Jethro and his company encamped near the river's edge. They had not yet decided whether to cross the desert or continue their voyage via water.

They had the option between two courses: the traders generally crossed the desert, taking with them their lighter and more valuable goods, the heavier items made a long detour by boat, traveling in large fleets both for protection from the locals and for mutual assistance in conquering the rapids that had to be faced. It was easy to rent a different boat because it was the usual practice to unload here, as the Egyptian boatmen wanted to avoid entering Meroe. So, beyond this point, the journey was in the hands of the area's people.

When he met with the traders congregated at Semneh, Jethro discovered that it was not essential to travel up the river to the city of Meroe and then eastward through Axoum, the capital of Abyssinia, to the sea but that a much shorter path was available from the easternmost point of the bend of the river straight to the sea. There were, in fact, several large Egyptian towns along the Red Sea, and from these, a prosperous trade was conducted with Meroe and Abyssinia; and the first merchant to whom Jethro spoke was stunned to find that he didn't know about the route described.

The voyage, though difficult, was said to be no worse than that from Meroe to Axoum, while the distance to cover was small in comparison. After much deliberation, it was decided that the best course of action was to get rid of the goods they had brought with them to one of the traders heading south, keeping only enough to pay the men they would need for protection on the trip. Jethro had no problem doing this, saying that he found that the expenses to Meroe would be much higher than the amount he had estimated, and therefore he had decided not to go any further. They thought it best to wait six months from when they left Thebes before entering any major Egyptian city, so they stayed for almost two months at Semneh. Then when they discovered that a group of boats was ready to go up the river, they agreed with some boatmen to hire their vessels up to where they would leave the river and start their journey again.

The journey posed significant challenges. After traversing around sixty miles, they reached rapids more treacherous than any they had encountered before. It took the group more than two weeks to pass through them, with only four to five boats handled daily using joint effort from the crews. Nevertheless, there was much rejoicing when the last boat made it up the rapids, and the boatmen celebrated with a feast that evening.

The area had a bad reputation, so the group took extra precautions. All the cargo was hauled up by hand and arranged to form a barricade. As the night fell, several sentries were on watch to ward off potential attacks from the desert dwellers. It had been decided that the men from the boats each day would perform sentinel duty that night, and Jethro and his companions were among them. Several boats had already left Semneh ahead of them, so they were among the last to arrive at the foot of the rapids and, consequently, were part of the previous group.

As owners, they were exempt from the labor of hauling up the boats and had spent much of their time during the enforced delay in hunting. They had acquired dogs and guides from the village at the base of the rapids and enjoyed good sport among the ibex abundant in the rocky hills. The girls had rarely left their cabin after departing from Semneh. It was not uncommon for women to be present in a boat that went further up the river, as many of the traders took their wives with them on their journeys. However, they left them at Semneh when they traveled beyond it since the danger and hardships of the desert journey were too much for them to deal with, and it was thus thought best that the girls should remain in seclusion.

Jethro, Amuba, and Chebron were standing together at one corner of the encampment when the former abruptly exclaimed:

"I can see people or animals moving on that steep hill! I

thought I heard the sound of stones being moved a few times. I heard them then." He turned and raised his voice: "I can hear noises from the hill. It would be wise for everyone to arm themselves and prepare to defend themselves against an attack."

In an instant, song and laughter died away amongst the groups gathered around the fires, and each man grabbed their weapons. There was a sharp ringing sound beside Jethro, and bending down, he picked up an arrow that had landed close to him.

"It's an attacker!" he yelled. "Form a line by the barricade and prepare for their approach. Extinguish the fires and extinguish the blazing brands quickly. They can spot us while we can't see them."

As he spoke, a loud and terrifying scream rose from the hillside, and a multitude of arrows was sent into the encampment. Several men were hit, but Jethro's orders were followed, and the fires were quickly extinguished.

"Duck behind the barricade," Jethro shouted, "until they are close enough to aim at them. Then, have your spears ready to hold them back when they attack."

Although Jethro didn't have any authority which would entitle him to give commands, his orders were followed as if he was the leader. It was evident to the men, just by the composure of his voice, that he was used to warfare, and they readily obeyed him. After a minute or two, a group of figures could be seen moving towards them, and the Egyptians, jumping to their feet, released a volley of arrows. The shrieks and screams which followed revealed the devastation of the enemy forces, but they continued to move forward. The Egyptians launched their arrows as quickly as possible during the few moments they had left, and then, as the natives charged the barricade, they threw away their bows and, raising their spears, maces, swords, axes, and staffs, facing their foe bravely.

For a short while, the fight was uncertain, but with encouragement from Jethro's shouts, which could be heard above the natives' yells, the Egyptians defended their position with strength and courage. Whenever the natives attempted to climb the makeshift barricade of products, they were stabbed or cut down. Then, after ten minutes of intense battle, the attack ceased abruptly, and the battlefield was suddenly silent.

"Job well done, comrades," Jethro declared. "We were able to fend off our attackers, but it would be wise to stay on alert for a while. I don't think they'll be back since they were surprised by our strength and preparedness. Nonetheless, we should remain vigilant since we don't know what they may do."

An hour later, with no sign of the enemy, the fires were reignited, and the injured received treatment. Arrows killed sixteen men from the attackers; around fifty were wounded by the same projectiles, while eighteen were killed in the hand-to-hand barricade combat. Thirty-seven natives were found dead inside. The defenders never knew how many had been killed by their arrows since the attackers had taken away the dead and wounded who had fallen outside the enclosure. As soon as the fighting was done, Chebron ran to the boat to calm the fears of the girls and assure them that no one in their party had been badly hurt, apart from Jethro, who had been struck in the ribs by a spear, but it had only caused a flesh wound which he dismissed as insignificant.

"Why didn't Amuba come with you?" Mysa inquired. "Are you sure they didn't hurt him?"

"I can guarantee that he is unharmed, Mysa, but we still need to be vigilant, just in case the enemy might return, though we hope the lesson was learned."

"Did you get scared, Chebron?"

"I was apprehensive as they approached, but when it came to hand-to-hand combat, I was so focused I couldn't think about the danger. Plus, I was standing between Jethro and Amuba, and they'd both been in serious battles before and were so composed that I couldn't feel anything else. Jethro was in charge of everyone, and the rest followed his orders without hesitation. But I should go back to my station. Jethro told me to slip away to tell you we were all right, but I would not like to be absent from my position if they attack again."

"I have often pondered, Ruth," Mysa said as Chebron left them, "what would have come to pass if it wasn't for Jethro and Amuba? If not for them, I would have been forced to marry Plexo, and Chebron probably would have been apprehended and killed in Thebes. They seem able to handle anything and never appear to be afraid."

"I think your brother is courageous, too," Ruth replied, "and they always check in with him about their plans."

"Indeed, but it's all their doing," Mysa responded. "Chebron, before they arrived, only thought of reading and was gentle and tranquil. I heard one of the slaves tell the other that he was more like a girl than a boy, but being with Amuba has changed him. Of course, he is not as strong as Amuba, but he can run, sprint, and take aim with an arrow and javelin nearly as well as Amuba can, yet he doesn't have the same enthusiasm. Amuba always speaks decisively, while Chebron hesitates to make a suggestion."

"But your brother has much more knowledge than Amuba, so his opinion ought to be more valuable, Mysa."

"Oh, yes, if it were about history or science; for anything of that sort, of course, it would, Ruth, but not about other things. Naturally, they should be different since Amuba is the son of a king."

"The son of a king?" Ruth asked in surprise.

"Yes, I heard it when he first arrived; only father said it wasn't to be mentioned because if it were known, he would be taken away from us and kept as a royal slave at the palace. But he is the son of a king, and as his father is no longer alive, he will be king when he returns to his own country."

"And Jethro is one of the same people, right?" Ruth inquired.

"Oh, yes! They are both Rebu. I think Jethro was one of the king's warriors."

"That explains," Ruth said, "what has puzzled me. Jethro is much older than the rest of us, and he's always been the leader, yet I have noticed that he always speaks to Amuba as if the Amuba was the chief.

"I hadn't noticed that," Mysa responded, shaking her head, "but since you mention it, I see that he always asks Amuba's opinion before giving his own."

"I've seen it countless times, Mysa, and I was puzzled that since he and Amuba were your father's slaves, he always sought Amuba's advice rather than your brother's; but I understand now. That also justifies Amuba giving his opinion so firmly. In his homeland, Amuba was used to having his way. I'm pleased about that because I greatly admire Amuba, and it annoyed me sometimes to observe him making decisions when Jethro is so much older. And you think he will be king if he ever returns to his homeland?"

"I'm not sure," Mysa said doubtfully. "Of course, he should be. There's another king now, and he might not be willing to give in to Amuba."

"I don't think we'll ever get there," Ruth stated. "Amuba said the other day that this country is much further than the land my people came from a long time ago."

"But that's not so far away, Ruth. You said that the caravans took six or seven days to get from that part of Egypt where you lived to the east side of the Great Sea from which your ancestors came."

"But we are a long way from there, Mysa."

"But if it's only a six or seven-day journey, why didn't your people return, Ruth?"

"They always dreamed of returning one day, Mysa, but I doubt their captors would have allowed them to. Remember, they were useful for building, excavating canals, and performing other tasks. Plus, other people now live in the country they came from and wouldn't want to leave unless they were defeated in battle. My people aren't used to fighting; they've been here for so long that they've started to act like the Egyptians. Most of them speak your language, although some still remember their own. They worship your gods, and I think if they weren't made to work against their will, they'd rather stay in Egypt in comfort and luxury than venture into an unknown place of which they know nothing other than that their ancestors came from it hundreds of years ago. But here come the others," she broke off as the boat lurched suddenly as someone hopped aboard. "We'll hear more about the fighting now."

The following day, the expedition continued and reached the town where the group would disembark from the river and head towards the shore. Jethro rented a small house until plans were made for their journey to the nearby coast. El Makrif was a minor city. Some trade happened with the coast, but most merchants dealing with Meroe chose the longer, safer route through Axoum. Nevertheless, parties of travelers frequently went up and down and took a boat there for Meroe; however, there were no temples or impressive structures like the ones seen in Thebes and Semneh.

Jethro, after investigation, discovered that there were wells at the campsites along the route. The people living in the area were wild and fierce, with Egyptian power only reaching from the shoreline to the base of the hills - a distance of around fifteen miles. Occasionally, expeditions were organized to punish mountain dwellers for raids on the cultivated coastline. The troops rarely managed to catch them, as they were familiar with every nook and cranny of the mountains and could easily avoid their heavily-armored pursuers. Jethro learned that merchants traveling through the region would pay a predetermined sum in goods as a toll for the right of passage. Two chiefs claimed power over the road, and a messenger was sent to the closest one with the offer of the usual payment and a plea for an escort.

Four wild-looking people arrived at the house a week later, saying they were ready to lead the travelers through their leader's territory. Jethro had already worked out a deal with the head of the area to get twelve men to carry the provisions needed for the journey, and the following day the group set out. Mysa and Ruth wore boys' clothing as Jethro had realized that while traders might bring the women of their family to Semneh or even take them further up the river by boat, it would be highly unusual to expose them to the rigors of a trek across the mountains. This meant that the arrival of two girls in the Egyptian town on the coast would definitely draw attention and possibly an investigation by the authorities.

For the first few hours, the girls enjoyed the change from the long confinement on the boat, but before nightfall, they longed for the snug cushions and easy life they had left behind. The bearers, heavy laden as they were, proceeded at a steady pace that taxed the strength of the girls after the first few miles were done. The heat of the sun was intense. After just a short distance, the country became barren and desolate. They weren't thirsty, for one of the bearers carried an ample supply of fruit, but their limbs ached, and their feet, unused to walking, became tender and painful.

"Can't we stop for a while, Jethro?" Mysa begged.

Jethro shook his head.

"We have to go to the wells. They are still two hours away. They told us in the beginning that the first day was six hours of steady walking."

Mysa was about to say that she couldn't go any further when Ruth whispered in her ear:

"We can't give up, Mysa. We promised to go through everything without complaining if they took us with them."

Ruth's advice had the right effect. Mysa was ashamed that she had almost given up on the first day of their real journey, but both girls were utterly drained when they got to the wells. They were rewarded, however, when Jethro praised them for their efforts.

"You both struggled like heroes," he said, "for I could see you were exhausted. I'm afraid it will continue to be very hard at first, but it will get easier after that. Tomorrow's journey is shorter."

It was a good thing that they stopped, for the girls were struggling to keep going and required the help of Jethro and the boys to make it to the next camp. As soon as the tent, split into two sections by curtains, was set up, they collapsed onto their cushions, unsure if they could handle another day like the one they had just survived.

Jethro noticed this and told their escorts they must take a break the next day because his children had been in the boat so long that they were utterly exhausted. He showed his appreciation by giving presents to each of the four men.

The guards, paid by the day, didn't object, and the porters were more than happy to take a break.

The day's rest was highly beneficial to the girls, although it wasn't enough to fully heal their feet. They wrapped their feet in bandages before setting off again, following what would have been a stream in wetter conditions. The hills on either side of the path sometimes receded and sometimes rose almost straight up, leaving the girls to pick their way between boulders and rocks. This was less taxing than walking along a level terrain; their feet didn't hurt as much as when they wore sandals. By the journey's end, the girls were in much better condition.

"It's all behind you now," Jethro said to them encouragingly. "You'll find each day's journey will get easier and easier. You have done better than I expected, and I am more optimistic that we can make it to the end of our trip without any problems than I did the night I agreed to take you with us."

As they were going through some of the ravines, the group was highly entertained by the actions of the troops of apes. At times they would sit peacefully on the side of the hill, the adults critically observing the small caravan, the younger apes jumping around with no worries. At times they would stay with them for an extended period, slowly making their way over the rocky terrain of the hill but still keeping up with the people walking below.

As the ape was seen as a sacred creature in Egypt, Mysa was pleased to see them and saw it as a positive sign of the success of their trip. The men who accompanied them said the apes would never attack voyagers if left alone. Still, if provoked, they would immediately come together and fight with such strength that even four or five individuals together would have a slim chance of escaping with their lives. During the first week's travel, they saw no other animals, although at night, they heard the yelps of hyenas, who often came nearby the encampment, and once or twice a roar which their guide said was from a lion.

On the seventh day, though, shortly after they had left on their march, the sound of breaking branches was heard among some trees a short distance up the hillside, and right after, the heads of four or five giant beasts appeared above the mimosa bushes which connected the wood to the bottom of the hill. The bearers screamed out of fear, and dropping their loads, they ran away. The four men of the escort were hesitant. Although none of Jethro's party had ever seen an elephant before, they knew what these colossal animals were from pictures, engravings, and the giant statues on the Island of Elephanta.

"Are they going to attack us?" Jethro asked the men.

"They usually don't," one of them responded. "Though occasionally they come and devastate the fields in the villages and can sometimes harm anyone they encounter. However, it's best to stay out of their way."

Jethro singled out some of the more valuable items, and lugging them, they ventured into the bushes on the other side of the hill and tried to make their way through them as far as possible. This, however, only got them a short distance, as the shrubs were full of sharp thorns and offered a great challenge for them to pass. As a result, everyone in the party got multiple wounds, and their clothes were torn to shreds as they advanced into the bush for merely twenty yards.

"That's all that is necessary," Jethro said. "We'll be torn to shreds if we go any further, and we're as hidden from sight here as we would be another hundred yards further. I'll see what they're up to."

Rising and inspecting cautiously through the veil of feathery leaves, Jethro saw that the elephants were immobile. Their big ears were erect, and their trunks outstretched as if taking in the air. Then, after two or three minutes hesitation, they kept going down the hill.

"Are they afraid of humans?" Jethro asked one of the escorts.

"Sometimes they're seized with fear and flee at the approach of a human being, but if provoked, they will attack any number without hesitation."

"Do you ever hunt them?"

"Sometimes we have to deal with a large number of elephants; shooting at them isn't practical. The best way is to sneak up on them from behind and cut the backs of their legs, which takes a strong man and a sharp sword. Even after that, it's an uphill task to finish them off. Generally, we can drive them away from our villages by lighting large fires and making loud noises. Single elephants are more dangerous than groups, capable of killing a dozen people by picking them up with their trunks and tossing them high into the sky, smashing them on the ground, or simply crushing them with their weight.

The elephants had now reached the bottom of the valley, and the chief escort gestured for complete quiet. If the elephants followed them into the brush, they were determined to fight since they had nowhere else to retreat. Amuba and Chebron had loaded their arrows and unsheathed their swords while the four natives had drawn their short, heavy swords. Jethro held his trusty ax tightly, whispering to the boys, "Remember, the only effective spot to aim for is the back of the legs; if they come forward, split up, and if they head towards the girls, position yourselves behind them and break the formation apart."

A long pause of anticipation occurred. Then, finally, the elephants could be heard making a low snorting sound with their trunks; Jethro eventually lifted himself sufficiently to peek through the foliage at what was happening. The elephants were inspecting the bundles that had been dropped.

"I believe that they are eating up our food," he mumbled as he sat down again. Thirty minutes passed, and then there was a sound of the bushes being trampled.

Jethro once more peered out. "Thank the gods!" he exclaimed, "they are departing once more."

Trampling the mimosa thicket like grass, the elephants climbed the hill on the other side and eventually returned to the woods they'd left earlier. The fugitives paused for fifteen minutes, then left the thicket with Jethro cutting through the thorns with his axe. They were taken aback when they reached the open ground. All of their supplies were strewn around in total disarray. Every parcel had been opened, and tents, articles of clothing, and rugs were hung on the bushes as if the animals had tossed them aside, deeming them inedible. Every edible item had disappeared. The fruit, grain, and vegetables had been thoroughly devoured. The wineskins had been punctured; their contents had been savored as none remained in the rocks' cracks.

"What insatiable creatures!" Mysa exclaimed in anger, "they have not left us anything."

"They don't often get an opportunity of such delicious sustenance," Amuba said. "I don't think we should blame them, particularly as they do not appear to have caused much damage to our other belongings." "Look how they have stamped over the shrubs as they passed through. I wish their hides were as fragile as mine," Mysa said as she wiped away the blood from a deep cut on her cheek; "they would then remain in their forests and not come down to plunder travelers."

"Well, Mysa, we should be grateful that the elephants didn't pursue us further," Chebron said. "We wouldn't have had any chance to get away or fight back if we were stuck in these bushes. Jethro told us to circle and attack them from behind, but that's easier said than done in this thicket. We'd be a mess of scrapes and scratches within two minutes of trying to move."

It took a few hours before the bearers returned one by one. They were rebuked harshly by Jethro for the cowardice that caused them to lose all the food. He dismissed four of them immediately, as there was nothing more for them to carry. The remaining bearers would have left if not for the guard, who threatened them with death if they didn't pick up their loads and continue. This was because Jethro had been generous with his supplies, and they were just as angry as he was about the sudden lack of rations.

Three days later, they arrived at a small village, which marked the beginning of the territory of the second chief through whom the road was running. Here the escort and carriers left, and natives of the village replaced them. It was easy to get a supply of grain and goats'-milk cheese, but these were not as good as the food the elephants had eaten. Nevertheless, they were just grateful for making it halfway through the arduous journey, so they continued. Finally, after another two weeks of traveling, they reached the lower slopes of the hills and saw the vast expanse of the sea in the sun from a wide flat area.

Two more days' journey and they arrived at the Egyptian trading station. This was situated on a small peninsula connected to the mainland by a narrow neck of land, protected by a massive wall from the frequent attacks of the wild tribesmen who would often come and ruin the cultivated fields up to the wall. As soon as they entered the town, Jethro was asked by an official to come with him to the governor's house, and he took Chebron with him. Amuba was in charge of finding a small place they could use while they stayed.

The governor inquired about the nation's condition, the behavior of the tribesmen along the path, the condition of the wells, and the number of supplies obtainable along the route. "There are a group of Arab merchants from the other side who desire to pass up to bring their goods either to Semneh or Meroe, but I have detained them until news should reach me from up above, for if any harm should befall them, their countrymen may hold us accountable for their deaths, and this could lead to quarrels and loss of trade; however, since you have traveled through with such a small group there is no need to worry, and they can discuss with the people who brought you down regarding the amount to be paid to the chiefs for free passage."

He asked Jethro why he traveled over the mountains rather than take the Nile. Jethro replied that he had gotten a great offer for his merchandise and sold it to a trader heading to Meroe. The Nile had already gone down, and the risks of passing through the rapids were too significant, so he thought it would be better to take the shorter land route and sail to Lower Egypt instead.

Additionally, he wanted to see if it would be more beneficial on his next venture to ship the merchandise down the Nile and start the journey from the coast of Meroe.

"It would be better without a doubt," the governor remarked, "but it would be wiser to sail another two days along the coast and then head up to Axoum."

A week of rest replenished the girls' stamina, and Jethro then booked passage on a trading ship that planned to make stops at various small harbors on its journey north.

CHAPTER XVIII

The Desert Journey

The voyage was a lengthy one. The winds were often so gentle that the ships scarcely moved, and the temperature was higher than anything they had experienced during their voyage. They stopped at many minor ports on the Arabian side; the captain traded with the locals — selling items of Egyptian production to them and procuring the region's wares for sale in Egypt. Before leaving, the group decided to disembark at Ælana, a city situated at the top of the gulf of the same name, constituting the eastern arm of the Red Sea. By doing this, they would evade the journey through Lower Egypt.

After much discussion, the question was decided. By traveling from Arsinoe to Pelusium, they could find a Phoenician trader to take them to a port in northern Syria. After that, they could go across Asia Minor towards the Caspian Sea. Jethro favored this route since it would lessen the hardship the two girls would endure traveling through Syria. Despite this, they were still willing to face any challenge instead of running the risk of being discovered either when they arrived at Arsinoe or during their journey north.

They all acknowledged that it had been a long time since the authorities were on the lookout for them. Still, because a scribe would come on board and list down the passengers' place of birth and occupation for registration, it would be difficult to provide answers without arousing suspicion.

When the vessel arrived at the entrance of the long and narrow gulf, the party was in awe of the majestic mountains that jutted up from the water's edge on their left.

The captain informed them that the largest of these peaks was Mount Sinai, and even though the landscape appeared to be barren and desolate, it contained valleys with sheep grazing and wandering tribes that got by. No one had informed the captain that the voyage would be cut short at any of the Arabian ports, for that would have been an unusual move for a trader traveling with his family. As they sailed up the gulf, Mysa began to complain of feeling unwell, and she was so overcome by the heat that she was not exaggerating. When they reached Ælana, Jethro took her to land, obtained a house there, and stayed on land while the ship remained in port.

A small Egyptian military contingent was stationed in the town and conducted a thriving business with Moab and the region to the east. No one noticed the merchants who arrived and departed since the land beyond the town walls was outside Egyptian control. The coming and going of people in the harbor were of no consequence to the authorities. Two days later, Jethro went back on board and reported that his son was so sick that he could not continue their travels and that they would have to forfeit the passage money they had paid to Arsinoe.

He mentioned that due to the time it could take for another boat to arrive, he would try to finance his journey by trading with the locals, and he desired to buy a portion of his remaining merchandise suitable for this job. Seeing that he could conserve supplies for five people for the six weeks the voyage would last and, at the same time, dispose of some of his excess cargo, the captain immediately agreed to Jethro's plan. Several bales of goods were assembled, featuring textiles of different fabrics and colors from Egypt, ornamentations, and various weapons.

These were unloaded, and two days later, the boat set sail.

Jethro visited the Egyptian commander and immediately got his assistance in his venture by giving him a generous gift. He expressed that since his son's sickness had detained him and it might take some time for a vessel to come, he thought of getting rid of the other items he had brought with him by trading with the people of Moab.

"You could do that if you reach Moab," the Egyptian mentioned, "traders are always welcomed, but the trip from here is not without dangers. It is an area without a ruler; the people have no fixed dwellings, moving around depending on where they can find food for their animals, sometimes among the valleys of Sinai, sometimes in the desert to the east. These individuals pillage anyone they come across, and not content with looting, might murder or take you away as slaves. However, once you have traversed up to Moab, you are safe, as you would also be if you traveled west of the Salt Lake, into which the river Jordan runs. Many clans, aggressive and courageous people live in cities, among whom you would be safe. We have had many wars with them, not always to our benefit. But between us is some kind of truce— they don't bother our military units marching alongside the seacoast, nor do we go up among their hills to interfere with them. These are the people who, at one point, conquered a portion of Lower Egypt and ruled over it for many generations until, fortunately, we rose and expelled them."

"Is the journey between this and the Salt Lake you talk about a daunting one?"

"It's not a difficult journey, except it would be wise to bring along water because there are not many wells, and they can quickly run dry. The terrain is mostly flat, and there is a belief that this gulf used to reach as far north as the Salt Lake. The road is bumpy and rough, but it presents no major obstacles. I'd suggest that if you decide to go, you should leave your son behind."

"It's better for him to travel than stay here without me," Jethro replied. "If we go up through the people you spoke of to the west of this lake and river, it won't take long to make our way down to a port on the Great Sea. From there, we'd be able to find a ship to take us back to Pelusium and make it home before we'd even find a ship to take us from here."

"That is right," the Egyptian said. "The winds are so unpredictable on these seas that, as far as time goes, you could take the course you suggest and reach Egypt quicker than you would if you got on a ship right away. The danger lies mostly in the initial part of your journey. The caravans from here go once or twice a year through Moab to Palmyra are numerous and well-armed, capable of fending off an assault from these bandit tribesmen. But one left a few weeks back, and it may be some months before another one departs."

"What animals do you recommend I take with me?"

"Most definitely, camels are the best. They are used hardly at all in this country but come down sometimes with the caravans from Palmyra, and I understand that there is currently in the city an Arab who owns six or seven of them. He came down with the last caravan but got sick and could not go back with it. No doubt you could make a deal with him. I will send a soldier with you to the house he is living in."

Jethro discovered that the man was eager to return to his homeland, which lay on the borders of Media, and so was in the direction Jethro wanted to go. He was, however, unwilling to make the journey without a caravan, having intended to wait for the next convoy, but the amount that Jethro offered him for the hire of his animals as far as Palmyra eventually persuaded him to agree to take the journey right away, but stipulated that a band of ten armed men should be hired as an escort as far as the borders of Moab. Thrilled with the results of his investigations, Jethro returned home and informed his companions of the arrangements he had made.

"I have only organized our trip as far as Palmyra," he said, "because it would have seemed suspicious if I had reserved him for our trip to Media; of course, he will willingly keep the agreement for the whole journey. He negotiated for a guard of ten individuals, but we will take twenty. There is still a considerable amount of your father's gold left over, and we have not spent much since selling our possessions when we left. The boat covered all our expenses for the voyage up the Nile. Therefore, since this appears to be the riskiest part of our trip, we will not be thrifty when providing for it securely. I told him that we should leave in a week. It would not be a good idea to go away sooner. You should not heal too quickly from your sickness. In the meantime, I will select several well-trained fighters as our guard."

In this, the Egyptian captain was of great help, recommending men whose families lived in Ælana, therefore serving as surety for their dedication. It was needed, for a decent amount of the people in the little town were native tribesmen who had camped not far from its walls and had come to buy horses or the wool from their flocks for the fabrics of Egypt. Such men as these would have been a threat instead of protection. By the end of the week, he had brought together a group of twenty men, all of whom were to provide their own horses. The sum agreed upon for their escort was to be paid into the hands of the Egyptian officer, who was to give it to them on their return, with a document signed by Jethro indicating that they had fulfilled the conditions of their agreement.

Jethro discovered that the escort cost was lower than he had predicted. When the men realized that the party would be powerful, thus capable of protecting itself on the journey and on its way back, they asked for a reasonable sum for their services. Moreover, when the owner of the camels learned that they had determined to go east of the Salt Lake, he urged them to take the path east of the mountain range bordering the valleys rather than following the valley of Ælana to the Salt Lake, where it would be hard to acquire water. This was the route taken by all the caravans. As a result, villages would be found at short intervals, and there would be no difficulties concerning water.

"My camels," he said, "can travel long distances without water and could take the valley route; however, the horses would be greatly affected."

Jethro was glad to learn that the journey was likely less strenuous than he had expected; all the arrangements had been concluded, and the group set off shortly after sunrise on the designated day.

The girls were still in male clothing and rode in substantial baskets, hanging one on each side of a camel. The camel driver walked at the head of the animal, controlling it by a rope. Its companions followed in a lengthy line, each secured to the one in front. Jethro, Amuba, and Chebron, armed with bows, arrows, and swords, rode alongside the girls' camel. Half the escort went ahead; the other half constituted the rear guard.

"What is the most dangerous segment of the journey?" Jethro inquired of the camel driver.

"The area we're entering now," he replied. "Once we reach Petra, we will be relatively safe; however, our route now runs through an uninhabited and harsh land, with nomadic tribesmen traveling to and from the meadows by Mount Sinai. The steep hills on our left make a good hiding place and lookout. From there, they can watch for travelers traveling along this road and attack them."

"How long will it take us to get to Petra?"

"It should take three days if we travel at a comfortable pace; however, if we travel well into the evening, we should get there in two days. After that, we can take it easy; the villages are only a few miles away from each other."

"Let's go on, then, by all means," Jethro declared. "We can spend a day at Petra to give the animals a rest, but let's get through this desolate and dangerous terrain as soon as possible."

The girls had been highly entertained at the start at the sight of the odd animal that was carrying them, but they soon realized that the swaying motion was incredibly tiring, and they would have been delighted to get down and walk.

Unfortunately, Jethro said that this wasn't possible, for the animal's pace, although deliberate, was still too fast for them to keep up with on foot, and it was essential for the first two days to go as quickly as possible.

The blazing sun was fierce, and its reflection off the hills' black rocks and the plain's white sand seemed almost unbearable. Finally, after traveling for three hours, they stopped, and Jethro used the poles and cloths to create a shelter over the baskets where the girls were riding. The camels settled down as soon as they halted, and the girls jumped into the baskets before they could get up again. As the animal rose, they yelped in surprise - they had braced themselves for it to rise with its front legs, but when its hindquarters suddenly lifted in the air, they almost fell out of their baskets.

"I don't like this creature at all," Mysa said as they continued. "Who would have thought he'd start in the wrong direction? Not to mention why he's still grumbling. Ruth and I shouldn't be such a heavy load for him, right? If the driver hadn't pulled his rope, he would have bitten us when we got on. I'm sure riding a horse would be much nicer. It looks simple enough."

"It's not as easy as it looks, Mysa," Chebron replied; "besides, you know women never ride horses."

"In our country, they do," Amuba said. "When we get there, Mysa, I'll teach you how to do it."

"Ah! It's a long way away, Amuba," Mysa responded, "and I believe this creature will try to shake us to pieces as soon as he can."

"Don't sit rigidly," Jethro advised. "Relax and sway gently with the motion of the basket. You'll soon be used to it and find you can doze off like a rocking chair."

They continued until the sunset, then made camp for the night. Each horse was given a small drink from the skins of water they had brought. A few handfuls of grain were also given to each. The drivers drove their spears into the ground and secured the horses to them. The camels were made to kneel in a square formation. In the center of this, the girls' tent was pitched, with the horses arranged in a circle outside.

All the men had brought flat cakes and ate their meal using these and a few dates. There was no need to light a fire as Jethro's group had brought plenty of pre-cooked food. Very soon, the camp was silent. The journey had been hot and exhausting, and the men, wrapping themselves in their cloaks, lay down with their spears, each one sleeping, apart from four on sentry duty. Jethro had planned with Amuba and Chebron to share the night watch between them.

The men of the escort thought it highly unlikely that they would be attacked before morning, even if watched from the surrounding hills.

"They have no hope of catching us off guard, for they should be certain that we would post a guard in the darkness. They could not make their way down the hills without making some noise; they also think the forces of evil are powerful at night and rarely go out of their camps after sunset. So it will likely be just before dawn if we are provoked."

Therefore, Jethro had arranged for Chebron to take the first watch, Amuba the second, and that he would take charge four hours before dawn.

The night passed without cause for alarm, and as soon as morning dawned, the camp was already in motion. The horses were given another ration of water and grain, and the men quickly ate a hasty meal before continuing on their journey. After traveling half a mile, a large group of around a hundred people was spotted behind a hill. About twenty of them were mounted, and the rest were on foot. The travelers stopped and had a brief discussion before Jethro, accompanied by one of the escorts, rode out to meet the approaching party, carrying a white cloth as a sign of peace. Two of the Arabs rode out to greet them. After some time, Jethro finally returned to the anxiously waiting party.

"What did they say, Jethro?" Amuba asked as he rode up.

"He proposed, to begin with, that we should have bought from him the authorization to travel across the country. I said I would willingly have given a reasonable amount had I realized that such was necessary, but since he was not in Ælana, I could not be aware that he was claiming such a right. At the same time,

I was ready to offer four rolls of Egyptian cloth. After a lengthy conversation, he refused the offer scornfully. He made it quite clear that he meant to take all our possessions and animals and that we should consider ourselves lucky to continue along our route on foot. I said I would consult my friends; if they accepted his terms, we would keep the white flag flying; if we declined them, we would lower it."

"That is true. However, we would lose our seven camel-loads of goods, and we need them for trading as we go," Jethro said. "I suggest that we form the camels into a square like we did last night; that you two and six of the guys armed with bows and arrows should inhabit it and take care of the girls while the rest of us charge the Arabs. The men on foot will likely retreat if we can defeat the horsemen. Still, while we are doing that, some of those who walk may move forward and attack you. We will take care not to pursue, and you can trust that we will come to your aid as soon as you are attacked."

"I think that is the best plan, Jethro. We can repel them for some time with our bows and arrows, for certainly Chebron and I can bring down a person with each shot at a hundred yards."

Jethro selected six of the men who proclaimed themselves proficient archers. He tied their horses' legs and placed them just beyond the square formed by the camels on their knees. The girls were instructed to lie down, and the saddles and bales were placed around the camels to protect them from any possible attack. When everything was in place, the white flag was lowered, and Jethro, with his fourteen men, charged at full speed against the Arabs.

Believing they had the advantage in numbers, the Arab horsemen moved to confront them. Still, Jethro's party, following his orders to remain in a cohesive line with their spears aimed forward, rode right through the Arabs, who were scattered and unorganized. Men and horses fell together, with several of the latter impaled by the horsemen's spears. Jethro called for his men to stop and face the Arabs.

Several of the latter escaped to the infantry, who advanced to assist, yet were still chased and slain. Others continued to battle until the bitter end in silence and determination, but these, too, were killed. As soon as the infantry came close, they let loose a rain of stones and slingshots. Jethro rallied his troops and put them in formation again, and at the head of his men, charged the Arabs. The latter fought bravely. Retreating momentarily, they surrounded the small group of riders, hurling spears and slicing at them with their swords. Jethro spurred his horse into their midst, wielding his heavy ax and swinging to the left and the right. His companions followed him and cut their way through their enemies after a tough fight.

Repeatedly, the maneuver was carried out, the Arabs' resistance waning, as most of their skilled combatants had been slain. At the same time, the bulky shields toted by the riders repelled most of the objects they pushed at them. A further minute or two and the Arabs turned tail and fled from the hills, leaving over twenty of their number on the ground, in addition to all of their mounted men. Jethro could now look around and observed for the first time that he had not, as he assumed, been the whole group of enemies. While about fifty of them had attacked him, the remainder had directed for the camels and were now grouped around them.

With a roar to his men to accompany him, Jethro raced at full speed toward the Arabs and, with a roar, flung himself upon them, hacking his way through them with his ax. He was just in time. A severe conflict was taking place across the camels. At one point, a number of the Arabs had broken into the square, and these were fought by Amuba, Chebron, and one of the men, while the remaining ones still blocked the Arabs on the other side. The arrival of Jethro, rapidly trailed by the rest of his men, without delay stopped the conflict.

"You made it just in time, Jethro," Amuba said.

"I did," Jethro replied. "I was too busy fighting off the footmen to realize that a party had moved away to attack you. You and Chebron are badly injured, I'm afraid. Are the girls okay?"

Mysa and Ruth both stood up after the attack was over.

"We're both safe," Mysa said. "But look at how hurt you both are, and Jethro too!"

"My injury is nothing," Jethro said. "Let's take care of Chebron's wounds first," for Chebron had sat down against one of the camels.

"Don't worry," Chebron said weakly. "I think it's just blood loss; my shield protected the rest of my body."

"All right, girls," Jethro said, "go ahead and open one of the bales of cloth and rip it up into strips for bandages. Let me take a look at these two."

After examining their wounds, Jethro determined that none would have serious consequences. Chebron had been wounded in the leg with a javelin and had a sword cut on the side of the face, while a spear had cut through the flesh and grazed the ribs on the right side of Amuba's body. Amuba's most serious injury had been caused by a javelin that had passed through his back, below both shoulder blades, and had broken off. Jethro cut off the ragged end, grabbed the point that had stuck out behind the left arm, and pulled it through. Then, he used some of the bandages the girls provided to wrap up all the wounds before taking a look at the men who were tending to their comrades' injuries. Sadly, one of the square's defenders had died, and three others were severely wounded.

Of Jethro's party, two had been injured, and all had received some form of wounds, ranging in severity. Had it not been for the shields that guarded their bodies, few would have survived the fight; however, these shields provided them with a significant advantage over the Arabs, none of whom had any form of protection. Moreover, the owner of the camels had managed to stay hidden during the battle, hidden beneath a pile of bales. The camels were freed and allowed to stand up as soon as the wounds had been treated and a glass of wine and water had been given to each of them.

Three men with the worst injuries, unable to ride their horses, were placed on top of the bales carried by camels, and the party restarted their journey. It was fortunate that they had to travel at the same speed as the camels, as several of the men could barely stay on their horses and would not have been able to manage a faster pace.

"All right, Amuba, tell me what happened in the fight," Jethro said. "I haven't had the chance to ask about it yet."

"Not much to tell," Amuba replied. "We saw you race down upon their horsemen and defeat them, then go straight into the middle of their infantry. A group of about thirty quickly split off and charged at us. We began shooting as soon as they were in range, and I got four of them before they could reach us. Chebron must have done the same, but the men with us shot poorly, so they probably didn't take out more than seven or eight. That was roughly half their number, leaving around fifteen to fight us in hand-to-hand combat. Our makeshift barrier was doing its job, and we were holding them back pretty well. But eventually, they managed to jump over, and though we were fighting back hard, a few of us had been injured. We would have been in a tough spot in a minute or two if you hadn't come to the rescue. Now, what were you doing?"

Jethro then recounted the encounter he and his group had with the footmen.

"They battle well, these Arabs," he said, "and it was fortunate that we all had shields; for had we not done so, they would have overcome us with their javelins. As you can see, I had a close call; had that dart that went through my ear been an inch or two to the right, it would have pierced my eye. I have two or three nasty lacerations with their swords on my legs, and I believe that most of the other men were more injured than I was. Fortunately, they did not attack the horses, but I suppose they wanted them, and so refrained from causing injury to them. It was an intense fight, and we are fortunate to have come out unscathed. I hope I won't be called on to use my battle-axe again until I am fighting in the ranks of the Rebu."

CHAPTER XIX

Home at Last

As they approached Petra, a horn sounded, and people were observed running around the dwellings.

"They must think we are a group of Arabs," one of the riders commented. "Since I've been to the town a few times and am known by some folk here, I can, if you'd like, speed ahead and inform them that we are harmless voyagers."

The party paused for a few minutes and then continued forward. When they arrived in the town, news of their trading status spread, and the people emerged from their houses. These homes were tiny, constructed of solid stone, and only one story high. The roof was flat, with a low wall surrounding it, and each house had only one relatively low and narrow entrance, making it an ideal place to defend against intruders. Furthermore, as the town was situated on the side of the hill, the lower houses were easily visible from the higher ones, making it an even more effective place to defend against raids.

The head of the town welcomed the travelers and brought them to an empty house to use, offering them a gift of chickens, dates, and wine. The news that a significant defeat had been inflicted upon one of the roaming bands was met with great satisfaction. Their interference hindered the town's prosperity, making it difficult for the people to trade with Ælana unless they traveled in large groups. Nevertheless, the townspeople showed the party every hospitality, tending to their wounds and applying medicinal herbs to the more severe cases.

Petra, at that point, was nothing more than a large village. However, it later rose to become a place of great importance. The travelers stayed there for a week, by the end of which only two couldn't continue the journey.

Without any other obstacle, the journey continued toward Moab. Upon arriving there, the escort was dismissed, each man getting a gift in addition to the predetermined pay to be given to them on their return to Ælana.

Moab was a well-established region. It didn't have any large towns; however, the considerable population was gathered in small villages of low-stone-built houses, similar to those in Petra. The inhabitants were eager to trade. Their language was unfamiliar to Jethro and Amuba, but it was closely related to that spoken by Ruth, and she typically acted as a translator between Jethro and the locals. After traveling through Moab, they took the caravan route across the desert to the northeast, passing through the oasis of Palmyra, a large and prosperous city, and then ventured along the Euphrates. They were now in the country of the Assyrians, and not wanting to draw attention or unwanted questions, they steered clear of Nineveh and the other great cities and kept progressing northward until they reached the mountainous region located between Assyria and the Caspian.

They encountered many setbacks along the way. It was six months after departing from Ælana; after traveling through a part of Persia, they reached the area populated by the various tribes referred to as Medes, related to the Rebu. Thotmes had taken control of this region previously, resulting in many of the tribes submitting to Egypt and paying tribute to the country, with Egyptian troops being stationed in various places.

Jethro and Amuba were now in a familiar environment, but they decided to keep their identities hidden until they had a better understanding of what was going on in their home country. As a result, they posed as Persian traders, having sold the goods they brought with them long before arriving in Persia and purchasing Persian-made items in their stead. They moved through the villages alongside Persian traders, never being challenged as trade in the area was exclusively conducted by Persian merchants, whose civilization was already quite advanced. The Median tribes, despite having become more sedentary, still hadn't learned the arts of peace. The party journeyed in the company of some Persian merchants, gradually making their way north until they arrived at the first Rebu village.

They had discussed at length the role they should play and decided it would be best to maintain their guise as Persian traders until they better understood the political situation. To keep up the façade, they had acquired a fresh supply of Persian merchandise at the last village they had stopped at. Had Jethro been alone, he could have revealed his identity and would have been welcomed back from his captivity in Egypt. However, Amuba would have been in danger until they knew whether or not the person on the throne was hostile. It was unlikely that Amuba would have been recognized, as it had been four years since he had been taken, and he had grown into a strong young man. Furthermore, had Jethro been identified, Amuba's identity may have been revealed, too, as he was known to have accompanied the young prince.

As for Amuba, he had no ambition to take the throne of the Rebu and wished only to live peacefully in his homeland. The sizable sum Ameres had entrusted to Jethro had been significantly reduced with their expenses on the long journey. However, there was still enough to give them a comfortable life in a country where money was scarce.

On their travels through Persia, they had picked up many Persian words different from those of the Rebu, which they used to pass as traders with a good grasp of the local dialect. They soon discovered that an Egyptian army still held control of the capital and that the people suffered from the financial demands to cover the annual tribute. Moreover, General Amusis seized the throne after the main Egyptian army left and was now close with the Egyptian officials, making him extremely unpopular among the people. He had also executed all potential rivals for the throne and would not hesitate to eliminate Amuba if he suspected his return from Egypt.

Amuba had several long talks with Jethro about his plans. He repeated his conversation with his father the day before the battle in which he was killed. He explained how his father had warned him against Amusis' ambition and suggested collecting a group of supporters and finding a new home in the west. However, Jethro believed that while this advice was sound, the chances of success were better if they stayed and fought to reclaim Amuba's rightful throne.

"First and foremost, Amuba, when you were sixteen, we were in the midst of a war with Egypt, and people were likely to favor a seasoned and capable general over an inexperienced boy to lead them in battle. Now you are a man with a wealth of knowledge and experience. You are well-acquainted with our oppressors' customs and practices. You could do much for the people if you were in a position of power - introducing new farming techniques and elements of Egyptian civilization.

"Furthermore, in the four years that have passed, Amusis has had time to make himself loathed. Having to levy high taxes to pay the tribute has earned him a bad reputation, not to mention that he is seemingly on close terms with our foreign conquerors. Therefore, the outcome of the succession would be heavily in your favor."

"But I'm not interested in being king," Amuba replied. "I want to live a life of peace and contentment."

"You're destined to be king, Prince Amuba," Jethro said; "it's not a matter of choice. Furthermore, the usurper must be overthrown and the rightful dynasty restored for the people's welfare. But, that aside, it's apparent that you can't live in peace, as you may be identified and your life is taken away. And I'm sure your father would not have wanted the original plan to be followed in light of the changed circumstances. Besides, I think you've had enough of wandering and turmoil.

"On top of that, I don't think you would want to drag Mysa with you on your journey to an unknown country, knowing that many trials and struggles would await before you even start to build a new settlement. But, I'm guessing," he said, smiling, "that you have other intentions for her."

Amuba was silent for quite some time.

"Egypt is, as we have discovered, a very long way off. Now and then, a ruler with a taste for conquest emerges, permitting their forces to be deployed to distant lands and bringing many countries into their control. Yet, such episodes rarely occur, and we are situated on the furthest edges of their dominion. Thotmes has already achieved great fame. He was away from his homeland for years, and on his return, he reaped the rewards of his conquests. It is unlikely that he would once more embark on a long journey just to bring this far-off corner of the land back under the control of Egypt. The land has been deprived of wealth, and there is nothing to compensate for the hard work or the resources required to undertake such a mission. It could be decades before another monarch rises, eager for glory like Thotmes and ready to abandon the comforts of Egypt in search of distant conquests.

"In addition, Egypt has already experienced, to their detriment, that the Rebu cannot be easily defeated and that their chances of coming out on top are just as slim as the odds of being conquered. Therefore, you need not be afraid of Egypt's retaliation. In other ways, the Rebu's occupation is in your favor, allowing you to be presented to the people as their legitimate king and liberator from the despised Egyptian rule."

"You are correct, Jethro," Amuba stated after a long pause; "it is my obligation to assert my rights and to bring the land back to freedom. I've made up my mind. What is your counsel on the subject?"

"I would make my way through the land until we reach a port by the sea often visited by Persian merchants and would leave the two girls there in the care of the family of some merchant in that country; there they can remain in peace until matters are settled. Chebron will, I'm confident, insist on sharing our fortunes. Our long travels have made a man of him, too. They have not only augmented his frame and toughened his constitution but also given firmness to his character. He is reflective and reasonable, and his advice will always be of value, while of his bravery, I have no more doubt than yours. Once you have secured your kingdom, you will discover in Chebron a wise consultant, one on whom you can depend in all times of difficulty.

"When we have left the girls behind, we will carry on our voyage through the land and slowly put ourselves into communication with the governors of towns and other individuals of influence as we may learn to be discontented with the current situation so that when we make our strike the entire country will declare for you at once. As we travel, we will gather a body of determined men to attack the capital. Many of my old friends and comrades must still survive, and there should be no difficulty in collecting a force capable of capturing the city by surprise."

Jethro accomplished his plans, and the girls were put under the care of the wife of a Persian trader in a port near the Persia border; the others then started on their journey, still pretending to be Persians. Jethro didn't have much difficulty discovering most people's feelings in the towns they passed. He first introduced himself to them as a Persian trader wanting their protection while traveling through the country, but he soon revealed his real identity.

A lot of them knew him either personally or by reputation. He informed them that he had fled from Egypt with Amuba, but he led them to think that his companion was waiting in Persian land until he knew from him that the country was ready for his arrival; for he felt it was best not to tell anyone that Amuba was with him, in case some of the people he spoke to tried to get rewards from the king by betraying him. Nevertheless, the news was welcomed joyfully everywhere. In many cases, Jethro was urged to immediately send for Amuba and show him to the people, for then the whole country would rise in his support.

Jethro, nevertheless, said that Amuba would await his time because a premature revelation would let the king summon a portion of the army that had formerly battled under his command and that, with the help of the Egyptians, he could potentially succeed in putting down a popular revolt.

"My intention," he said, "if feasible, is to collect a small force to grab the usurper by surprise and stop the resistance. After that, there would only be the Egyptians to cope with, and these would be worn down from their fortress long before any help could get to them."

After visiting most of the towns, Jethro and his friends traveled through the remote villages beyond the capital. There, the king's power was barely experienced apart from when troops arrived annually to collect the taxes. As a result, Jethro had no problem making himself known and began enrolling people in his cause. The message that an immediate effort was being made to overthrow the intruder and evacuate the land from the Egyptians and that the rightful ruler would appear at the right time and lead the command was welcomed with great excitement.

In each valley they went through, all the young men joined, receiving instructions to stay quiet and fabricate weapons until a messenger called them to meet at a rendezvous on a specified date.

In six weeks, the numbers of those enrolled in the enterprise had grown to the point deemed necessary, and a date was set for them to assemble in the hills just a few miles from the town. On the appointed day, the bands began arriving, and Jethro quickly got to work. He purchased cattle and provisions, organized each band into companies, and established leaders.

As the evening approached, all of the contingents had arrived, and Jethro was pleased with their enthusiasm and the practical, if a bit rough, weapons they had crafted. He then gathered them together, giving an inspiring speech that stirred their patriotic feelings. Finally, leading Amuba out of the tent, he introduced him to the group as their king.

During his travels, he uncovered arms and armor fit for a high-ranking person, which had been hidden since the Egyptians conquered the area. Amuba put on this armor when he stepped out of his tent, and the troops erupted with a wild cheer. They broke formation and threw themselves on the ground, hailing him as their king and pledging their loyalty.

The excitement eventually died, and Amuba addressed his followers, vowing to free them from Egyptian rule and the oppressive taxation they had long suffered under.

They spent the week organizing and creating discipline within the camp, placing guards around the perimeter to keep strangers from entering and leaving to share the news with the city. Finally, they sent some of their most trusted people to the city to determine what was happening. They returned with the information that reports of the late king's son had been received—that he had escaped captivity in Egypt and was coming to reclaim his throne—but it was being met with disbelief. The king and his Egyptian allies had taken over the country so successfully that the garrison wasn't even taking any precautions. No one kept watch, and the city gates rarely closed at night.

The plans were now finally arranged. With a band of two hundred men, Jethro would enter the town in the daytime; some going down to the next port and arriving by sea, others entering one by one through the gates. They would assemble in the square next to the palace at midnight, which would be suddenly attacked. Amuba, with the main body, would approach the city late in the evening and station themselves near one of the gates.

Jethro was appointed to launch the assault to determine whether the gate was open and unguarded. If he discovered it was closed and guarded by an Egyptian, he would order fifty of his soldiers to attack, overpower the Egyptians, and throw open the gate when they heard the trumpet. The trumpet was the signal for the attack on the palace. Jethro's contingent was, thus, the first to begin, leaving in small groups, some to the adjacent ports, others directly to the city. Jethro himself was the last to depart, having personally given instructions to each gathering when they left regarding their ways and where they would enter the city and the meeting point where they were to gather. He also planned that if they heard his call on the horn at any time, which would be repeated by three or four of his supporters, who were provided with similar instruments, they would rush to the spot at full speed.

"You never know," he told Amuba, relaying his orders, "what could happen. I'm sure everyone here is loyal to you, but there's always a chance for one traitor in the crowd; even without that, a careless comment from one of them, an altercation with the king's men or the Egyptians, and the number of armed men in the city could be exposed. Then, others would rush in to help their comrade, and the situation would become heated until everyone was involved. Other factors could make it smart to act earlier than I planned."

"I don't think that's the case," Amuba replied. "If anything were to cause things to speed up, it would be a terrible idea. You and your small army would surely be overwhelmed by the large group of people the king keeps in his palace, let alone the Egyptians. Not only would you lose your lives, but you would alert them so much that our nighttime mission would have little chance of succeeding."

"That is accurate," Jethro said, "and I do not intend to alter the plan we agreed on unless I am forced to do so. Still, it is prudent to be prepared for everything."

"I know that you won't do anything reckless, Jethro. After being my guide and advisor for all these years, I know that you wouldn't do anything to jeopardize our success now that it seems almost certain."

Jethro had a motivation for wanting to be able to assemble his people quickly, which he had not mentioned to Amuba. He believed it conceivable that, as he had said, the plan might be exposed at the final moment in one way or another. And his thought was that if that were the case, he would quickly gather his supporters and attack the palace, relying on surprise and his knowledge of the construction in the effort to fight his way to the sovereign's residence and kill him there, even if he and his men were later encircled and slaughtered. The impostor once removed, Jethro did not doubt that the entire nation would gladly acknowledge Amuba, who would have only the Egyptian garrison to contend with.

No accidents happened, however. The men went into the town and went unnoticed. Most people who had come by boat were from villages near the shore and stayed in the lower town by the shore. Those that entered the gates walked around the town by themselves or with a partner and, as their weapons were hidden, they were overlooked as they seemed like people who had come from the countryside to sell their produce or hunting spoils or to get what they needed. Jethro went straight to his old friend's house to whom he had already sent a messenger.

The house was located in an open area facing the palace. Now and then, he was updated by his sub-leaders that all was going fine. Rumors had been circulating in the country about the possible return of the late king's son, causing some concern to the usurper. As a result, the usurper arrested several influential people loyal to the late king that morning. It was unlikely that Amuba was returning, yet the possibility of an impostor using his name for selfish gain couldn't be ruled out.

Several groups had been dispatched from the town to the sites of these rumors to investigate the rumors and put down any attempts to challenge the king's authority. This news pleased Jethro, as it demonstrated that the king was unaware of any threats to his capital and reduced the number of fighters in the palace to a figure slightly less than his forces.

Jethro didn't leave the house until the evening since his face was well known in the city and could have been recognized at any moment. When it got dark, he went out with his companion and walked around the town. He noticed that some changes had taken place since his last visit. The Egyptians had completely removed the huts at the end of the cliff furthest from the sea and built large structures for the government, officers, and soldiers. In addition, they had erected a wall between the two walls, completely separating their area from the rest of the city. Jethro's friend informed him that the construction of these buildings had increased the hatred the Egyptians received since the people had been forced to work on them by the thousands and had to labor for many months.

Jethro discovered that soon after the internal wall was finished, the Egyptians quit monitoring the entryways of the city walls altogether. Yet, for quite a while, they had kept a watchful eye on the entrance that led to their quarters through the new divider. For the most recent year, in any case, they had lowered their alertness because of the nonappearance of any insurgents among the Rebu and their trust in the fellowship of the ruler.

By nine, the town was tranquil. Jethro sent a courier on the same route Amuba's force would come, advising him that the city walls were unguarded and that he should enter by the gate a half-hour before midnight rather than waiting until he heard the sign for assault. At that point, he could move his men up near the Egyptian divider with the goal that he would have the option to assault that entryway when the sign was given; or else the Egyptians would be put on high caution by the sound of fighting at the royal residence before he could arrive at their entryway.

At the appointed time, Jethro went to the gate by which Amuba was to enter and soon heard a faint confused noise. A minute or two later, a dark mass of men was at the gate path led by Amuba. Jethro explained to him the exact position, and he placed a guard by Amuba's side to act as his guide to the Egyptian wall.

Jethro then returned to the rendezvous, where his men were already drawn up in order. Midnight was now close at hand. Quietly the band crossed the square to the palace gate; then

Jethro gave a loud blast of his horn, and in an instant, a party of men armed with heavy axes rushed forward and began to break down the gate. Then, as the thundering noise rose on the night air, they heard cries of terror and the shouts of officers within the royal enclosure. Then men came hurrying along the wall, and arrows began to fall among the attackers, but by this time, the work of the axmen was nearly done, and in five minutes after the strike of the first blow, the massive gates splintered and fell, and Jethro rushed in at the head of his band.

The garrison, led by Amusis, the usurper, attempted to repel the oncoming force; however, taken off-guard, half-equipped, and unaware of their adversaries' numbers, they could not resist the relentless onslaught of Jethro's troops. Finally, Jethro himself pushed his way through the crowd of combatants and engaged in hand-to-hand combat with the usurper, who, consumed with rage and despair at the unexpected capture of the palace, fought recklessly, and Jethro's hefty ax brought the battle to an end by slicing cleanly through helmet and skull.

The usurper's downfall went unnoticed in the darkness and chaos, but Jethro shouted to his men to lay down their arms and move back. He then asked the garrison to surrender, informing them that Amusis had fallen, and Amuba, the son of Phrases, had come to power and was now the Rebu king.

"We are not at war with our people. The Egyptians are our only enemies. Some of you may recognize me. I am Jethro, and I implore you to join us and stand together against the Egyptians, who are undergoing an attack from our young king."

The garrison was only too eager to accept the terms. Fear had driven them to Amusis, and they were relieved to escape the imminent danger of death and to pledge their allegiance to their rightful king. As Jethro finished speaking, shouts of "Long live Amuba, king of the Rebu!" echoed throughout.

"Form up in order immediately under your captains," Jethro ordered, "and follow us."

The battle had been so quick that when Jethro led his force, now doubled in size, to Amuba's aid, not more than ten minutes had passed since he had sounded the horn of attack. Upon arriving at the wall which separated the Egyptian barracks from the rest of the town, he discovered that Amuba had gone in without resistance and had seized two or three adjacent buildings, taking their occupants by surprise; but he had made no further progress. The Egyptians were experienced combatants, and after that initial shock of surprise, they soon regained their composure and showered such a barrage of arrows across the empty areas between the buildings that the Rebu couldn't advance.

Jethro instructed the forces who had just joined him, all armed with bows and arrows, to scale the walls and launch an attack on the buildings inhabited by the Egyptians. Then he and his army joined Amuba. "Everything has gone according to plan," he said. "The palace has been taken, and Amusis killed. I don't want to take any further risks tonight. The Egyptians number four thousand, while we only have half of that. It would be too risky to attempt to attack them now. I will immediately send out messengers to the governors of all the towns and to our allies there to inform them that the usurper has been slain, that you have been declared king and are currently laying siege to the Egyptians in their territory, and ordering them to march here at once with every able-bodied man.

"In three days, we will have twenty thousand men here, and the Egyptians, realizing their situation is hopeless, will surrender; however, if you attack now, we may be pushed back, and you may be killed, and then the country, without a leader, will fall back into slavery."

Amuba, whose armor had already been struck by a few arrows and bleeding heavily, was eventually convinced by Jethro to take his advice. He ultimately recognized that it was the wisest plan to take, and orders were immediately given to the men to cease any more assaults but to merely defend against any onslaughts the Egyptians might make.

The Egyptians, however, were unaware of their assailants' strength, so they were not in a position to initiate an attack.

Until morning, both sides kept firing arrows at one another's strongholds. Then, at dawn, Amuba ordered some green branches to be raised on the flat terrace of the house he was occupying. The Egyptians picked up this sign, and the firing ceased. Soon after, Jethro made his presence known on the terrace, and a few minutes later, the Egyptian governor also appeared on the balcony of the opposite building. He was utterly taken aback to hear himself addressed in his language.

"By the decree of King Amuba, son of King Phrases and rightful ruler of the Rebu, I, Jethro, his general, demand your surrender. The usurper Amusis is dead, and the nation has joined forces against you. Our military supremacy is unsurpassable— fighting will only lead to the demise of all Egyptian subjects under your jurisdiction. Moreover, if we choose, we can starve you out, as we know that your storehouses are only stocked with a week's worth of provisions."

"It is impossible for help to come to you. No messenger can make it through the guards in the plains; even if they could, the nearest army is hundreds of miles away and is not strong enough to march over here. But, in the king's name, I offer to allow you to leave, taking your weapons and flags with you. The king has been to your land. He knows how great and powerful your nation is and wishes to be friends with it, so he will not treat you with disrespect. The tax your king put on the land is too much to be paid, but the king will be willing to send a tribute of gold and jewels, a fifth of the value of what was taken from the land each year, to the nearest army on the border. This will show his respect for your powerful nation. The king told me that you have until tomorrow morning to consider this offer. If you reject it, the entire garrison will be killed."

With that, Jethro descended from the terrace, leaving the Egyptians to consider his proposed offer.

CHAPTER XX

The King of the Rebu

Amuba's plan was strategic, and two objectives drove him to offer a delay of twenty-four hours before providing an answer. Primarily, he was confident that his forces would be tripled in strength by the end of that time, and should the Egyptians decline the offer, he would be able to repel any attempts they might make to flee until he had such a powerful force that he could take their positions by storm or, as he planned, lay siege to them until starvation forced them to surrender.

Additionally, he suspected that if the Egyptians answered immediately, it would likely be a refusal; however, the time for contemplation would allow them to examine their predicament and acknowledge its direness. On one side would be inevitable defeat and death, but on the other, their commander would lead out his troops unscathed and without dishonor. Even though he had threatened to slaughter the garrison if they refused, Amuba had no intention of following through. Instead, he had determined that even if the Egyptians were compelled to surrender due to starvation, he would generously grant them the same terms he was now offering.

He was aware of the arrogant and conceited nature of the Egyptians and that the news of the destruction of a vast garrison and the triumphant uprising of a vassal state would arouse such strong emotions that sooner or later, an army would be sent to avenge the calamity. Nevertheless, if the garrison left the country with their weapons and flags, no humiliation would be meted out to the national arms. As a tribute, however, diminished, they would still be compensated, and they could still consider the Rebu as under their domination. The decrease in the tribute would be virtually unnoticeable in the revenue of Egypt.

Leaving Jethro in command of the siege, Amuba, accompanied by Chebron, who had been by his side during the fighting, and a small guard, returned to the town. News of his arrival had already spread, and the inhabitants, who had been in a state of terror during the mysterious commotion of the night, had now flooded into the streets, with the large area in front of the palace swarming with people. As Amuba approached, an overwhelming shout of welcome was heard; the gates of the prisons had been opened, and those arrested the day before, as well as many of the principal captains of his father's army, flocked around him and hailed him as their king.

With great effort, a path was cleared to the gate of the royal area. Amuba, after crossing the threshold, climbed up the wall and addressed a few words to the people. He informed them that, against all odds, he had escaped from his captivity in Egypt and had made his way back to his homeland, not to claim his rightful place but to free them from the power of their oppressors. He assured them that he would always honor their rights and customs and try to follow in his father's footsteps. Then he retired to the palace, where he held a council with the captains and principal members of the city. Immediately, orders were given for every man capable of bearing arms to arm himself with some kind of weapon and meet in the gate area.

A comprehensive list of all remaining officers from the previous army still inhabiting the town was compiled. When the meeting began at noon, these were assigned to form the men into companies, appoint sub-officers, assess the condition of the arms, and replenish any necessary items. Much to everyone's surprise, a larger proportion of the three thousand men in attendance had already been equipped with weaponry. Although it had been historically documented that all arms had been surrendered to the Egyptians, many spears, arrowheads, swords, and axes had been buried. Shafts were made quickly to fit the spears, and bows used for hunting were now used for combat.

Hundreds of spears and swords were discovered in the palace stores, and when these were distributed to the men, most of them had some kind of weapon. They were quickly brought up to the Egyptian enclosure, with those possessing bows and arrows placed on the walls and the rest massed near the gate to provide support if the Egyptians attempted to break out. Amuba's forces had now grown to exceed the Egyptians in number, though he was aware that the better arms and training of the Egyptians could make them successful in a sortie, should they choose to do so.

The women of the town were instructed to start grinding the grain being handed out from the palace and to bake bread for the warriors who were already there and those who were expected to arrive. By midday, the groups from the cities started coming in regularly. At the same time, the shepherds and villagers began to appear randomly as soon as they heard about what had happened the night before. By the time night fell, around ten thousand men had gathered, and since the Egyptians had been calm all day, Amuba was sure they would accept the terms he had proposed, which would make it so that there was no need for any more fighting. Nevertheless, the army stayed alert throughout the night, prepared to repel any attack. The following day Amuba and Jethro rode up to the terrace of the building where the negotiations had taken place the day before.

A few moments later, the Egyptian governor and a contingent of his men appeared on the other side of the house.

"This is King Amuba," Jethro declared loudly. "He has come to affirm yesterday's terms and receive your response."

"We are ready," the Egyptian governor said, "to withdraw beyond your borders, taking our weapons, banners, and valuables with us, understanding that we are making no surrender and that we are marching out on equal footing, knowing that we could, if we wished, cut our way out regardless of any opposition."

"You may hold that belief," Amuba replied, and the Egyptian was astonished to discover that both the king and his general could converse in the Egyptian language. "And, given that I recognize and respect the valor of the Egyptian troops, it's possible that, although with great losses, you may make it out - but you won't be able to do any more than that. You could not hold the country, for the entire nation stands against you. It's uncertain whether you could even reach the border. Clearly, it would be better for you to leave with dignity without suffering any losses."

"As far as the tribute you offer is concerned," the Egyptian commander said, "I do not have the authority to agree to a reduction of the terms imposed by the king. If it is his wish that an army is sent to invade your country and enforce the earlier terms, then I, with the troops here, must march as commanded without any accusations of betrayal."

"That is clearly understood," Amuba stated; "however, I hope that you, having witnessed for yourself how impoverished our country is and how we are incapable of continuing to pay the previously demanded tribute which has left us destitute, will report the same in your messages to your king, and will intercede on our behalf in gaining a favorable assessment from him. I guarantee that the tribute shall be paid without fail. I consider Egypt the most powerful nation in the world, and I earnestly wish to stay in friendly ties with it, and I swear to you that I will make sure that no grievances will reach you from us."

Amuba's speech was carefully crafted to appease the Egyptians. Although he spoke confidently, he knew it would be no simple task for his forces to make their way through the gateway held by the Rebu, let alone reach their border while being harassed. However, if he returned with his troops unharmed and in good condition, he could minimize any potential blame or discredit and be delighted with the prospect of finishing his military service in good standing. He thus accepted Amuba's proposal, and after a brief discussion, the details of the Egyptian withdrawal from the town were settled.

Amuba consented to pull back his troops from the structures they had seized, and also from the entryway, and to position them all on the dividers, sparing the Egyptians the humiliation of going through lines of armed men and evading the danger of a disagreement emerging between the soldiers. He quickly gave the necessary requests, and the Rebu withdrew to the walls, where they could shield themselves if there should arise an occurrence of any treachery on the part of the Egyptians, and the locals of the city were all arranged back from the street prompting from the passageway to the Egyptian confine to the entryway in the city dividers. An hour later, the Egyptians arrived all together in their enclosure.

Each man carried enough food for a week's sustenance. In addition, Amuba had arranged for cattle to be sent ahead to each rest stop on their way to the wilderness so that a herd would wait for them and provide for their nourishment during their march to the closest Egyptian garrison. Then, in an orderly and resolute fashion, the Egyptians marched out. They carried the images and symbols of the gods high, and their stance was proud and bold, for they, too, had doubts about whether the Rebu could be trusted to honor their terms. As soon as the rear of the column left through the city gate, the Rebu joyfully streamed down from the walls, and the city erupted in celebration.

Jethro promptly dispatched messengers to ensure the oxen were brought to the predetermined spots and to issue commands for the people along the path of the march to evacuate before the arrival of the Egyptians, who may have been enticed to take them away as slaves in their retreat.

Over the next few days, Amuba was entirely consumed with

accepting delegations from the numerous towns and regions, appointing new officers, and putting in place plans for the people to be rearmed and organized into groups so that the country could put up a fierce defense if the Egyptians made a move to reclaim it. It was clear that many months would pass by before any force able to attempt the invasion could be mobilized from Egypt; however, Amuba resolved that no time should be wasted in making preparations, and he concluded that some of the strategies and order of the Egyptians should be adopted into the Rebu army.

On the evening of the surprise, he sent a message to the girls to let them know he had been successful and that neither he nor Chebron had been hurt. After working tirelessly to finish his most urgent tasks, he left Jethro –officially appointed general-in-chief – to continue the work. He set off with Chebron to bring the girls to his new capital. He was now expected to travel with a certain level of grandeur and was accompanied by twenty of the leading Rebu in chariots and a group of light cavalry as an escort. As he journeyed from town to town, he was welcomed with exuberant cheers and celebrated as the king and savior of the nation.

Two days after beginning, he arrived at the tiny coastal town. After being welcomed by the locals and hosting a meeting where he greeted the main occupants who came to offer their fidelity, he ventured to the abode of the Persian trader where he had placed the young ladies. As his chariot stopped at the doorstep, the merchant showed up and bowed deeply. Until Amuba showed up in the city, he had no idea that the individuals who had put the young ladies under his care were anything other than what they appeared. He knew obviously from their unawareness of his language that the young ladies were not Persians, yet accepted that they were female slaves who had been brought from a remote spot, with an end goal, perhaps, of being presented as an offering to the ruler.

After talking with him for a moment, Amuba and Chebron entered the house and headed to the room that had been saved for the young ladies. They stood shyly at one side of the room, and both bowed profoundly as he entered. Amuba stopped for a second in amazement and, at that point, burst into laughter.

"Is this your sister, Chebron, greeting her old friend with such respect? Am I myself or someone else?"

"You are King Amuba," Mysa said, half-smiling but with tears.

"That is true, Mysa, but I was always a prince. So there is nothing extraordinary about that."

"There is still a notable distinction," Mysa said, "and it is only right to recognize a difference in rank."

"Mysa, there doesn't need to be a difference in our rank for much longer," Amuba said, stepping forward and taking her hand. "Chebron, your brother, who is also like a brother to me, has given me his approval, and it's up to you whether you will become queen of the Rebu and my wife. If I hadn't managed to gain a throne, I would have asked you to come with me in exile, and I think you would have said yes. Don't let this moment of triumph be spoiled by saying no. If you do, I'll use my royal authority seriously and marry you whether you want it or not."

But Mysa did not say no, and six weeks later, the capital held a royal wedding. Amuba had immediately provided one of the largest houses in the royal grounds for Chebron and Mysa, then left to travel throughout his country, receiving homage, hearing complaints, and ensuring preparations for the country's defense were underway. Upon his return, the wedding was celebrated in grand style, with the religious ceremonies somewhat abbreviated and Amuba abstaining from offering a sacrifice on the altars of the gods. The ceremony was double, as Chebron was also united to Ruth.

For the following year, the Rebu army went through intense preparations for war and eventually achieved great competency. Amuba and Jethro were sure that it could successfully resist any attack from Egypt, and, as they had anticipated, Egypt didn't attempt to reclaim its far-away land but was content to rank the Rebu's land among its list of tribute-paying countries and accept the reduced payment.

After preparing for war, Amuba shifted his focus to the country's internal affairs. He adopted many of the methods of government used in ancient Egypt, such as irrigation on a large scale and replacing mud with stone in the towns. In addition, he introduced transportation methods similar to those used in Egypt, such as wagons and carts instead of pack animals. He also implemented improved methods of agriculture and ensured that justice was enforced throughout the land, leading to a more content and prosperous population.

Chebron stayed Amuba's chief minister, advisor, and ally, and through their joint efforts, the Rebu transformed from a settled tribe to a small yet flourishing nation.

Another transformation occurred but at a slower pace. Shortly after his ascension, Amuba called together many of the country's leading men and chief priests and explained his and Chebron's beliefs: that only one God was governing the world and that this knowledge was the peak of Egyptian wisdom. He made it clear that he had no desire to demolish the temples or hinder the worship of the former gods. Instead, he wanted to ensure people wouldn't stay ignorant and should be taught that the gods they revered were symbols and images of the sole Supreme. He said he had no intention of coercing people to accept his beliefs and that he and Chebron would always be open to different ways of worship.

Amuba encountered much opposition in this endeavor and would have faced severe consequences had he not been so beloved by the people. The Rebu were devoted to him, and as the priests gradually realized that the change would not undermine their power, their opposition dissipated. Many of the younger men were swayed by Amuba and Mysa's arguments and spread the new religion passionately. It wasn't until after many years had passed that Amuba was finally gratified to witness the one God being worshipped among his people. He was aware that this success was partly due to Mysa and Ruth's earnest efforts to reach out to the wives and daughters of the nobility.

"It is amazing how things turn out," Chebron remarked one

decade after arriving in the land when the little group who had journeyed together for so long assembled in a palace room. "At one point, it seemed like that ill-fated shot of mine would not only bring about the downfall of all associated with me but also be a source of distress for me to the end of my days. Yet, now I witness that, apart from my father's death, it was the most fortunate occurrence in my life. Had it not been for that, I would have stayed devoted to the deities of Egypt throughout my lifetime; had it not been for that, while Amuba and Jethro could have possibly made their escape, Mysa and I would have certainly never left Egypt, never experienced the life of blissfulness and usefulness that we now enjoy. I credit this to the lucky shot that killed the Cat of Bubastes."

◆ ◆ ◆

ACKNOWLEDGEMENT

Simply rewriting a book is a labor of love. First and foremost, I would like to express my gratitude to G.A. Henty, a man who dedicated his life to the pursuit of history, and relating it to the younger generation in an engaging way. I could never have done the same dedicated research.

To my daughter Ruth (editor and designer), thank you for tolerating my pestering. And recreating fussy designs that aren't "current", but to satisfy your "not current" mother. And most of all, my husband Jim, who puts up with me going down the rabbit hole and hearing about ancient battles even before breakfast.

Finally, I would like to thank the readers who dive into this book. Your interest in history makes this endeavor worthwhile, and I hope this book sparks a new curiosity and appreciation for the past. It will be one more tool in your history toolbox.

Printed in Great Britain
by Amazon